AFTER THE GUNS FELL SILENT

Books by A. A. Hoehling

The Fierce Lambs
The Last Voyage of the *Lusitania (with Mary Hoehling)*
Last Train from Atlanta
A Whisper of Eternity
Lonely Command
The Great Epidemic
Home Front USA
Who Destroyed the *Hindenburg*?
The Great War at Sea
They Sailed into Oblivion
America's Road to War, 1939–1941
Thunder at Hampton Roads
Vicksburg, 47 Days of Siege
The *Franklin* Comes Home
The *Lexington* Goes Down
The *Jeannette* Expedition
The Week before Pearl Harbor
The Day Richmond Died *(with Mary Hoehling)*
Epics of the Sea
Disaster: Major American Catastrophes
Women Who Spied
Great Ship Disasters
Lost at Sea
Damn the Torpedoes! Naval Incidents of the Civil War
The Fighting Liberty Ships: A Memoir

AFTER THE GUNS FELL SILENT

A Post-Appomattox Narrative,
April 1865–March 1866

A. A. Hoehling

MADISON BOOKS
Lanham • New York • London

Published by Madison Books
4720 Boston Way
Lanham, Maryland 20706

3 Henrietta Street
London WC2E 8LU England

Distributed by National Book Network

5   4   3   2   1

Library of Congress Cataloging-in-Publication Data

Hoehling, A. A. (Adolph A.)
   After the guns fell silent : a post-Appomattox
narrative, April 1865-March 1866 / A. A. Hoehling.
     p.   cm.
   Includes bibliographical references.
   1. United States—History—1865-1898.
2. Lincoln, Abraham, 1809-1865—Assassination.
3. United States—History—Civil War, 1861-1865—
Peace.   I. Title.

E666.H62 1990
973.8'1—dc20   90-31749 CIP

ISBN 0–8191–7805–5

British Cataloging in Publication Information Available

This book is dedicated to Mary Surratt. Her illegal execution by the government of the United States endures as a vile blot on the character and soul of the nation. In death, she haunted the perpetrators of this crime and thus indirectly altered the course of immediate post–Civil War history.

CONTENTS

Ten pages of photographs follow page 140.

FOREWORD

O n April 3, 1865, Richmond, Virginia, fell. Early that Monday, seemingly endless columns of exultant federal troops surged into the capital of the Confederacy past block upon block of burning buildings or their embers. The fires had been set, ostensibly in warehouses, by the defenders.

Although the capitulation after four wasting, devastating years of war was scarcely unexpected, the people nonetheless were stunned. Many were deep in grief. Those churches whose ministers had not fled with the retreating soldiers became a haven for the heavy-hearted.

"I never knew anything more painful and touching than that . . . when the Litany was sobbed out by the whole congregation," wrote Constance Cary, a young beauty and chronicler of the war years. She continued: "I then, with a tremendous struggle for self-control, stood up in the corner of the pew and sang alone. At the words, 'Thou Saviour see'st the tears I shed,' there was again a great burst of crying and sobbing all over the church. I wanted to break down dreadfully, but I held on and carried the hymn to the end. When the rector prayed for 'the sick and wounded soldiers and all in distress of mind or body,' there was a brief pause, filled with a sound of weeping all over the church. He then gave out the hymn: 'when gathering clouds around I view.' There was no organ and a voice that started the hymn broke down in tears. Another took it up, and failed likewise."

Yet "through all this strain of anguish ran like a gleam of gold the mad, vain hope that Lee would yet make a stand somewhere—that Lee's dear soldiers would give us back our liberty."

Connie wrote of St. Paul's Episcopal Church and the impassioned

German-born minister, the Reverend Charles G. Minnigerode, both a believer and a firm, sometimes unshaven personality who frequently lapsed into his native tongue for whole, incomprehensible sentences to the hushed bafflement of his flock.

The imposing brick place of worship raised its familiar lofty spire beside Capitol Square as though in competition with the handsome State House itself. Perhaps in spite of rather than because of its pastor, St. Paul's had drawn capacity congregations throughout the war. Counted in the number were Confederate statesmen and soldiers, including Robert E. Lee and the relatively short-lived Jeb Stuart.

President Jefferson Davis was himself worshipping there Sunday, April 2, when he received word that the defenses before Petersburg were crumbling. Considering the depletion of the Southern forces, the news should have come as no surprise.

The days as they ticked away were "eminently of leisure," observed John Leyburn, a young man of the city. "Nobody had anything to do. All business was brought to a sudden standstill. Few had any money; my own stock amounted to an old-fashioned three-cent piece. Some of us spent most of the time sitting on the front steps talking over the past, the present, and the most uncertain future.

"At length, one night my host informed me that the sentinel near our door had just told him that General Lee had surrendered. Though we did not credit it, it seemed worth inquiring into. On further interrogation, we were assured that the news was official; and soon all remaining doubts were dispelled by the salvos of artillery from the Capitol Square saluting the tidings."

Connie Cary knew it was true when "our streets were filled up again with the gray uniforms of soldiers on parole, dusty, threadbare, with tarnished buttons and insignia . . . The war was over."

"They seemed almost heartbroken," added Hannah Garlick Rawlings, from Orange County, Virginia. "Tears flowed . . . Their trembling lips could scarcely utter a word." When Hannah observed to a neighbor that "the dead calm oppressed me," he replied, " 'I wish to heaven I could hear 40,000 [cannon] burst out at once!' "

There were, too, the prisoners returning from the North, streaming into Richmond, "homeless, penniless, hungry, ragged," wrote Mary Stanard, "almost—or quite—barefoot, they came; but still singing the old southern melodies, fighting battles over again in reminiscent talk, sparkling with quip and jest, whenever two or more of them came together, and laughingly telling one another how they had 'worn themselves out' whipping the Yankees."

A Georgian, George W. Lamar, expressed a common reaction of the secessionists in a letter to "Dear Cousin": "The termination of the war has caused such a shock upon my self respect that I am unable to make comments."

The old familiar patterns were abruptly changed. Connie Cary, Hannah Rawlings, Mary Stanard, John Leyburn, and George Lamar were just some of many thousands who had to accept the reality that 1861 was gone, forever.

Physically, socially, emotionally, the South had no alternative but to start anew.

The Union, looking toward fresh horizons, had emerged as a powerful industrial nation that, suddenly, commanded worldwide attention and, surely, respect. Even proud Great Britain had to admit it had bet on a loser.

The North and Midwest not only had effected strides in weaponry and in the forging of a respectable navy, boasting innovative *Monitors* and ironclads, but also had scored telling advances in peacetime industry and science. These included mechanized agriculture, clothing manufacture (through the increasing employment of the sewing machine), bridge building, railway operation, education, and even aeronautics in the form of ballooning.

In Pennsylvania, petroleum, little more than a curiosity during the past century, surged into volume production, heralding new industry and fresh scientific applications, notably the internal combustion engine and, ultimately, synthetics. The transcontinental railroad arrowed westward at an accelerated pace.

The *Great Eastern* streamed hundreds of miles of the transatlantic cable.

Immigration rates of Europe's "Your tired, your poor" rose to new records as fast steamships such as the Cunarder *Scotia* brought the Old World no more distant than eight days' voyage. A mighty explosive, nitroglycerin, was introduced by Alfred Nobel which would literally move mountains and also make war more terrible.

All of this in the twelve months following Appomattox.

But the South was bankrupt in every respect. Not only was its currency worthless, its communications and food supply inadequate, and its industry ruined, but the late Confederacy was deprived of its primary source of labor: slaves.

This loss was devastating. Involved was a black population in the eleven seceded states generally put at three and a half million, in contrast to some five and a half million whites. The attrition of the younger white males dead in battle from wounds and from disease was estimated to amount to as many as 258,000. Confederate statistics, however, remained unreliable since what government records existed had been burned or dumped into canals during the evacuation of Richmond.

No attempt was made to keep count of civilian dead during the four war years. In the winter of 1862–63, there was a serious epidemic of smallpox. Pneumonia, influenza, typhoid, measles, and dysentery ravaged the South throughout the whole rebellion. There were also ill-diagnosed maladies such as swamp fever and bilious fever, so labeled, in desperation, for want of better medical terminology or knowledge.

Sherman and Sheridan had become rampaging devils in the Southern mind. They ripped up farms and plantations, the business hearts of cities. They burned barns and newly harvested crops and led off or ate the cattle from the Shenandoah to Georgia. Grant presided over the slaughter of the Confederacy's finest young men, along with those of the Union, in wasting, rash frontal assaults.

But here was the anomaly. "Unconditional Surrender" Grant was not hated with the same white heat as William Tecumseh Sherman or Phil Sheridan. The conclusion appeared self evident: the loss of material possessions—"things"—must have hurt more than the loss of human beings.

The ruin in the Shenandoah was particularly bad. "From Winchester to Harrisonburg," a traveler wrote, "scarce a crop, fence, chicken, horse, cow, or pig was in sight. Extreme destitution prevailed throughout the entire valley." The same general area, by the measure of Alexander Stephens, the vice president of the Confederacy, was "horrible to behold!"

Farther south, the condition of the railroads bespoke the ruin that had been visited upon the land. In the heart of Alabama, an engineer reported "114 miles almost entirely destroyed, except the roadbed and iron rails and they in very bad condition—every bridge and trestle destroyed, crossties rotten, buildings burned, watertanks gone, ditches filled up, and track grown up in weeds and bushes; not a sawmill near the line; the labor systems of the country gone. About 40 miles of track was burned, crossties entirely destroyed, and rails bent and twisted in such manner as to require great labor to straighten, and a large portion of them requiring renewal.

"That portion of the road [in Mississippi] not having received any attention since 1862, it became enveloped with briers, bushes, and grass, the undisturbed growth of three years, thus causing the decay of the pine timber used in its construction. There was scarcely a single bridge on that section that was not wholly or in part destroyed by fire or rendered unfit for use by decay."

Out of 49 locomotives, 37 passenger cars, and 550 freight cars, only one of each survived. On other rights-of-way, burned-out locomotives and cars stretched like mileposts as far as the eye could see.

The aparthy described by John Leyburn—"nobody had anything to do"—was the shock effect attending the immediate cessation of hostilities. The sound of hammers, the rasping of saws, the song of train whistles, and the vibrant obbligato of industry would be heard again. And the molds for rebirth would take shape in the first twelve months following Appomattox. Here already were the seeds of the twentieth century.

Much, aside from the ending of the war, happened in those months. Lincoln was assassinated, projecting an ill-qualified, crude man into the White House, a man rendered the more ineffective by the fury of his enemies. People for the first time shared a national grief as the funeral train tolled in agony westward. Booth's conspirators were tried and a woman executed who would, or should, forever haunt the country's conscience. In many ways, in death she dominated the immediate postwar years.

Washington, now a world capital, witnessed a grand review of the disbanding army of a magnitude that would not be approximated even after the world wars, decades in the future. Jeff Davis was captured but would not be "hung on a sour apple tree" or any other species. There was, nonetheless, considerable executive and legislative sentiment to the contrary.

Many pieces remained to be picked up and sorted in war's cluttered aftermath.

This account, however, is not a military, social, or political history of twelve months as such, nor does it attempt to offer an academic focus on reconstruction or, surely, to be encyclopedia or all-inclusive.

Rather, it aims at recapturing the dimension of a brief but dramatic postwar period as many of the participants saw, heard, and felt it. This is their story, that of some familiar figures, but mostly of the unknown, the little people. It is the presentation of vignettes as painted by them or, in some cases, longer and broader canvases, bequeathed to future generations in the intimacy and, sometimes, passion of their diaries, letters, and published memoirs.

These broader canvases, however, are scarce treasure. After the fevered emotions of the war years, the ink ran dry even in the pens of inveterate diarists such as Mary Boykin Chesnut. Entries became more spasmodic after April 1865. There were gaps of weeks, months, or even years, attesting to the letdown.

Everyone was tired. In the North and Midwest, the story was quite different. Families had lost members but not property. They were not hungry. And if they hurt, they hurt in a different fashion from their Southern brothers and sisters.

Whatever their emotions, few in the nonseceding states confided them to posterity. Federal soldiers, who would commence a virtual avalanche of memoirs, returned to a life that proved humdrum. "Mustered out" was an invariable amen. None thought his grandchildren would be much interested in the postwar currents of life in Wilton, Maine, or Xenia, Ohio, after the headiness of Shiloh, the Wilderness, or, most certainly, the carnage of Cold Harbor or Chancellorsville.

In the wake of horror, these postwar months were dramatic, if in a different, a conceivably lower, softer key. The spectrum, however, reveals no dead history. The hopes and fears of an ancestral citizenry have found their counterparts in succeeding generations that were also doomed to repeat the folly of war.

1865

APRIL

It's a Canard

On Saturday afternoon, April 15, the Confederacy's general-in-chief returned to Richmond. It was just six days after he had surrendered the Army of Northern Virginia to Ulysses S. Grant at an improbable, generally unknown county seat, Appomattox Court House. The place was sixty-eight miles west of Richmond.

There was no advance word of the general's visit, other than an oblique request a courier had brought earlier in the day to the federal quartermaster. A terse note merely asked for "forage and stabling of 20 horses on General Lee's behalf."

Thus the citizenry was taken by surprise when the gray-bearded but erect figure of Robert E. Lee, accompanied by five aides, rode over the pontoon bridge from Manchester. All permanent spans across the broad James had been burned the night of the evacuation, April 2–3. The city yet smelled of smoke and charred timbers.

One of the aides, Colonel Walter H. Taylor, who happened to have been married in Richmond by the light of the flaming buildings after midnight that fateful Monday morning, April 3, noted, "The general quietly proceeded to the house on Franklin Street then occupied by his family . . . All was quiet and no demonstration attended General Lee's return."

But others witnessing this postscript to history that afternoon saw the defeated warrior's reception in a somewhat different, more dramatic perspective. Among them was the correspondent for the New York *Herald,*

3

William H. Merriam, who looked at his watch and timed the general's party off the bridge and into the city at precisely 3:00 P.M.

An "immense crowd," which somehow had learned of the arrival, was present, according to Merriam: ". . . He was greeted with cheers upon cheers." Even Union officers, on occupation, "raised their caps."

Lee "crossed the river and turned onto Cary Street," wrote a resident, John Southall. "He was riding Traveler and looked neither to the right nor to the left, but straight ahead. The streets were filled with debris . . . and it was very difficult to make your way through, even in the middle of the roadway."

Edward A. Pollard, assistant editor of the padlocked Richmond *Examiner,* watched the familiar gray-uniformed officer who "passed on rapidly, as if to escape notice," and he added, "blackened ruins threw their shadows across the way; strange faces were on the streets; but it was impossible for his commanding figure to pass without the challenge of curiosity, and there presently ran along the sidewalks the shout: 'It's General Lee!' "

Then, "instantly" there commended "a wild chase after the party of horsemen." Yet it was not a trained reporter but an elderly resident, Julia Page Pleasants, who reported Lee's return with especial depth and sensitivity. Having observed the scene from her porch, she penned: "He rode Traveler and was, as usual, a commanding figure, though the gray coat was dingy from hard service, and both he and his horse looked tired and dispirited. His expression, though calm, was unutterably sad. With him came his staff, gaunt and pallid, in ragged uniform, on bony, weary old horses. Dilapidated army wagons creaked after them. One of these was covered with an old quilt in place of the customary canvas. Not a very inspiring cavalcade, it would seem."

On the other hand, Merriam, the reporter, thought Lee "looked exceedingly robust . . . with fair forehead, gray hair, burned countenance and military beard."

Then, as Julia Pleasants listened to the cheers, "loud and prolonged," the general acknowledged them "by gravely lifting his hat."

The crowd, Merriam continued, "increased in numbers and the cheers grew louder." Julia thought the acclaim came in waves, "again and again," and each time Lee doffed his hat. When he reached his house on Franklin Street, which was still occupied by his ailing wife, Mary Custis, he dismounted, evidencing "anxiety," it appeared to editor Pollard, "to retire inside."

But the multitude still barred the way to his door, as "so many as could get near his person shook him heartily by the hand," according to the New York *Herald* correspondent. "Men in blue," Julia noted, were as numerous as those of the Confederate gray, seeking the privilege. "One rebel officer," wrote Merriam, "seized him by the extremity of his coat."

The recent commander of the Army of Northern Virginia somehow "backed up the stone steps on his house and through its door, which closed behind him." He had passed, Pollard added as a postscript, "into the fondly-desired retirement of his simple home."

But he would not be permitted to relax long. Lee was seated in the front parlor with Mary Custis when a friend entered, bearing unanticipated news: President Lincoln had been slain.

Described by those with him as "deeply shocked," the general stared for some moments at the floor, then exclaimed, "This is the hardest blow the South has yet received!"

Only that morning, at 7:22, Abraham Lincoln, the sixteenth president, had succumbed to a single bullet wound. The night before, which had also marked the damp, waning hours of Good Friday, April 14, the chief executive had sought to relax at Ford's Theatre, in Washington. There the popular actress Laura Keene was performing in the frothy comedy *Our American Cousin*.

In the presidential party, in addition to the first lady, Mary Todd Lincoln, was a tall and handsome army officer, Major Henry R. Rathbone and his fiancée, Clara Harris. She was the daughter of Senator Ira Harris, of New York, and also the stepsister of the major.

Lieutenant General Grant had been scheduled to accompany the group. In mid-afternoon, he apologized for not being able to attend and departed with his wife, Julia Dent, on the late train for Baltimore. After changing in that city, the couple went on to Philadelphia. It was a predictable decision. The victor over the Army of Northern Virginia wished to see his children in Burlington, New Jersey. Nor was he any patron of the theater. A military band concert, perhaps, would have sufficed.

The presidential box at Ford's was festooned with flags. Lincoln entered and seated himself in a large, overstuffed plush armchair, as Major Rathbone recalled, "nearest the audience, but farthest from the stage." This "he occupied during the whole of the evening, with one exception, when he got up and put on his coat, and returned and sat down again."

Seated in the audience was James P. Ferguson, who operated a restaurant next door to the theater. Big Jim naturally knew all the actors who played the circuit. Thus it did not surprise him when about 10:00 P.M., during the second scene of the third act, he saw John Wilkes Booth "pass along near the [presidential] box, and then stop, and lean against the wall. He stood there a moment."

(Ferguson, like others associated in any way with the theater or its audiences, knew Booth as an uncommonly bad actor who refused to memorize his lines. He endeavored to compensate for the lack with wild histrionics or rambling, often irrelevant ad-libs. Sometimes he recited poetry.)

Ferguson shrugged and returned his attention to the play. Actors and actresses, invariably according the courtesy of the house, were ever wandering about the theater, like any visitors, often studying the effectiveness and tonal qualities of fellow performers' deliveries, as well as the acoustics. But then something caused Ferguson to look back, ". . . and [I] saw him [Booth] step down one step, put his hands to the floor, and his knee against it, and push the door open, the first door that goes into the box . . . I saw the flash of the pistol."

Much closer, Henry Rathbone "heard the discharge of a pistol behind me, and, looking 'round, saw through the smoke a man between the door and the President. At the same time I heard him shout some word, which I thought was 'freedom!' "

Strong and lithe, the young officer leapt up and seized the intruder who "wrestled himself away from my grasp, and made a violent thrust at my breast with a large knife. I parried the blow by striking it up, and received a wound several inches deep in my left arm." As his assailant raced across the box for the stage, Rathbone cried out, "Stop that man!"

Bleeding in gushes, the major nonetheless grabbed Booth again, tearing some of his outer garments and causing the actor to lose his balance as he vaulted over the rail. His left leg snarled in the flags which draped the box—probably in the Treasury Guards flag—and he fell heavily onto the stage, a spur torn off his boot clattering down beside him. Ferguson heard Booth exclaim; "Sic semper tyrannis!"

Ferguson would report that Booth then "ran right directly across the stage to the opposite door where the actors come in." Booth was limping from a fractured bone in his right leg. Even so, he made good his escape out of the theater's rear exit.

There he had left his horse in the care of the scenery carpenter and sometime stable hand, Edward Spangler. However, Spangler, a notorious alcoholic, had turned the reins over to a dull-witted backstage choreboy, "Peanut John" Burroughs, and gone off for a drink. In his haste, the wildly excited Booth knocked the youth down and painfully hauled himself up onto the steed.

And so the crazed actor galloped off down the alley, into the night—and history.

Rathbone now "turned to the President. His position was not changed; his head was slightly bent forward, and his eyes were closed. I saw that he was unconscious and, supposing him mortally wounded, rushed to the door for the purpose of calling medical aid."

Dr. Charles A. Leale, a young surgeon in the audience, was the first into the box. Leale would observe that "he appeared to be dead . . . I placed my finger on the President's right radial pulse but could perceive no movement of the artery." Shortly, he would judge that "his wound is mortal."

Lincoln was carried by soldiers across the street from Ford's to the home of a tailor, William Peterson. Medical men and cabinet officers soon congregated in a cramped, stuffy first-floor bedroom where the unconscious leader was breathing heavily. Absent was Secretary of State William H. Seward, who, as he slept, had been knifed by a hulking accomplice of Booth's, Lewis Payne.

Seward, by chance, had suffered a broken jaw in a recent accident. Seward's son, Frederick, assistant secretary of state, was severely slashed as Payne forced his way upstairs. A second son, Major Augustus Seward, was less seriously beaten.

The irascible, controversial secretary of war, Edwin M. Stanton, and Navy Secretary Gideon Welles, who was rather the emotional opposite of Stanton, were among the first in the Peterson house. Welles, distinguished by a shaggy beard and immense wig that deceived no one, was a former Hartford publisher and lawyer. He had built up the federal fleet, pushed the construction of ironclads, and tightened the blockade of Southern ports. The starvation strategy had in itself shortened the Confederacy's ability to hold out.

"The giant sufferer lay extended diagonally across the bed, which was not long enough for him," Welles confided to his meticulously kept diary. "He had been stripped of his clothes. His large arms, which were occasionally exposed, were of a size one would scarce have expected from his spare appearance. His slow, full respiration lifted the clothes with each breath that he took. His features were calm and striking. I had never seen them to appear to better advantage than for the first hour, perhaps, that I was there. After that, his right eye began to swell and that [side] of his face became discolored." This would have been because of the bullet wound in the back of his head.

Welles found the small room greatly "overcrowded," when only the surgeons and "members of the Cabinet" should have been in attendance. Yet people filled the narrow halls and spilled into additional rooms on other floors of the little building.

The secretary of the navy might have settled for almost anyone but Stanton in the sick cubicle. His dislike for the secretary of war was obsessive, on occasions almost irrational. At best, he considered Edwin McMasters Stanton "fond of power . . . ungracious and rough . . . bearish . . . [with] little moral courage nor much self-reliance."

Nonetheless, according to Assistant Secretary of War Charles A. Dana, summoned because of his stenographic skills, "Mr. Stanton alone was in full activity." The remainder "within this little chamber" appeared to be "as much paralyzed as the unconscious sufferer."

This was Stanton's moment. He furiously dictated telegrams: to Vice President Andrew Johnson, presumably sleeping in the Kirkwood House, down Pennsylvania Avenue; to the newly appointed chief justice, Salmon P. Chase, warning him to be prepared for delivering an oath to the seventeenth president; to General Grant in Philadelphia; to the president of the Baltimore and Ohio Railroad, asking that he provide a special train for returning the general-in-chief of the Armies of the United States from Philadelphia to Washington; and to Colonel Lafayette C. Baker, Stanton's chief detective and henchman in New York.

Stanton ordered troops with fixed bayonets to guard all roads leading into Washington and rail traffic to the south halted. The latter was quite unnecessary since few trains moved beyond Alexandria, on the Potomac, or Centreville, to the west. The tracks persisted in disrepair.

His drumroll of commands and "advisories," as though the war secretary were actually acting chief executive, seemed endless. He even ordered John T. Ford (the theater owner), Laura Keene, and the entire cast of *Our American Cousin* placed under arrest. From time to time Stanton dictated bulletins on the dying President's condition. Thus, with reason, did some dub Stanton the Great Energy.

While Dana scribbled feverishly, using his battered beaver hat as a table, Mrs. Lincoln tiptoed in and out, "about once an hour," Welles estimated. Yet another witness, Brigadier General Thomas M. Vincent, an assistant adjutant general, would write, "I cannot recall a more pitiful picture than that of poor Mrs. Lincoln almost insane with sudden agony, moaning and sobbing out that terrible night."

And another present, James Tanner, quoted the president's wife as crying, "O my God, and have I given my husband to die!" Tanner, who had lost both legs at Second Manassas and was assisting Dana with messages, added, "And I tell you I never heard so much agony in so few words."

She was too much for Stanton. "Take that woman out of here," he was heard to order, "and don't let her in again!"

There would arise a question as to when or even whether Vice President Johnson visited the Peterson house. Welles made no mention of his presence. Tanner at first thought he saw the vice president but later admitted he was not at all certain. The *National Intelligencer* reported that "the Vice President has been to see him." There was, however, no evidence that the newspaper had a reporter present.

Johnson knew of the shooting within minutes. Leonard I. Farwell, a former governor of Wisconsin, who had been in the audience at Ford's, raced the three blocks to the Kirkwood House, at 12th Street and Pennsylvania Avenue, to awaken the vice president in suite 68, on the second floor, and warn him for his own safety. Shortly, Major James R. O'Beirne, provost marshal for the District of Columbia, arrived and threw a cordon of guards around the hotel.

Amid confusion and conflicting evidence, the notion would persist that Johnson, accompanied by O'Beirne and so heavily cloaked as to virtually defy recognition, paid a very brief call around 2:00 A.M. Then, uncertain as to the propriety of his presence, he hurriedly departed. But O'Beirne, who would receive the Medal of Honor for earlier gallantry at Fair Oaks, filed no report of the supposed visit.

Senator Charles P. Sumner, of Massachusetts, among those present, would later write to his friend John Bright, a radical member of Parliament, in London, "Mr. Johnson was at the bedside of the dying President only two minutes, about 2 o'clock in the morning." (Sumner was a man of giant stature and influence, a fiery abolitionist and advocate of "punishing" the secessionists. He was among the most radical of the "Radical Republicans.)

And this was not the sole mystery surrounding Johnson in the immediate hours past. Only that afternoon, Booth had called at the Kirkwood and left an oblique note: "Don't wish to disturb you. Are you home?"

According to the *Evening Star,* a houseboy had informed the actor that the vice president was indeed in his room, but Booth continued on his way. Johnson would not attempt to clarify the ambiguities arising from such a compromising caller and his message.

(Gossip, fueled by his political foes, darkly hinted that Andy Johnson, as military governor of Tennessee, at Nashville, met Booth when he was performing at a local theater. Furthermore, it was whispered that the statesman and actor kept company with two prostitute sisters. That Mrs. (Eliza) Johnson had long been an invalid and her husband something of a carouser supposedly lent credence to such a damaging accusation. Johnson's enemies and, later, skeptical historians would continue to sniff and bay over this trail of suspicion until it became as cold as death itself.)

In tailor Peterson's bedroom the long, unreal hours passed, "dark, cloudy and damp," Welles would recall. About six o'clock, rain pattered down onto a porch just outside the little room. A door had been left open in what was perhaps a vain effort to introduce fresh air.

Welles, who had been seated for almost two hours on a chair at the foot of the bed, without moving, "experienced a feeling of faintness" and went outside for "a walk in the open air." He encountered "large groups of people . . . all anxious and solicitous." They kept inquiring of the navy secretary the condition of the patient, only to manifest "intense grief" when he told them the president could survive "but a short time." He found "the colored people especially . . . overwhelmed by grief."

About 7:00 A.M., Saturday, after the cabinet officer had returned inside, the "death-struggle" was apparent as "the respiration . . . became suspended at intervals." Mary Todd Lincoln paid her last visit and, it appeared to General Vincent, was assisted out in a fainting state. Robert Todd Lincoln, the twenty-two-year-old son, stood at the head of the bed and "bore himself well, but on two occasions gave way to overpowering grief and sobbed aloud, leaning on the shoulder of Senator Sumner."

At this time, the firm resolve of Secretary Stanton deserted him. According to Colonel A. F. Rockwell, one of his aides, his superior "stood quite motionless, leaning his chin upon his left hand, his right hand holding his hat and supporting his left elbow, the tears falling continually." Considering Stanton's very full beard, the spectacle was the most incongruous, like some furry animal dissolved in tears.

Tanner himself would add, "Secretary Stanton was there trying every way to be calm and yet he was very much moved. The utmost silence prevailed, broken only by the sound of strong men's sobs."

It became Sumner's turn. One of those present, unidentified, was nonetheless quoted as observing, "Sumner was seated on the right of the President's couch, near the head, holding the right hand of the President in his own. He was sobbing like a woman, with head bowed down almost to the pillow of the bed on which the President was lying . . . All cabinet ministers . . . were bathed in tears, not excepting Mr. Stanton, the War Secretary with iron will and nerve."

At 7:22 A.M. it became obvious to the several medical men present that the president had ceased to breathe. Surgeon General Joseph K. Barnes "tenderly" drew a sheet over the familiar craggy head, the head that had long been an inspiration for grotesque and often rabid political cartoons.

During the next few minutes there were blank spots in memories as well as contradictions about what those present may have said or how they reacted. According to Colonel Rockwell, for one, "Mr. Stanton slowly and with apparent deliberation straightened out his right arm, placed his hat for an instant on his head and then, as deliberately, returned it to its original position."

A few saw Stanton "darkening the windows," then pausing to pronounce a requiem, which they heard as "he now belongs to the ages." Others, including Welles, did not hear the secretary of war say any such thing but thought Senator Sumner had stated something to the effect that finally Lincoln was out of the reach of his enemies. Certainly Stanton himself, a Jacksonian Democrat who was attorney general in President Buchanan's cabinet, could not necessarily be excluded from that number, any more than Sumner, the abolitionist. An Ohio lawyer, Stanton had been chosen by Lincoln as a successor to Simon Cameron largely because of his (Stanton's) staunch opposition to secession and slavery.

There was, however, general agreement that Dr. Phineas Gurley, the popular pastor of the Presbyterian Church on New York Avenue attended by Lincoln and other Washington leaders, had offered a prayer. Yet none, not excepting even the minister, could recall the exact words. Tanner thought the prayer "very impressive" and would have written it down except "my pencil had been broken in my pocket."

The room was emptied. General Vincent was left in charge of moving the remains to the White House. Before summoning soldiers to assist him, the adjutant drew back the sheet from Abraham Lincoln's face to reveal opened eyes, "producing a sensation that will be vivid in my mind as long as I live." Then, "after pressing and smoothing the eyes of the dead President, I placed coins on them to close them for a last long slumber."

Dr. Leale, his ministrations finished, walked outside, a "cold drizzling rain dropping on my head . . . My clothing was stained with blood. I had not been seated since I first sprang to the President's aid; I was cold, weary and sad."

Gideon Welles went home for breakfast before making his way to the White House in "the cheerless cold rain" through crowds of people, "mostly women and children, weeping and wailing their loss." There he encountered Lincoln's son, Tad, who had been looking out of a window. Suddenly, the twelve-year-old boy "cried aloud in his tears, 'oh, Mr. Welles, who killed my father?' "

Two days later, Easter Monday, the seventeenth, Major General William Tecumseh Sherman was about to board a train at Raleigh. The leader of the powerful Military Division of the Mississippi had been resting in the North Carolina capital from his devastating campaign to "make Georgia howl." To this promise he had added South Carolina, as he swept "like a besom of destruction" through Charleston and Columbia following his triumphs at Atlanta and Savannah.

The hour was 8:00 A.M. It was "raining torrents" here also. The general was en route to Durham to confer with an old adversary, General Joseph E. Johnston, commander of the last major Confederate force in the field, the Army of Tennessee. On the thirteenth, which was Maundy Thursday and the day before the tragedy in Ford's Theatre, Johnston had hurried off a note to Sherman, suggesting a meeting in the interests of stemming "the further effusion of blood."

Steam was up and wood cinders poured out of the special locomotive's bulbous funnel. Then, "just as we were entering the car," Sherman would recall, "the telegraph operator, whose office was upstairs in the depot building, ran down to me and said that he was at that instant of time receiving a most important dispatch in cipher from Morehead City, which I ought to see.

"I held the train for nearly half an hour, when he returned with the message translated and written out." From Secretary Stanton, it read: "The distressing duty has devolved upon the Secretary of War to announce to the Armies of the United States that at 7:22 o'clock on the morning of Saturday the 15th day of April, 1865, Abraham Lincoln, President of the United States, died of a mortal wound, inflicted upon him by an assassin . . . the headquarters of every department, post, station, fort and arsenal will be draped in mourning for thirty days, and appropriate funeral honors will be paid by every Army, and in every department and at every military post . . ."

Sherman asked the operator if anyone else had seen the message. When the operator replied in the negative, the general ordered him "not to reveal the contents by word or look" until the general's return.

In the early afternoon, the rain abated. Sherman met with Johnston, his foe in the early stages of the Atlanta campaign, in the house of "a Mrs. Bennett," near Hillsboro. It was their first encounter face to face. Sherman added, "He was some twelve or more years my senior; but we knew enough of each other to be well acquainted at once."

The two West Pointers presented a contrast. Sherman (class of 1840) was tall, lean, with a shock of sparse red hair itself lending an appearance of unruliness. Johnston (class of 1829) was noticeably short, immaculate, his dominant physical characteristic being a well-trained goatee. A more appropriate environment might have been a campus or salon of diplomacy. The wounds he had sustained at Seven Pines (or Fair Oaks) during McClellan's Peninsular campaign told on Joe Johnston. He could no longer manifest the sort of sturdiness that die-stamped tireless Old Tecumseh.

When the two were alone, the Union commander showed Johnston the telegram from Stanton and "watched him closely." At once, "the perspiration came out in large drops on his forehead, and he did not attempt to conceal his distress. He denounced the act as a disgrace to the age."

Sherman then "told Johnston that he must be convinced that he could not oppose my army, and that, since Lee had surrendered, he could do the same with honor and propriety. He plainly and repeatedly admitted this, and added that any further fighting would be 'murder.' "

The meeting was concluded, to be resumed the following day after both generals conferred with their staffs. In Sherman's mind, there was little if anything further to be resolved. Johnston, on the other hand, found that the existing armistice had "produced great uneasiness in the army" since "it was very commonly believed among the soldiers that there was to be a surrender, by which they would be prisoners of war, to which they were very averse."

Whereas General Sherman had anticipated that some of the Confederates might start "breaking up into guerrilla bands," the opposite was happening. Rather than risk capture, Johnston's troops commenced deserting, abandoning their weapons as they "rode off artillery horses and mules belonging to the baggage trains." In a very few hours, "not less than four thousand" Confederates had left the ranks of artillery, infantry, and cavalry.

On Tuesday, the eighteenth, Sherman, "punctually at noon," was back at the Bennett house. Impatiently, he waited for two hours for Johnston. When Johnston arrived, he explained that the delay was occasioned in part by discussion over his officers' "political rights." He had also brought along Davis's last secretary of war, John Cabell Breckinridge. Although the Union commander evinced misgivings over the presence of a Confederate cabinet officer, Johnston pointed out that Breckinridge had fought in the war as a major general and his role was that of a soldier.

Sherman also remembered that the tall, moustached Breckinridge had been vice president under James Buchanan, and that, too, bothered him. The federal general, however, soon was conversing over a bottle of bourbon (no stranger to either officer's saddlebags) in friendly fashion with this personable member of a fallen cabinet. He went so far as to suggest that Breckinridge had "better get away as the feeling of our people was utterly hostile to the political element of the South!"

Sherman pointed out that Breckinridge faced especially serious consequences, reminding him that he had acknowledged "Mr. Lincoln . . . the properly elected President of the United States," then "openly rebelled and taken up arms against the Government."

Somewhat abashed, Breckinridge "answered me that he surely would give us no more trouble, and intimated that he would speedily leave the country forever." Then Sherman, obviously warming to his subject, "may have also advised him that Mr. Davis too should get abroad as soon as possible."

General Sherman obviously was enjoying his whiskey. His counsel was tantamount to a warden advising his prisoners that a jailbreak would be an advisable course.

Soon, the Union general "sat down at the table and wrote of the terms which I thought concisely expressed his [Lincoln's] views and wishes . . ." But in his welling mood of camaraderie and forgiveness, Sherman went too far. Exceeding Grant's conditions for Lee's surrender, Sherman guaranteed, for example, the southern states' "political rights and franchises, as well as their rights of person and property." There also arose some ambiguity about the number of Confederate troops who could keep "arms and ammunition" in order to "maintain peace and order."

Moreover, Johnston had "assured" Sherman that he exercised control "over all the Confederate armies," a military prerogative for which not even Jefferson Davis could fully vouch. His precise command was the Army of Tennessee, nothing more.

With "full faith" that his opponent would keep the interim truce, however, Sherman sent off the signed terms of surrender, via telegraph and coastal steamer, to Washington. All present in the little Bennett house "rejoiced," or so Tecumseh would confide to his notes.

The news of Lincoln's assassination had consumed two full days in reaching Sherman's headquarters, even though it had been wired into Richmond on Saturday afternoon. It arrived in Charlotte, North Carolina, even as the ink was drying on the general's overly generous terms of surrender. Fleeing there with his cabinet from Danville, Virginia, his previous short-term capital in exile, Jefferson Davis received word "at the moment of dismounting."

Unlike Sherman, Davis was unable to keep the news suppressed. In an instant, "some troopers" nearby were cheering, "not appreciating the evil it portended." Davis, who at once sensed the implications of the tragedy, would write, "For an enemy so relentless in the war for our subjugation, we could not be expected to mourn; yet in view of the political consequences, it could not be regarded otherwise than as a great misfortune to the South. He had power over the northern people, and was without personal malignity toward the people of the South . . ." On the other hand, Davis thought that Andrew Johnson was "the embodiment of malignity" toward the same Southern citizenry.

He turned to his navy secretary, Stephen R. Mallory, to observe rather laconically, "There are a great many men of whose end I would much rather have heard than he. I fear it will be disastrous to our people, and I regret it deeply."

This Tuesday, the eighteenth of April, the assassination tidings, like ominous storm clouds, were rolling through the Carolinas. Mary Boykin Chesnut learned in Chester, South Carolina. Mrs. Chesnut, wife of Brigadier General James Chesnut, Jr., sometime aide to Davis, was frustrated at the fragmentary details: "Murdered . . . why? by whom?" Then the tireless, often vitriolic wartime diarist prophesied: "The death of Lincoln I call a warning to tyrants. He will not be the last President put to death in the Capital, though he is the first."

In northern Georgia, Eliza "Fanny" Andrews heard the news in a railroad station, as Sherman had. The twenty-five-year-old schoolteacher from Washington, Georgia, in the eastern part of the state, was en route home from a several-month stay in Albany, Georgia. She had been not only visiting family and friends but dodging Sherman's "great black tide of destruction" as it surged toward Savannah, ripping up railroads and plantations. Here and there sections of track survived along with some old locomotives and cars to creak and rattle over them.

Thus Fanny found herself in the little town of Camack, about one hundred miles east of Atlanta and but eighteen miles south of her home, Washington. She had been traveling with friends, over remnants of the Central of Georgia and Georgia lines "but little faster than our mule team." While she was waiting for her car to be hooked onto the train from Augusta, itself thirty-six miles east of Camack, somebody clomped across the platform and "thrust his head in at the window and shouted, 'Lincoln's been assassinated!' "

Fanny smiled and would observe, "We heard so many absurd rumors that at first we were all inclined to regard this as a jest. Somebody laughed and asked if the people of Camack didn't know that April Fools' Day was past . . .

"But soon the truth of the report was confirmed. Some fools laughed and applauded, but wise people looked grave and held their peace. It is a terrible blow to the South, for it places that vulgar renegade Andy Johnson in power, and will give the Yankees an excuse for charging us with a crime which was in reality only the deed of an irresponsible madman . . .

"About one o'clock we reached Barnett, where I used to feel as much at home as in Washington itself, but there was such a crowd, such a rush, such a hurrying to and fro at the quiet little depot, that I could hardly recognize it. The train on our Washington branch was crammed with soldiers; I saw no familiar face except Mr. Edmundson, the conductor. There is so much travel over this route now that three or four trains are run between Washington and Barnett daily . . . We looked out eagerly for the first glimpse of home, and when the old town clock came into view a shout of joy went up from us returning wanderers. When we drew up at the depot amid all the bustle and confusion of an important military post, I could hardly believe that this was the same quiet little village we had left sleeping in the winter sunshine five months ago.*

"Long trains of government wagons were filing through the streets and we ran against squads of soldiers at every turn. Father met us at the depot, delighted to have us under protection once more, and the rest of the family, with old Toby frisking and barking for joy, were waiting for us at the street gate."

In Griffin, thirty miles due south of Atlanta, Kate Cumming, who had been a nurse in several Georgia military hospitals, decided she did not believe "any of the rumors," including the "mythical report of the surrender of General Lee's army." Nevertheless, she placed firm credence in current gossip that "the French fleet has had a battle with the Federal fleet, and whipped it, and taken New Orleans. All are much rejoiced. . . !"

Sixty miles southeast of Atlanta, at Macon, Virginia Clay and her husband, Clement C. Clay, had especial reason to evince shock at the word of Lincoln's murder. Formerly a senator from Alabama in the U.S. Congress, Clay had served in a similar capacity in the Confederacy and, as well, had been on missions to Canada for Jefferson Davis. His name had been associated with a mare's nest of lurid plots, including the burning of New York, the rescue of Confederate prisoners, and, most incredible of all, the poisoning of President Lincoln "with yellow fever germs."

Small wonder that "a kind of horror seized my husband when he realized the truth of the reports," his wife would write. "At first he had refused to credit them.

" 'It's a canard!' he said; but when at least he could no longer doubt, he exclaimed, 'God help us . . . if that be true, it is the worst blow that yet has struck at the South!' "

---

*On a sentimental journey to Washington, Georgia, the author searched in vain for "the old town clock" as well as the depot that long ago evoked "a shout of joy" from Fanny Andrews. At least one very elderly resident professed to have known Fanny but could not pinpoint her place of burial.

And in Atlanta, or what was left of that once thriving hub, S. P. Richards, a bookseller, wrote in his generally well-kept diary, "I fear it will prove the worst thing for the South that could have been done at this juncture. I am sorry that he was killed, but would to God that he had never been born. . . !"

The stun was felt equally throughout the Union. The reaction of a schoolgirl in Canandaigua, New York, was typical. Caroline Cowles Richards had first suspected that something was wrong when she looked out of the window "and saw a group of men listening to the reading of the morning papers . . . I feared from their silent, motionless interest that something dreadful had happened . . . oh, how horrible it is!"

She went downtown later in the morning to hear "everybody, small or great, rich or poor . . . talking low, with sad and anxious looks." But the passing hours did not dull her emotions.

"I have felt sick over it all day," she continued in her diary, "and so has everyone that I have seen. All seem to feel as though they had lost a personal friend, and tears flow plenteously. How soon has sorrow followed upon the heels of joy! One week ago tonight we were celebrating our victories with loud acclamations of mirth and good cheer. Now everyone is silent and sad and the earth and heavens seem clothed in sackcloth.

"The bells have been tolling this afternoon. The flags are all at half-mast, draped with mourning, and on every store and dwelling house some sign of the nation's loss is visible."

Then, the next morning, a cold "disagreeable" Easter, she went to church to find the pulpit and choir loft draped with flags and black crepe. After the singing of "Oh God Our Help in Ages Past," the minister, Mr. Daggett, "alluded so beautifully to the nation's loss, and prayed so fervently that the God of our fathers might still be our God through every calamity or affliction, however severe or mysterious. All seemed so deeply affected as though each one had been suddenly bereft of his best friend."

Similar grief and incredulity was manifested by Gideon Welles. Seated before his desk, four nights following Lincoln's death, he penned, "I have tried to write something consecutively . . . but I have no heart for it . . . sad and painful, wearied and irksome . . . the incidents are fresh in my mind and may pass away with me but cannot ever be by me forgotten."

Washington remained in shock. Colonel Henry L. Burnett, a judge advocate brought from Ohio to Washington by his mentor, Secretary Stanton, would report on the unreality of the scene that greeted him in the national capital: "All the public buildings and a large portion of the private houses were heavily draped in black. The people moved about the streets with bowed heads and sorrow-stricken faces as though some Herod had robbed each home of its first-born."

Finally, on Wednesday, April 19, the funeral: "imposing, sad, and sorrowful," it appeared to Gideon Welles. "All felt solemnity, and sorrowed as if they had lost one of their own household . . . Business was everywhere suspended and the people crowded the streets.

"The Cabinet met by arrangement in the room occupied by the President at the Treasury. We left a few minutes before meridian so as to be in the East Room at precisely 12 o'clock, being the last to enter . . ."

There were not many who could be accommodated in the East Room, but it appeared to one Maine-born correspondent that "half of the North was out on the streets and sidewalks, as bells, great and small, tolled from the far reaches of the city, and minute guns were fired with solemn monotony. Three batteries had been moved into the city for this purpose, as if to add immediacy to the constant banging from the many forts surrounding the capital. Black predominated, including what appeared to be women's black crepe dresses hanging from windows." (Indeed, this author's grandmother, who lived to a great age, recalled having been spanked by her mother for cutting up her Sunday best for just such a show of mourning.)

Altogether, wrote Noah Brooks for the Sacramento *Union,* it was a "sight" that "probably never will be forgotten . . . Long before the services in the White House were over, the streets were blocked by crowds of people thronging to see the procession, which moved from the House precisely at two o'clock . . . The day was cloudless, and the sun shone brilliantly upon cavalry, infantry, artillery, Marines, associations, and societies, with draped banners, and accompanied in their slow march by mournful dirges from numerous bands . . . in gorgeous uniforms . . . [with] all the pomp and panoply . . . then the funeral car, a large structure canopied and covered with black cloth, somewhat like the catafalque which had been erected in the White House.

"The casket rested on a high platform eight or ten feet above the level of the street. As it passed, many shed tears, and all heads were uncovered. The car was enclosed in a hollow square formed by a guard of honor consisting of mounted non-commissioned officers of various light artillery companies . . . then came the carriages for the family . . . the President, the Cabinet, the diplomatic corps, both Houses of Congress, and others.

"One noticeable feature of the procession was the appearance of the colored societies which brought up the rear, humbly . . . The coffin was taken from the funeral car and placed on a catafalque within the rotunda of the Capitol, which had been darkened and draped in mourning."

Under the recently completed dome the coffin rested, open, for two days. Brooks, allowed up the winding stairway to the dome's top, would write: "The sight was weird and memorable. Directly beneath me lay the casket in which the dead President lay at full length, far, far below; and, like black atoms moving over a sheet of gray paper, the slow-moving mourners, seen from a perpendicular above them, crept silently in two dark lines across the pavement of the rotunda, forming an ellipse around the coffin and joining as they advanced toward the eastern portal and disappeared." (Brooks was personally involved. He would assert that he had been chosen to replace John G. Nicolay as a Lincoln secretary. Nicolay never confirmed this.)

Records were set that day, not only in the numbers of mourners but in the volume of words flashed over the telegraph to New York. Nine wires carried 14,000 words an hour, primarily to newspaper offices, for a total approaching 100,000 words by late afternoon. Battlefield transmissions even at the height of the Peninsular campaign or such vast encounters as Antietam or Gettysburg, the climactic moments of Vicksburg, or the forty-eight hours preceding the fall of Richmond did not approximate the concentrations of grief pouring over the wires that April 19.

For two days the president reposed in state, until Friday morning, the twenty-first. No one kept accurate count of those filing by, although it was said that 25,000 viewed the remains the first evening, and as many as 3,000 passed in some one-hour periods.

On Friday, at 6:00 A.M., one week after Lincoln had been shot in Ford's Theatre, Gideon Welles left for the Capitol.

Scheduled to ride with the secretary of war, Welles nonetheless ordered his own carriage. In understatement, the secretary of the navy opined that Stanton was "in some respects unreliable" and likely would be late. This proved to be the case, but Welles, attesting to his own unpredictability, waited anyhow. The pair rode together and reached the rotunda "just as Mr. Gurley was commencing an earnest and impressive prayer."

Accompanying Lincoln's remains would be those of Little Willie, disinterred from Oak Hill Cemetery. That son, then twelve, had died in February 1862 of typhoid. The loss projected the father into recurrent depressions from which he seemed never to fully recover. He was haunted by visions. Only ten days before the assassination, Lincoln told of dreaming that he had walked down the stairs to the East Room and saw "the President . . . wrapped in funeral vestments." Soldiers on guard explained to him in his dream that "he was killed by an assassin."

A special train of seven cars, six of them double-deckers, waited at the Baltimore and Ohio station, only a few blocks up Pennsylvania Avenue from the Capitol. The whole train, including the engine *Edward H. Jones,* was heavily draped in black cloth. Even the locomotive's brass had been painted over. On board but hardly publicized was a somber little group, members of a new profession: embalmers. It was their challenge to keep the corpse from deteriorating in the long days ahead so that it would be presentable to viewers.

At 7:30 A.M. the engine's bell tolled as the train, under a plume of smoke, slowly steamed out toward Baltimore and, Welles noted, "the great prairies of the West." Ahead, along the line, there sounded the doleful notes of church and school bells, in villages and from lone belfries in the countryside. At crossings, small knots of mourners stood silently as they waved black streamers. In Baltimore, the coffin was uncovered for viewing.

"Those who had never seen Mr. Lincoln in life," wrote Laurence Gobright, of the Associated Press, "now saw him in the stern, shuddering reality of death."

That same evening, thousands braved a cold rain to view the train in Harrisburg. On Sunday, some 200,000 passed the casket in Independence Hall, Philadelphia. Women fainted and were carried away. One woman suffered a broken ankle from the jostling. According to the New York *Herald,* a young child was supposed to have been crushed to death.

Then on to New York City, where the populace was strangely hushed and wide-eyed. A rowdy metropolis that viewed public hangings with relish, Manhattan was still rebuilding from the fiery, murderous draft riots of the summer of 1863. Now the roughest elements, dressed in Sunday best, silently waited.

Even as the train tolled northward before the long sweep out to Springfield, Illinois, the last vestiges of a beaten Confederacy were crumbling. In a private residence in Charlotte, while the tree toads in the garden below chorused a song of spring, Confederate naval chief Stephen Mallory was penning to Jefferson Davis an obituary for a lost cause.

The "struggle," he wrote, following a cabinet meeting, had become "hopeless." The people were "weary of the war and desire peace." There existed "a vast army of deserters and absentees," and with the whole coast "and our ports . . . in the enemy's hands."

Worse, "our currency is nearly worthless, and will become utterly so with further military disasters . . . the pacification of the country should be as speedy as practicable."

Such gloom, added to that of other cabinet officers, inspired Davis to hasten a dispatch to General Johnston, approving his surrender. He could not, however, know that Stanton and President Johnson had already canceled those terms and, in fact, hurried General Grant to Raleigh to negotiate a surrender that would be a blueprint of that signed at Appomattox.

Characteristically, Stanton read nonexistent implications into Sherman's generosity, letting Congress as well as the press know that he thought the general who had cracked in two the Deep South could be little less than a traitor. When Sherman the redhead learned of this, he burst into a rage that his staff would long remember. Grant, the diplomat and the general's great admirer, managed to soothe his friend's injured feelings and tailor terms that were signed by Johnston on April 26 and dealt solely with military matters: "All acts of war on the part of the troops under General Johnston's command to cease from this date.

"All arms and public property to be deposited at Greensboro and delivered to an ordnance officer of the United States Army. Rolls of all the officers and men to be made in duplicate . . . the sidearms of officers and their private horses and baggage to be retained . . ."

Included in the general parole were two unlikely and certainly dissimilar officers, Admiral Raphael Semmes and Captain Henry Wirz. Wirz was the commandant of the notorious prison camp at Andersonville, Georgia. Semmes earlier in the war had captained the merchant raider *Alabama* and had been responsible for the burning of fifty-seven ships and the ransoming of fourteen others. The colorful if imperious admiral had spent the final days of the rebellion defending Danville, Virginia, Davis's final capital, with a ragtag force of 250 soldiers and sailors.

In the early hours of that same day, April 26, another and different drama was being enacted not far from Port Royal, Virginia (some fifty miles south of Washington), at the farm of John W. Garrett. Here, this night, the tree toads, as in Charlotte, also chorused. Their song, however, was disturbed by the galloping of horses as a detachment of the Sixteenth New York Cavalry pounded in.

Lieutenant Edward P. Doherty, with twenty-six men, had departed Washington a day and a half before on an urgent mission. He was accompanied by two emissaries of Colonel Lafayette C. Baker, formerly a special agent, now chief of the infamous National Secret Service Bureau. Baker was Secretary Stanton's chief and extraordinary detective.

The colonel, whose villainy was rather effectively masked behind a distinguished beard and semibland expression, had been notorious throughout the war for locking up suspects, only to seek reasons, much less lodge formal charges, at a later date, often much later. The two emissaries with Doherty were Luther Baker, a cousin of Lafayette, and Everett Conger.

John Wilkes Booth and his "accomplice" David Herold had been reported to be "somewhere between the Potomac and Rappahannock Rivers."

Late in the evening of the twenty-fourth, the trail led to the Garrett property. Uncooperative at first, Garrett, a Confederate sympathizer, admitted that Booth was in the barn after Doherty threatened to shoot him. The structure was surrounded. "Considerable conversation" ensued between the lieutenant and the actor after the latter refused shouted commands to surrender. Threatening to "burn the barn down," Doherty gave the fugitive, who sounded "very defiant," ten minutes.

At that point Booth called out "oh captain, there is a man here who wants to surrender awful bad!" The lieutenant opened the door and pulled an unarmed David Herold out by the wrists. Events accelerated. Conger, taking advantage of the slightly opened door, tossed a flaming torch onto the hay, even though none had ordered him to do so. Also, quite on his own initiative, Sergeant Boston Corbett, a former inmate of an insane asylum and a Bible thumper, spying Booth, took aim and fired. There would remain doubt as to whether he used a musket or a revolver.

The assassin fell, pierced through the neck.

"I entered the barn as soon as the shot was fired," Doherty would report, "and found that Booth had fallen on his back. Messrs. Conger and Baker, with some of my men, entered the barn and took hold of Booth. I proceeded with Herold to find a rope to secure him, there being no irons for that purpose."

The mortally wounded Booth was carried to the porch of the Garrett farmhouse in the glow of the hotly burning barn. A doctor was summoned. Although Booth was semiconscious, in pain, and paralyzed, there was consensus that he spoke a few times. Witnesses agreed that he muttered, "Tell Mother I die for my country," and that he pleaded as well, "Kill me! kill me!" Some but not all of those present believed he had asked for his hands to be lifted up, then despaired, "Useless! useless!"

Booth expired at approximately 3:00 A.M., about two hours after he had been shot. Doherty personally "sewed up the body in a blanket," and the group started the long journey back to Washington.

John Wilkes Booth, theatrical to the end, breathed his last as if in flaming fulfillment of his own madness. That same night of April 26, far to the west, on the Mississippi, another postscript to a long and wasteful war was being written in a greater fire.

Just before midnight, the 1,700-ton side-wheeler *Sultana* was plowing up the river past Memphis. Aboard were approximately 1,900 released federal prisoners (many from the pesthole of Andersonville), a scattering of Confederate prisoners, 236 civilian passengers, and a dozen women from the Christian Commission who had served as nurses in Vicksburg's hospitals.

By 2:00 A.M. Thursday, April 27, the *Sultana* was about three miles north of the city, passing what were generally known as Paddy's Old Hen and Chickens islands. Almost all slept, including a group on an upper deck which had spent most of the evening harmonizing such popular hymns as "Sweet Hour of Prayer." At that moment there was a tremendous blast from the engine room, as if a boiler had burst, and the whole steamer was ablaze.

"The upper decks," twenty-one-year-old Sergeant Chester Berry, from South Creek, Pennsylvania, recalled, "were a complete wreck and the dry casings of the cabins, falling in upon the hot bed of coal, were burning like tinder . . . The flames swept fiercely through the light wood."

An Indiana lieutenant, Joseph Taylor Elliott, raced to the hurricane deck, where "one of the boat's chimneys was down, and all the men were in commotion . . . I saw the men were jumping from all parts of the boat into the river. Such screams I never heard, twenty or thirty men were jumping off at a time, many lighting on those already in the water—until the river became black with men, their heads bobbing up like corks, and many disappearing never to appear again."

Elliott was lucky. After he leapt and surfaced, he grabbed a large piece of wreckage—a staircase—and hung on. From this odd refuge he watched the *Sultana,* incandescent, drifting away into the night, lower and lower, those still on board "singed off like flies." Then, with a hissing, the side-wheeler partly sank beneath the muddy waters.

The toll would never be exactly known. Of the approximately 2,200 on board, however, only 800 survived. One woman alone lived. She was Mrs. Harvey Ennis, who, it was said, rode the broad back of a mule to shore. Her husband (a lieutenant in the navy), her child, and her sister all perished.

Years later, another U.S. naval officer, who had been aboard a gunboat at Memphis, wrote that he had learned on good authority that die-hard Confederate agents had placed explosives in the coal bunkers. This sort of sabotage was not unknown during the conflict.

Others in the South—both soldiers and civilians—more fortunate than those who had embarked on the *Sultana,* were also returning home. The "shattered remains of Lee's army are beginning to arrive," wrote Fanny Andrews, in Washington, Georgia. "There is an endless stream passing between the transportation office and the depot, and trains are going and coming at all hours. The soldiers bring all sorts of rumors and keep us stirred up in a state of never-ending excitement."

In Virginia, homeowners were coming back. Among them was Sara Pryor, who had lived in and around Richmond during the war years. She started for one of her previous abodes, Cottage Farm, near Petersburg, which had been briefly one of General Lee's field headquarters. Various federal officers, including staffers of General Sheridan, had temporarily resided there. The wife of a federal general whom she had befriended furnished Mrs. Pryor, whose husband was Brigadier General Roger A. Pryor, of the Confederate Army, with an ambulance and four horses, "and we departed in fine style."

En route, she encountered "a line of weary-looking dusty Confederate soldiers, limping along, on their way to their homes. They stood aside to let us pass. I was cut to the heart at the spectacle."

The returning troops were all the shabbier as a result of a federal policy stripping them of uniform buttons, insignias, and, often, the uniform itself, which was as illegal as the Confederate flag. Sentries stood on street corners, with big scissors or their campaign knives in hand, waiting for the sight of the hated brass symbols of rebellion.

The adjutant general in Norfolk, for example, had issued orders "strictly" prohibiting the Southerners "from wearing any clothing, emblem or badge ever adopted, worn or ordered in or for any of the insurgent forces of the United States," and "every vestige of such emblem or badge" must be removed, with only forty-eight hours allowed for assuming "citizens dress." Since clothing was virtually unobtainable, the result was a mob of dejected, beaten soldiers wearing buttonless jackets, threadbare trousers, and other outer garments that had been hanging in someone's closet since 1861.

When Sara reached Cottage Farm she found a home "that no soldier, however forlorn, could have envied me." She continued: "A scene of desolation met my eyes. The earth was ploughed and trampled, the grass and flowers were gone, the carcasses of six dead cows lay in the yard, and filth unspeakable had gathered in the corners of the house. The evening air was heavy with the odor of decaying flesh. As the front door opened, millions of flies swarmed forth.

"Within was dirt and desolation. Pieces of fat pork lay on the floors, molasses trickled from the library shelves, where bottles lay uncorked. Nothing . . . was left in the house, except one chair out of which the bottom had been cut and one bedstead fastened together with bayonets. Picture frames were piled against the wall. I eagerly examined them. Every one was empty. One family portrait of an old lady was hanging on the wall with a sabre cut across her face."

In Charleston there were not only shattered and despoiled homes but also starvation. Colonel William Gurney, 127th New York Infantry, military commander of that half-ruined South Carolina city, wrote of the "influx" of people "from the interior" who had "consumed" virtually all food stocks, especially rice. In pursuing the unusual expedient of appealing "in the name of humanity" to the Produce Exchange of New York, Gurney stated, "Unless aid and money, food and clothing is sent to these people from the North, the suffering and destitution will be incalculable. The armies passing through the interior have, of necessity, either consumed or destroyed the wealth, the produce, and the very sustenance of the country."

And so April, a month unequalled in America's history, drew to a close. The Lincoln funeral train was moving ever nearer to its destination. All along the route were placards, banners, and hand-lettered signs frequently more eloquent in their emotion than in artistic execution. They ranged from simple statements—"The Nation Mourns"—to quotations from the Great Emancipator's second inaugural address.

The opening of his final paragraph had already gripped the Northern psyche: "With malice toward none, with charity for all, while firmness in the right as God gives us to see the right . . ."

A great deal of the traveling was at night. No matter the hour, according to Laurence Gobright, the Associated Press reporter, "crowds gathered on the roads to see the train on its onward progress; and whenever we halted, flowers were brought into the funeral car, and placed upon the coffin by delicate hands which had culled them for this purpose."

The buildings in Cleveland had been draped "heavily" in black, another observer reported. "The immense crowd was hourly added to by the trains and steamers arriving from different points.

"The scene when the procession started was very solemn and impressive. A slight rain fell, falling like tears on the remains of the good man."

From Friday the twenty-eighth through Sunday the thirtieth, the last day of April, the familiar tableaus were repeated as the train progressed under continuing rain: from Cleveland to Columbus, from Urbana, Ohio, to Richmond, Indiana, and on to Indianapolis. At Indianapolis, on Sunday, the correspondent for the Chicago *Tribune* listened to "the sweet, sad sounds of musical dirges, the occasional mutterings of muffled drums," while watching "the human figures passing and repassing . . . like spectres as the glare of lamps and torchlights send their shadows across the pale faces . . ."

The train wailed past the stabbings of habitation which were little known beyond the borders of Ohio and Indiana: Scioto, Hilliards, Pleasant Valley, Unionville, Milford, Woodstock, Valkenburgh, Cambridge, Dublin . . . Their names read like a history of the westward sweep of civilization, like the dreams and fears, like America itself.

> A lonesome train on a lonesome track
> Seven coaches painted black
> A slow train, a quiet train,
> Carrying Lincoln home again . . .
> —Millard Lampell

MAY

A Mournful Silence Is Abroad

At 1:17 A.M. Monday, May 1, the correspondent for the New York *Times* accompanying the funeral train would write, "We are now slowly passing the village of Whitestown. At least 200 persons including a number of young ladies are drawn up in line. The latter are dressed in white, with black sashes. Large bonfires are burning in the drizzling rain. This place is 21 miles from Indianapolis, and is the residence of farmers and drovers."

Just twenty minutes later he filed, "The people here have hung over the track, suspended from two uprights, a hundred variegated Chinese lanterns. Bonfires are also burning . . ." They cast their yellow glow, too, in Lebanon, Thorntown, Colfax, Clarks Hill, and on until, three hours later, "it is now early dawn and the citizens can be seen before their dwellings, which wear the usual emblems of mourning." Many had waved beside these very tracks as Lincoln journeyed to Washington for his first inaugural.

In profound tribute to nostalgia, a few of the same locomotives that had sped the newly elected president east four years earlier had been located, greased, draped in black, then hooked up to the coaches. None was in the same condition as in 1861. The ceaseless operations of war had taken toll. But they ran, puffing, wheezing, and creaking. At least one displayed a large portrait of Lincoln above the cowcatcher, flags draped beside its headlight.

29

Coaches were switched, too, as honor to the participating railroads, at times increasing the total length of the train to eight coaches. Only two would not be changed: one bearing the casket, which constantly over-flowed with flowers brought in by weeping women, and the other the guard of honor.

Some of the original train crewmen were back, solemn and silent. A few, hauled out of retirement, wore their faded, shrunken uniforms.

North to Lafayette, passed before daybreak, where the engine was changed: "Thousands were assembled . . . houses well illuminated; badges of mourning and draped flags were abundant; the bells were tolled, bonfires lit, and the funeral strains, sweet and solemn, came from the choir of many voices."

Then Michigan City, Indiana, on the lakefront where "a temporary structure under which the train stopped was erected with a succession of arches in the Gothic style, and from the crowning central point floated a draped national flag at half-mast."

The tour de force of the extravaganza was a woman "almost hidden in the folds of the national flag" representing "the Genius of America." She was among some thirty-six other young women dressed in white and wearing black scarves as in Whitestown. All in all, as the anonymous chronicler of the Michigan City proceedings concluded, "the military and civil" present were "affected to tears."

The same morning the train continued along Lake Michigan, past smoky, evil-smelling foundries and density of population squalor, leading almost without interruption or relief into Chicago. There throngs were already milling about the Court House—the simply curious, the overly morbid, and those, too, genuinely and unabashedly sorrowing, even as it had been the past eleven days since Washington. His fellow citizens of Illinois would have forty-eight hours to say goodbye to the Great Eman-cipator before Wednesday, when the casket would be borne the final miles south to Springfield, and home.

The heavily curtained White House remained shrouded in black, a somber tribute to the sixteenth president. The mood of Andrew Johnson, yet to take up residence in the executive mansion, was equally dark. On May 2, he offered rewards totaling almost $200,000 for the apprehension of Jefferson Davis and four other alleged conspirators. His proclamation, accorded wide distribution, read: "Whereas it appears from evidence in the Bureau of Military Justice that the atrocious murder of the late

President Abraham Lincoln and the attempted assassination of the Honorable Wm. H. Seward, Secretary of State, were incited, concerted and procured by and between Jefferson Davis, late of Richmond, Virginia, and Jacob Thompson, Clement C. Clay, Beverly Tucker, George N. Saunders, William C. Cleary and other rebels and traitors against the Government of the United States, harbored in Canada now therefore I Andrew Johnson, President of the United States, do offer and promise for the arrest of said persons or either of them within the limits of the United States so that they can be brought to trial . . ."

The reward for seizing Davis—$100,000—was tempting. Twenty-five thousand dollars was offered for each of the others, except for Cleary, "late clerk of Clement Clay," for whom a modest $10,000 was promised.

But who were these targets of presidential wrath, other than Davis and the less-known Clay, the onetime U.S. senator from Alabama?

Thompson, former U.S. secretary of the interior, had been the Confederacy's commissioner to Canada. Tucker had served as consul in Liverpool and in Paris. This was an unofficial post since neither Great Britain nor France maintained diplomatic relations with Richmond. Both governments had hedged the issue from the inception, hoping to reap the best out of both worlds: trade with North and South. Saunders had recently been on potential peace missions to Canada.

But Secretary Stanton saw nothing of a normal diplomatic nature in the dealings of Clay, Thompson, Tucker, and Saunders. He had convinced Johnson that all or most of the four men had met in Canada with the freewheeling Booth. Booth was reported to have been in much of the eastern United States and Canada, even in Nashville, if briefly, during Johnson's military governorship.

The news of the wanted persons radiated from Washington at least as speedily as that of Lincoln's murder. The Clement Clays heard it the next day in La Grange, Georgia, where Virginia Clay was boarding a train for Atlanta and, ultimately, Huntsville, Alabama, their family homestead. She was accompanied by a friend, Henrietta Hill, the wife of a former Georgia senator, Benjamin H. Hill, and their young son, Benny.

It was, as a matter of fact, not merely coincidence that General Sherman and Fanny Andrews, for just two other examples, had learned of major tidings in railway depots. Not only did the stations persist as crossroads of personal communications but, certainly in the South, these structures were virtually the only locations of telegraph offices.

"As the train swept into the city with a shrill scream," wrote Virginia Clay, "it was crowded with men and women of both races; so over-crowded, rather, that many clung to the platforms. There were shouts and a general Babel, which I did not understand and, as debarkation began, to these was added the bedlam of drunken laughter. When as near to the cars as the carriage would permit, I directed Benny Hill to go forward to the conductor and ask, 'what currency is needed to get to Macon?'

"The men seemed to understand that I had prompted the question, and called to me, 'gold or paperbacks, Madam?' "

The conductor then volunteered that both Macon and Atlanta were in federal hands. The former had been surrendered; the latter, having been abandoned by Sherman in December 1864, was now reoccupied. The trainman next proclaimed, certainly as a non sequitur, "One hundred thousand dollars is offered for Clement C. Clay, of Alabama!"

Then a "trembling" seized Virginia. She would not take the train to Atlanta. Instead, she hurried back to the Hill residence, where the Clays had been staying, to tell her husband. She found Clement "sitting quietly, deep in the conning of a thick volume." Present also was Secretary Mallory, who had been in Abbeville, a few miles north, where, as a matter of fact, he had just written his letter of resignation.

Though at first the senator "blanched" at the news, he recovered his composure and finally declared, "As I am conscious of my innocence, my judgment is that I should at once surrender to the nearest Federal authorities."

Virginia found that she "could not restrain my sobs."

The others sought in the proclamation heard it in Montreal and reacted with affronted innocence. "I did not know that any such person as J. Wilkes Booth existed," Tucker replied on May 4 in a letter to the Montreal *Leader*. He and Saunders added, in a joint letter, "Your [Andrew John-son's] proclamation is a living, burning lie, known to be such by yourself, and all your surroundings, and all the hired perjurers in Christendom shall not deter us from exhibiting to the civilized world your hellish plot to murder our Christian president . . . !"

Then the pair, along with William Cleary, the clerk, left for Nova Scotia. However, even without these three, Clement Clay, or the enfant terrible of the conspiracy quest, Jefferson Davis, the machinery of justice—or revenge?—was turning in Washington. Six in addition to David Herold, captured at the Garrett farm, and Mrs. Mary Surratt, boardinghouse owner, had been arrested in connection with the assassination. They were held manacled and, most of the time, hooded. Trial before a military court was scheduled to commence in a week.

But first the dead must be laid to rest. And this happened on Thursday, May 4, in a vault in Oak Ridge Cemetery, Springfield, Illinois. Under bright, warm skies, tens of thousands stood silently "as the corpse was borne from the State House . . . amid tears and sorrow . . . There were double- and single-starred generals who had won distinction on many diverse and hotly-fought fields. . . ," according to one of those present, B. F. Morris. Curiously, the marshal-in-chief of the procession was one of the president's least successful military leaders, the unpredictable Major General Joseph Hooker, of Massachusetts, removed from command of the Army of the Potomac following the debacle at Chancellorsville in 1863. In a fit of temperament, Fighting Joe the next year stamped out of an incomplete Atlanta campaign.

The waiting vault was built of hard, white limestone, quarried in the area, with one immense slab serving as the hinged door. Situated on the left bank of a brook, it fit well into the pastoral aspect of the area, which was distinguished by farms, orchards, and gardens shaded by many towering elms and smaller oaks.

"On the high bank above the vault," Morris continued, "were thousands upon thousands of people, and on the hillside across the stream from the vault there were as many more, and then the narrow valley was overflown with 'a sea of upturned faces.' On the left of the vault sat the choir of two hundred voices, and on the right was the platform, upon which sat the clergy who were to conduct the exercises. Facing the vault were the congressional and Illinois committees, Governors of States and other delegations, and nearer still the pallbearers and family friends, and on either side of the door the relatives . . .

"The coffin, in a receptacle of plain black walnut and resting in the centre of its black bier, was hidden in the beauty of flowers."

When the strains of Handel's "Dead March" from the oratorio *Saul* at last were stilled, the obsequies commenced, with both clergy and laity participating. The Reverend Matthew Simpson, bishop of the Methodist Episcopal Church and a familiar visitor to the White House, delivered the principal eulogy. It proved an exceedingly long one, the preacher-educator being known for his powerful if seemingly interminable sermons. It was the apogee of his ministry, for how often was Caesar laid to rest?

From the bishop's Niagara of hyperbole, however, one phrase stuck in the memories of many who were yet listening: "A mournful silence is abroad upon the land . . ."

Finally, Lincoln's minister, Dr. Phineas Gurley, who had been at the bedside when the president expired, pronounced benediction. The services were over. With the last words and the final notes, a fevered chapter, though not yet an era—or decade—in American history was clapped shut forever.

And far to the east that Thursday night, a different sort of amen was sounded as regiment after regiment of the Army of the Potomac noisily broke camp preparatory to marching through Richmond, where the flags were at half mast, and homeward. The spectacle commenced the next morning and would continue for ten days, ending with the climactic passage of General Sherman's sinewy army.

It was, as a reporter for the Richmond *Whig* wrote, "the grandest, most imposing and at the same time the most pleasing of anything witnessed by the citizens . . . since the war began." Many people stood on the streets to observe the "Blue Line," the historian Asbury Christian would write, which "stretched from Manchester [south of the James River] across the pontoon bridge on Seventeenth Street, up Main and out Broad. They marched nearly all day."

But not all agreed with the gentleman from the federalized *Whig*. Some, perhaps many, residents of the fallen citadel of the Confederacy remained behind shuttered windows, even as they had during the first hours of the occupation. Others stood on the dirt sidewalks to watch impassively. Yet others pursued their daily activities, such as trying to find food, seemingly oblivious to the tramping legions. A very few would later boast that they had spat upon their conquerors, then somehow eluded the provost marshal who sought to punish them for their impudence.

For two days in cold, driving rain, according to Lieutenant Millett S. Thompson, a twenty-eight-year-old officer with the Thirteenth New Hampshire Regiment, there thumped through Richmond "an almost uninterrupted stream of cavalry, artillery, infantry teams and ambulances. A warworn and weather-beaten host—about 40,000 troops are in Richmond.

"Many of these troops having no arms march with old brooms, and hundreds of little broom-corn clothes brushes are stuck in the muzzles of muskets and borne aloft—the broom the emblem of the clean sweep. War songs are sung in the very grandest of choruses—by the victorious warriors themselves."

On Saturday the sixth, from 9:00 A.M. to 5:00 P.M., in spite of the fact that "the movement is very slow," about 50,000 additional troops marched through the city . . . On Monday Sherman's hardened fighters started arriving and occupied three days in their passage; "they have many pack mules with them carrying the men's baggage as well as that of the officers. On one of these mules are riding two little girls, with light hair, blue eyes and fair complexion—liberated slaves to be taken north and educated."

Crowds of Richmonders, black and white, on balconies and even rooftops listened to the bands play such stirring songs as "Old John Brown" and "Marching through Georgia."

Dignified and quiet, too imposing physically to be inconspicuous, Sherman spent a night at the Spotswood Hotel. He brought along his own whiskey, with no confidence in the depleted stocks of that famed hostelry. At the head of some 9,000 cavalrymen, was a man if not Sherman's rival, certainly his equal as a fighter; the flamboyant Philip H. "Little Phil" Sheridan.

Though many of the South agreed with Dr. John H. Claiborne, Confederate surgeon in charge of the Petersburg hospitals, that "desolation was left in the wake of the Federal Army," he also experienced mixed emotions at the departure of this disciplined body. He wrote: "I saw the last file of these Federal troops leave the city with regret, and when I expressed my regret to a friend, he seemed surprised, and said that he could not understand my position. I asked him to await events."

His neighbor Sara Pryor reflected somewhat the same emotion, taking note of the emptiness which had come into their existence: "We found it almost impossible to take up our lives again. All the cords binding us to the past were severed, beyond the hope of reunion. We sat silently looking out on a landscape marked here and there by chimneys standing sentinel over blackened heaps, where our neighbors had made happy homes. Only one remained, Mr. Green's, beyond a little ravine across the road."

She was echoed by an acquaintance, Mary Boykin Chesnut, now in Camden, South Carolina, with her husband, General James Chesnut. Mrs. Chesnut saw "nothing but solitude, nothing but tall blackened chimneys to show that any man has ever trod the road before. This is Sherman's track. It is hard not to curse him. I wept incessantly at first. The roses of the gardens are already hiding the ruins.

"My husband said nature is a wonderful renovator. He tried to say something else and then I shut my eyes and made a vow that if we were a crushed people, crushed by weight, I would never be a whimpering, pining slave . . ."

Left behind in Raleigh, Major General Jacob D. Cox, Sherman's Twenty-third Corps commander, assessing the mood of the North Carolinians, wrote on May 8: "I find the people here have been divided into the following classes. First, the original secessionists who were very few in this State. Second, the class of conservative politicians who were opposed to secession but who thought they must go with their State, and who became violent rebels when the war was once begun. Third, a class of still more conservative men who have remained firm in their opposition to the rebel government, though they have not dared to avow adherence to the United States. Fourth, the truly and openly loyal. This last class has been very small indeed—all prominent men of that way of thinking being driven from the State or imprisoned.

"I have no doubt, however, that a large part, probably a large majority of the people of North Carolina were opposed to secession and have remained so at heart . . . All the people here admit that slavery is ended . . . The great cause of the war being removed and the institutions of the country made homogeneous, there is no danger that anything can disturb the Government again, and it can therefore afford to be magnanimous."

Another ranking army officer, Major General Joshua L. Chamberlain, formerly in command of the Twentieth Maine Regiment, bivouacked his men for the night on his way to Washington and the Grand Review. Brevetted for his gallant fighting at Five Forks in the closing hours of the Petersburg campaign, in which he was severely wounded, Chamberlain was now leading the First Division of the Fifth Corps. His men had paused near Hanover Court House, near Richmond, scene of much bitter fighting in June 1862 during Major General George B. McClellan's abortive Peninsular campaign. He would write: "At about midnight when the tired camp was still, the sentinel in front of my bivouac spoke nervously, saying there was something strange going on about my horse not far away in the rear of us . . . amidst a little growth of scrubby pines . . . Before I reached him, my foot crushed through the breast bones of a body half buried by the fallen pine cones and needles so long undisturbed, now gone back mostly ashes to ashes.

"I found that the horse, pawing the earth within the scope of his picket rope, had rolled out two skulls and scattered the bones of bodies he had unearthed, and was gazing at the white skulls as if lost in doubt . . . It was a weird, uncanny scene, the straggling, uncompanionable pines, the night brooding still and chill; black, lowering clouds now massing, now rifting . . . the white skulls mocking life.

"The horse was not easily pacified—not until I had gathered up the menacing skulls and the outlying limbs too, and laid them where I saw glimmering amidst the dusky debris of the pines other bones as if adrift on a Sargasso sea."

In the morning, the soldiers packed up the bones in cracker boxes, along with personal trinkets, keepsakes, and shreds that might help in individual identification. No soldier, Union or Confederate, wore or carried identification badges or papers of any sort. Only his wallet or letters, usually unfinished, offered a clue. The dog tag was far, far over the horizon.

The troops continued northward. Other soldiers, left behind on garrison duty, were also tidying the final remains of war, according to the Richmond *Whig*: ". . . For some days past details have been made from the colored troops, who have been sent out with entrenching tools, to the battlefields around Richmond and employed in the burial of Union dead lying there exposed for a year past. Several hundred skeletons were put under the sod upon the battlegrounds of Gaines Mill (adjoining Hanover Court House) and Cold Harbor and other battlefields are being attended to in their turn."

And while the Army of the Potomac surged home, other events were taking place, to the north and to the south. In Washington, President Johnson, determined to crush every remaining vestige of the rebellion, issued a proclamation on May 10 ordering all "insurgent cruisers" to be rounded up, with a warning to other countries that might offer them sanctuary. There were but two of consequence: one, the ram *Stonewall*, happened to be en route to Havana to surrender, and the other, the big raider *Shenandoah*, oblivious to Appomattox, was on the prowl in the Pacific. Lieutenant Commander James Waddell, a hard-bitten North Carolinian, was certain that the Confederacy would be well pleased.

At the same time, Johnson revealed his interest in restoring Virginia to an active place in the Union. In addition to nullifying any wartime "acts and proceedings" on the part of Virginia's civilian or military officials, establishing federal post offices, and giving the U.S. secretaries of war and the navy appropriate jurisdictions, the president appointed Francis H. Pierpoint the state's interim administrator. Formerly governor of the newly created state of West Virginia, Pierpoint (his name is also spelled Pierpont) had been "waiting in the wings" in Alexandria for just such a mission.

The day of the provisional governor's arrival in Richmond, the windows of the Spotswood and Monumental hotels were described as "crowded" with women from the North waving handkerchiefs. The executive mansion, formerly Jefferson Davis's home, was decorated with flags and flowers. Die-hard Southerners meanwhile remained behind curtained windows as if, by one estimation, "in mourning."

Also on May 10, the military trial of eight persons charged in the assassination of President Lincoln commenced in the Washington (also called U.S.) arsenal grounds.

The national capital used two primary prisons: the Old Capitol and the Washington Penitentiary. The former, on First and A streets, N.E., across from the east front of the Capitol, traced its genesis to 1800, when it was a tavern and boardinghouse. After the British, in the War of 1812, put a torch to the Capitol, symbol of democracy, the tavern was renovated by popular subscription and enlarged. It would serve temporarily as the halls and chambers of Congress. James Monroe took the oath of office in 1817 before the structure's arched brick entrance, while painters and carpenters still were finishing work inside.

Known not without reason as Baker's Bastille, the Old Capitol had been fully booked throughout the war in testament to Lafayette Baker's ceaseless, frenetic angling for spies, federal deserters, officers charged with stealing U.S. government property, Confederates or their sympathizers, in fact anyone whose looks were unpalatable to Secretary Stanton or his zealous chief of detectives.

Habeas corpus had been suspended formally in 1863, although its effectiveness had become shaky with the fall of Fort Sumter. There was scant if any legal succor for those locked up and, as often happened, forgotten. Inevitably, the Old Capitol overflowed. Pressed into service was Carroll Annex, just across East Capitol Street, also facing First Street and the Capitol. It was named, inappropriately enough, for Charles Carroll, of Maryland, a signer of the Declaration of Independence.

Consisting of five well-built, joined houses, the confines were known by at least some of the inmates as Duff Greene's Row, perhaps for an officer temporarily in the Washington adjutant's office, Major Oliver Duff Greene. But the tag might as well have been dubiously honoring an old politician, Duff Greene. Speedily, Carroll Annex rivaled its mother warren in overcrowdedness, sparsity of even rudimentary furniture, meager nourishment, a soaring rat and roach population, and overall darkness and gloom by night and day.

A Baltimore woman, Virginia Lomax (who also used the pseudonym Maria Miller), spent a few weeks in Carroll, having been arrested merely because she was visiting a cousin. The prison, she would write, was "devoted to the use of such unfortunate females as aroused either the ire or suspicion of the Government, with the occasional addition of a southern governor and cotton-planter, prisoner of state. One wing of the building was appropriated [for families] and the other contained, for the most part, horse thieves, fraudulent contractors, unlucky blockade-runners,* and a variety of nondescripts; in short, a company more numerous than select. Such was Carroll prison."

The most notorious guest in Carroll and Old Capitol was the admitted Confederate spy Rose O'Neal Greenhow, who mobilized her social savoir faire and entrée to eavesdrop on Washington officialdom. The personable widow had been rather a favorite at the White House. But when it was learned that she had passed information on troop movements to Confederate General Pierre Beauregard before the debacle of Bull Run, in July 1861, Rebel Rose was placed under house arrest in her 16th Street mansion.

Even so, the premises became such a hotbed of intrigue, with those of a Southern mind coming and going at will, that it was known as Fort Greenhow. Lacking only were band concerts and morning colors. This was too much. Rose, with her nine-year-old daughter and namesake, was taken to Old Capitol.

She continued, with the use of a crude cipher, to communicate with

---

*This could have been true of U.S. captains, such as those trained at Annapolis, but the foreign-born were speedily repatriated. The ship and cargo, which were more important, were confiscated.

her beloved secessionists. Yet, with all his toughness and sometimes rabid defense of the Union, Stanton became queasy at the thought of bringing Rose Greenhow to the trial she had openly courted. Instead, in June 1862, he hustled her south, through enemy lines. She continued to England, where she wrote of her exploits.

Another who tarried at Old Capitol and its annex was the hillbilly from West Virginia Belle Boyd. She proved to be more of a flashy fabricator of cloak-and-dagger exploits than a true secret agent.

Far larger, and newer by some two decades than Old Capitol, the Washington Penitentiary was located within the high brick walls of the arsenal, on a jut of land known as Greenleaf Point, beside the Eastern Branch River (now the Anacostia), which flows into the Potomac.

Here the defendants faced their accusers. The former included David Herold, George A. Atzerodt, Lewis Payne (or Powell), Michael O'Laughlin, Edward Spangler, Samuel A. Arnold, Dr. Samuel Mudd, and Mary Surratt. She owned the shabby boardinghouse (still standing in what is now Washington's Chinatown) at 541 H Street, N.W., where, it was alleged, the plot had its inception under the aegis of a sometime visitor, John Wilkes Booth. All, according to the charges, were mortally tainted with rebellion.

Mary Surratt had been moved from Carroll Annex to a cell in the penitentiary. Although she was not hooded as the other prisoners were, she may have been manacled, or ironed. There was conflicting evidence on this. At Carroll Annex she had been treated better and allowed considerable freedom to move about. Virginia Lomax thought of her as "an angel of mercy," as she read newspapers to other prisoners, sometimes shared her own scanty rations, and generally tried to cheer them.

Her twenty-six-year-old daughter Anna, or Annie, a talented pianist who stayed at her mother's side, was far more nervous. Virginia lay awake nights listening to Anna's "pitter-patter" of footsteps.

Noah Brooks, among the reporters present as the trial began, entered "an old-fashioned brick building," then a "bare room on the ground floor, where sat a couple of staff officers receiving the credentials of those who applied for admission." He moved through successive checks of his personal pass to the third-floor courtroom. He continued: "It was an apartment about twenty-five feet wide and thirty feet long, the entrance being at the end opposite the penitentiary. Looking into the room, one saw that it was divided lengthwise into two parts, the portion on the right being occupied by the court, sitting around a long, green-covered table, General Hunter at one end, and Judge Advocate General Holt with his assistants at the other . . ."

Joseph Holt also headed the army's Bureau of Military Justice. There were many who thought its very name a contradiction and distortion. A Kentuckian and henchman of Secretary Stanton's, Holt had served not quite three months as secretary of war at the conclusion of President Buchanan's administration. He had been referred to, not idly, as a hanging judge; he was said to have observed, "There have not been enough Southern women hanged in this war."

Heading this special military commission—in effect a court-martial—was stern-faced Major General "Black" David Hunter, its president. Severely wounded at Bull Run, he distinguished himself, in a way, by plundering historic Washington College, at Lexington, Virginia, deep in the Shenandoah. His hard-riding cavalrymen carried off not only books and scientific instruments but also a laboratory skeleton, or so the irate college fathers charged.

Hunter, thought George Alfred Townsend, of the New York *World,* was at best "partisan . . . coarse." Nevertheless Hunter was a complex person who had, for example, provoked Southern enmity by integrating blacks into his units and forming all-Negro regiments.

Most recently, he had been the senior military officer on the funeral train. He was chosen, perhaps, because as a mere major he had escorted Lincoln from Springfield for the 1861 inaugural. As a general, however, he had incurred presidential displeasure by precipitately freeing slaves as his troops advanced. In the early days of the conflict, the White House reiterated that the primary purpose of the war was to preserve the Union.

Other members of the group included Major General Lewis "Lew" Wallace, described as "small, nervous"; Brevet Major General August V. Kautz, one of the first cavalry officers to reach Richmond; Brigadier General Robert S. Foster; Brevet Brigadier General James A. Elkins; Brigadier General T. M. Harris, distinguished by a remarkably long beard; Brevet Colonel C. H. Tompkins; and Lieutenant Colonel David R. Clendenin. None, at least of the officers of general rank, could be considered to be amply endowed with human kindness.

"The part of the room which was not occupied by the court," Noah Brooks continued, "was railed off, and was taken up with a few seats for reporters and spectators generally, who were crowded confusedly about, and rested as best they could against the bare, whitewashed walls of the room.

"At the farther end of the apartment was a wooden railing, behind which on a narrow, raised platform sat the accused men, all in a solemn row, with an armed soldier sitting between every two persons. At the left-hand corner behind them was a heavy iron door opening into the corridor along which were the cells of the prisoners. Each one of the accused was manacled hand and foot, and sat grimly against the wall, facing the court and the witnesses, the witness-stand being a raised box in the center of the room."

Both Brooks and fellow newsman Townsend, who used the name Gath in his war reporting, evinced consuming interest in the defendants' personalities. Townsend labeled the group "a clumsy set of knaves . . . Not one, if we except Dr. Mudd, seems to have intellect enough to conceive, carry on, or execute a plot of this kind."

Atzerodt (also known as Atzerot and Atzerodtt), Townsend was convinced, "is the meanest face of the lot . . . capable of crawling, damnable infamy, a vulgar and mercenary conspirator." Believed to have been assigned to murder Andrew Johnson, Atzerodt obtained no better pedigree from Noah Brooks: "small and sinewy, with long, dark-brown hair, dark blue and unsteady eyes . . . the complete personification of a low and cunning scoundrel."

The thirty-three-year-old Port Tobacco, Maryland, carriage-maker was known as a hard drinker. He had earned his living by ferrying both Northerners and Southerners across the Potomac as well as lesser waterways.

David Herold, twenty-three, perhaps younger, who surrendered at the Garrett farm, possessed the mind of a retarded child. He was a "boyish-looking young fellow . . . a kind of Plebian lot of followers," according to Townsend. He was, as well, "small, dark," by the measure of Brooks, with "a stooping figure, protruding teeth, and a vulgar face." Herold was unemployed, a "drifter."

Beside Herold sat Lewis Payne, or Lewis Powell, or Louis Paine Powell—he answered to several names. However one might address him or he labeled himself, this "young giant," as Brooks dubbed him, was doomed for his murderous attack on Secretary Seward. The youth, a preacher's son with a face, Brooks added, that would "defy the ordinary physiognomist," had been wounded in Pickett's charge at Gettysburg.

Taken prisoner, he walked out of a Union hospital in Baltimore, returned to the Confederate Army, then deserted.

His cardinal mistake would prove a mortal one. Carrying a pickax in the clumsy pose of an out-of-work laborer, Payne returned to the Surratt boardinghouse. One of the swarming detectives there arrested him. None could disagree with Townsend's profile: ". . . A desperado, ferocious, stolid, bestial . . . He seems to pay little attention to what goes on, manifests no emotion."

Unable to obtain employment, Payne found his sole diversion in hunting. His attention span was as diffuse and chancy as his several names and their inconstant spelling. Not surprisingly, he gravitated to the sharper intellect of Booth, whom he deferentially addressed as Cap.

Brooks speculated that a California vigilante committee, in 1849, probably would have hanged Michael O'Laughlin "on general principles." The supposition was that he had targeted Stanton or Grant for assassination, as Booth had Lincoln. "His large eyes, black and wild, were never still, but appeared to take in everything within the room."

And the reporter Townsend considered O'Laughlin "more of a southerner in appearance; his expression is dark and vindictive; he stands abundantly convicted of a general knowledge of the plot . . ." But it was apparent from the start that the generals and other officers, sitting fiercely in judgment, did not accord O'Laughlin the same degree of attention they did certain others brought before them.

Spangler, the alcoholic stage carpenter at Ford's Theatre, was in his middle years, "heavily-built, sandy in complexion and slovenly in appearance." Brooks added that he was "a weak creature . . . under the influence of imminent bodily fear." He was accused only because he held Booth's horse at various times. From this dual role as stable hand, Holt deduced that Spangler was at least an acquaintance of Booth's.

Samuel Arnold, twenty-eight, with the misfortune to have carried on a correspondence with Booth—"Dear Sam" letters were found in some quantity—had a habit, Brooks noticed, of "looking out of the window upon the pleasant sky and treetops beyond." It did not matter that one of Arnold's letters asserted he wished to "give up the job"; he remained "as uneasy as a caged whelp." Arnold, who had been seized at Fort Monroe, "leaned his head on the rail before him . . . lounged against the wall, or rested his chin on his breast."

It was generally understood that Arnold had been considered a player only in the original, fantastic plot, whereby Lincoln was to have been abducted rather than slain. Arnold would wait on stage and somehow catch the president after other conspirators had contrived to throw the tall man over the box.

Dr. Mudd, forty-five, who set Booth's fractured ankle, or leg bone, "had mild blue eyes, a good broad forehead, ruddy face, hair scanty and thin, a high head, and a sanguine temperament," according to Townsend. The physician sat in shirt sleeves, "with a white handkerchief knotted loosely about his neck, and attentively regarded the proceedings with the air of a man who felt sure of himself. Actually, Samuel Mudd was a southern Maryland farmer who had not practiced medicine for some years.

Mary Jenkins Surratt was the forty-eight-year-old widow of John Surratt, Sr., postmaster at Surrattsville, Maryland. He was a Southern sympathizer who had provided overnight lodgings to Confederate couriers en route to Canada. He died, primarily of alcoholism, early in 1862. Mary, deeply veiled, her face turned to the wall, was "slowly and constantly fanning herself," wrote Brooks. "She was a dark looking, fleshy, placid and matronly woman."

Although all but Arnold and O'Laughlin had met in Surratt's boarding-house, it could not be established that any of those charged as conspirators had actually been among her regular boarders. But one who was a resident, Louis Weichmann, a War Department clerk, was marked as a star witness for the prosecution.

The flamboyant Booth, who traveled extensively in the East and in Canada, preferred the more fashionable hostelries such as the Kirkwood or the National. His speculative ventures included the rapidly sprouting oilfields of Pennsylvania, near which he had become a familiar figure, especially in the bars. Herold, for one, would not have lodged at Surratt's since he spent more time in Baltimore than in the nation's capital.

In many ways, the military commission, appointed by Secretary Stanton and rubber-stamped by President Johnson as well as by Attorney General James Speed, presented no more impressive a mien than the defendants themselves. It is "to be regretted," mused Townsend, "that the War Department will put soldiers into the position of jurists."

These officers and Judge Holt, Noah Brooks added, "sat about in various negligent attitudes, and a general appearance of disorder was evident. Many ladies were present, and their irrepressible whispering was a continual nuisance to the reporters."

The preliminaries were over. The charges had been read. One by one, the prisoners, through those who represented them, plead not guilty. They did so even though Payne, Herold, and possibly Atzerodt understood but imperfectly why the state was angry with them, individually and collectively. The commission adjourned, with many long and weary days of testimony ahead.

Down the steps judges and spectators filed out into the dazzling sunshine of early May, where the robins sang. The prisoners were led through other exits to their cells, to their chains and their hoods. The latter nicety had been ordered by Edwin Stanton, although in a flickering gesture of humanity he consented to a hole being cut for breathing and eating—such as the prisoners were fed.

To the south, where it was already like summer, some leaders of the lost cause gave up willingly. Others had to be taken at gunpoint. Clement C. Clay made good his promise to seek out federal authorities. With his wife, he arrived in Atlanta, where Virginia found "the city a pandemonium: soldiers patrolling the streets, drums beating and vans, loaded with furniture, moving up and down the avenue . . . In our desire to proceed as rapidly as possible we accosted a soldier.

" 'Where is Colonel [Beroth B.] Eggleston?' Colonel Phillips [who accompanied the Clays] asked.

" 'There he is, within ten feet of you!' was the reply. Colonel Phillips thereupon approached the officer in command [of the post of Atlanta] and said to him, 'I have a distinguished friend here, Mr. Clement C. Clay, of Alabama, who is on his way, voluntarily, to surrender himself.'

"On hearing my husband's name, Colonel Eggleston approached us and held out his hand, saying: 'Is it possible, Mr. Clay, you are the man who is making such a stir in the land? I am not surprised at your surrender. I knew your record through my Senators, Pugh and Pendleton, of Ohio. You've done the right thing, sir, and I hope you'll soon be a free man.'

"Mr. Clay, surprised at the Federal Colonel's magnanimity, turned and presented him to me. He extended his hand. It took it. It was the first Yankee hand I had touched since we had left Minnesota, four years before. The colonel assured us it was impossible for us to proceed that night to Macon. 'It will be best for you,' he said, 'to spend the night at the Kimball House.' " (Virginia Clay's memory was playing tricks. The Kimball did not grace the modest skyline of Atlanta until the 1870s. She was a frequent visitor to the city during the next decades and, since she did not publish her memoirs until 1904, her confusion is not surprising.)

" 'But the city is in a tumult and, as Mrs. Clay is with you, I will have a guard that you may not be disturbed.' When we were ready to retire, two soldiers appeared, with muskets in hand, and took their stand, one at each side of our chamber door, where they remained until the next morning.

"Shortly after breakfast, Colonel Eggleston presented himself. His manner was courteous. 'As times are so turbulent,' he said, 'I think it best that I should detail a guard to accompany you to Macon.' "

With no inclination to surrender or, indeed, to offer any token of sacrifice, Jefferson Davis had been pushing through Georgia, aiming for Alabama, like a homing pigeon. With so large a reward—$100,000—for his delivery, the president who now boasted no domain had reason for flight. And it was scant solace that he was considered more desirable alive than in a pine box.

Accompanying him were his wife, children, Postmaster John R. Reagan, and former Texas governor Frank Lubbock, who had recently been on the gubernatorial staff. The flight southward was "no holiday excursion," according to Micajah H. Clark, a confidential secretary to Jefferson Davis, and "with the dusty roads, weary riding, and generally coarse fare . . . I saw the government, with its personnel, slowly but surely falling to pieces. Grief, sorrow and often indignation was felt and expressed by the immediate party among themselves, but the face of the Great Chief was serene, courteous and kind always, beguiling the tedium of the weary miles with cheerful conversation, reminiscences and anecdotes . . . I never heard one hasty or petulant expression escape his lips . . ."

By the evening of May 9, the party was encamped in a wooded area outside of Irwinville, some fifty miles east of Albany, Georgia, and eighty-five miles south of Macon. A light spring drizzle was falling.

Davis had abandoned his cavalry escort several days earlier since the horses "gave out." This in spite of rumors that "marauders" were dogging the group's tracks. They could be Southern bandits, or "bushwhackers," erstwhile Confederate soldiers or deserters, even "bummers" from Sherman's army who stayed behind to plunger. All were quite capable of murder.

Davis's pursuers, however, were of considerably higher caliber and in more formidable numbers than marauders. Two days earlier, on the seventh, in Macon, Major General James H. Wilson, commanding the Cavalry Corps of Sherman's Military Division of the Mississippi, had received intelligence that President Davis might be in the vicinity of Irwinville. The commander of his Second Division, Colonel Robert H. G. Minty, immediately ordered a detachment—about 450 officers and men—from the Fourth Michigan Cavalry, under Colonel Benjamin D. Pritchard, on the trail.

"At 5 a.m. of the 9th instant," Pritchard would report, "I moved my command out in the direction of Abbeville, which place I reached at 3 p.m., and where I discovered the first traces of the object of our search. Here I learned that a train of twelve wagons and two ambulances (as reported) had crossed the Ocmulgee River at Brown's Ferry, one mile and a half above Abbeville, about 12 o'clock on the previous night; had stopped at Abbeville long enough to feed their animals, and moved on again before daylight in the direction of Irwinville.

"I had met the lieutenant-colonel of the First Wisconsin Cavalry (Henry Harnden, I believe), who informed me that he with a force of 70 men was following on the track of the train, and that his men were from one to two hours in advance. As Colonel Harnden had ample force to cope with that supposed to be with the train, I decided not to move on the same road with him, and continued my course three miles farther down the river."

With 128 men and seven officers, Pritchard galloped off at 4:00 P.M. through a "blind woods road" toward Irwinville. He reached there about 1:00 A.M. on the tenth. Shortly afterward, Harnden, not aware of how close he was to Pritchard's forces, halted to graze his horses in the same area.

At dawn, Davis was awakened by cavalry deploying around his encampment. He informed his wife, who "implored me to leave her at once . . . I picked up what was supposed to be my 'raglan,' a waterproof light overcoat without sleeves. As I started, my wife thoughtfully threw over my head and shoulders a shawl."

At once, as Pritchard wrote, there was confusion, "firing about 100 rods in rear of the camp and across a narrow swamp. I immediately ordered all my forces forward."

Harnden did the same, resulting in an "unfortunate collision," as he would term it, of the two Union forces. Several of the troops were killed, others wounded.

Davis was captured, wearing his raglan, which inspired the belief that he was disguised as a woman. Reagan, the postmaster, brandished his revolver, then quickly decided that surrender was more prudent.

Thus ended the death agonies of the Confederate government, more in a whimper than even a gasp.

The captives were led first to Hawkinsville, four miles above Irwinville, where they camped the next afternoon, the eleventh. At Macon, lightly brushed by Sherman's legions, the derelicts of the Confederacy were joined by Clay; Alexander H. Stephens, late vice president; and others. Stephens, who had not seen Jefferson Davis since January, was no die-hard secessionist, in fact had gone along with fellow Southerners with heavy heart.

The party now embarked down the Savannah River on a tugboat for Hilton Head, South Carolina, where they would be transported up the coast to Fort Monroe. Then the ranking refugees would complete a wide, meandering circle that had commenced with the flight from Richmond.

"We were all crowded together in a small space on deck," wrote Stephens. "The night was cool, the air on the water damp, and I was suffering, as I had been for hours, from a severe headache. No mention was made of supper . . . Mrs. Davis sent us a mattress, and we made a joint bed in the open air on deck. I put the carpet bags under our heads. Strange to say, I slept sweetly and soundly."

Davis, accorded one of the few berths, appeared in the morning. Stephens continued, "much as I had disagreed with him, and much as I deplored the ruin which, I think, his acts helped to bring upon the whole country, as well as on himself, I could but deeply sympathize with him in his present condition. His salutation was not unfriendly, but it was far from cordial. We passed but few words; these were commonplace."

The losers were en route to imprisonment: Stephens and Reagan to Fort Warren, in Boston harbor; Davis and Clay to Fort Monroe; Alfred Trenholm, treasury secretary, and James A. Seddon, an early war secretary, to Fort Pulaski, Georgia, near Savannah. Other leaders remained on the loose.

There was not so much as one Confederate force now in the field to afford some meager solace to the erstwhile proconsuls of rebellion. Major General Edmund Kirby Smith, resourceful commander of the Trans-Mississippi Department, was completing surrender terms at Baton Rouge.

The victors, jubilant, were assembling by the tens of thousands in

Washington for the Grand Review. Multitudes were pouring in from the surrounding countryside and some from distant states.

Among the first to arrive, General Sherman spent the night of May 22 with an old friend, Senator Orville H. Browning, of Illinois. In an exceptionally garrulous mood, he reaffirmed what Southerners already understood: that, in a paraphrase of Browning, "he had made war as terrible as he could . . . but now he desired to see all restored to the rights of citizenship."

A "commodious" review stand, according to Brigadier General Horace Porter, aide to Grant, had been built in front of the White House. This historic May 23, a Tuesday, the weather was "absolutely perfect," Noah Brooks wrote. He added: ". . . All the conditions, barring the painful memories which even this inspiring sight recalled to many minds, were complete for the full enjoyment of the people's holiday. Two days of rain had cooled the air and laid the dust; and the streets of Washington, not always clean, were pleasant to march through. The air was bright, clear, and invigorating; as far as the eye could reach along the wide avenues through which the armed hosts moved with measured tread there was a blaze of color. Flags, banners, streamers, and all imaginable forms of patriotic device were lavishly spread to the air. The homecoming of the armies had been the signal for the removal of the somber badges of mourning that for more than a month had marked the grief of the city over the death of the beloved Lincoln."

Brooks's gaze wandered to the White House. Over its roof slates fluttered Old Glory, unfurled there for the first time since that gray April 15. Brooks wrote:

"Punctually at 9 A.M., General Porter smartly lowered his sword, and the signal gun was fired. The legions took up their march. They started from the Capitol, and moved briskly along Pennsylvania Avenue toward Georgetown, to the west. The width and location of the avenue made it an ideal thoroughfare for such a purpose. Martial music from scores of bands filled the air, and when familiar war-songs were played the spectators along the route joined in shouting the chorus. Those oftenest sung and most applauded were, 'When this cruel war is over,' 'When Johnny comes marching home,' and 'Tramp, tramp, tramp! the boys are marching.'"

This was the Army of the Potomac, which had taken so long to reach and, finally, capture Richmond. Of all the generals present, George

Armstrong Custer, "his long golden locks floating in the wind," was the most spectacular, evoking cries of "Custer! Custer!" His crimson necktie and buckskin breeches lent him the appearance of "half general and half scout," certainly of the flamboyant daredevil that was the twenty-five-year-old major general.*

Suddenly Custer's horse, frightened by a huge wreath of flowers tossed over its head, dashed off past the reviewing stand "like a tornado." Custer, however, brought his steed back to control, and again the spectators "screamed with delight."

Other officers experienced the same problem. Major General Joshua Chamberlain, who had remarked on "a tumult of sound and motion . . . all the way up the avenue," wrote: "A girlish form, robed white as her spirit, reaches up towards me a wreath of rare flowers, close-braided, fit for a Viking's arming, or victor's crown. How could I take it?"

Chamberlain managed to bring his horse to a kneeling position "and dropped my swordpoint almost to her feet, with a bow so low I could have touched her cheek."

To the squealing delight of young onlookers, mascots were brought along by the dozen: an eagle, a cat, a raccoon, cows, ponies, goats, a poodle, even "a chattering monkey."

The turn of the "mighty Army of the West"—that of General Sherman—was not until the next day. It was characterized, according to Colonel Elbridge J. Copp, of the Third New Hampshire Infantry, by "more of the swinging independent step." Old Tecumseh was already a legend, as his friend, Horace Porter made clear: "His tall spare figure, warworn face and martial bearing made him all that the people had pictured him. He had ridden but a little way before his body was decorated with flowery wreaths, and his horse enveloped in garlands. As he approached the reviewing-stand the bands struck up 'Marching through Georgia,' and played that stirring air with a will. This was the signal for renewed demonstrations of delight.

"When he had passed, he turned his horse into the White House grounds, dismounted, and strode rapidly to the platform. He advanced to where the President was standing, and the two shook hands. The members

---

*The youngest general in the army, Custer had distinguished himself in dashing cavalry charges at Gettysburg and Yellow Tavern and in the final assaults precipitating Appomattox.

of the cabinet then stepped up to greet him. He took their extended hands, and had a few pleasant words to say to each of them, until Stanton reached out his hand. Then, Sherman's whole manner changed in an instant; a cloud of anger overspread his features, and, smarting under the wrong the Secretary had done him in his published bulletins after the conditional treaty with Johnston, the general turned abruptly away. This rebuff became the sensation of the day."

Colonel Copp thought Sherman actually "brushed" aside the secretary of war, who thereupon slunk back to his seat like "a whipped child." Considering that this was the man who had created fact out of his boast to "make Georgia howl," the action was not surprising.

Prudently, the president ignored the animosity between the two. He kept doffing his hat in a manner which struck Porter, who found that Johnson had "a way of holding it by the brim with his right hand and waving it from left to right, and occasionally passing his right arm across his breast and resting the hat on his left shoulder. This manual of the hat was original, and had probably been practiced with good effect when its wearer was stumping East Tennessee."

The passage of Sherman's army proved a most unusual spectacle. As Copp related: "This army of General Sherman's had just completed a long march through the enemy's country, living chiefly upon the country they passed through; in this review it was the design of General Sherman not to put on a holiday appearance, but to give the President and the people a sight of his army as it really was. They had with them as they had upon their march through Georgia and the Carolinas, captured horses and mules, many negroes, women and children that had been army followers, the children on the backs of the mules and the negro women leading, making a most grotesque appearance; horses loaded down with cooking utensils; chickens, geese and other products of the country that 'Sherman's bummers' had captured."

But Sherman had had enough. He grew tired. As he attempted to descend from the reviewing stand, the crowd surged around him in a crushing swarm, attempting to shake his hand, pushing bouquets at him. Affable initially, the general soon was glowering.

"He pushed down step by step," Copp noted. "We could see that his patience was exhausted, and refusing the offered hands, forced his way down, brushing aside the men in front of him, finally angrily exclaiming, 'damn you, get out of my way! Get out of my way!'

"The crowd, concluding that he meant just what he said, gave way for him to descend, and mounting his horse, he rode away."

On the troops came, 67,000 strong, Senator Browning estimated, closer to 100,000, others counted, with perhaps twice that number of spectators. It was an obvious semirhetorical question that a "foreign diplomat" posed to Dr. Charles Leale, the surgeon who had attended Lincoln at the Peterson house: "What will become of these thousands of soldiers after discharge?"

That they would return to their homes throughout the land "and soon be at work doing their utmost to pay off the national debt" seemed to Dr. Leale a natural and, possibly, a prosaic answer. But the diplomat clapped his hands to exclaim, "Is it possible? No other country could expect such a result!"

Dusk came. Women carried sleeping infants wearily homeward. The sound of carriages began to replace the clomp of horses' hooves and the shuffle of soldiers' boots over the dusty, rutted streets.

"The shadows deepen," Chamberlain wrote. "It has passed—the splendid pageant; it is gone forever, the magnificent host that streamed from the mountains to the sea, that flaming bolt which cut the Confederacy in two—or shall we say that left its deep track upon the earth to mark the dark memories of those years; or to shine forever a token of saving grace in the galaxy of the midnight sky?"

Noah Brooks, as tired as everyone else, seconded, "The pageant faded. The men-at-arms who had spent their years and lavished their energies in camps or on fields of battle went from the National Capital to their own homes, to take up once more the arts of peace and the cares and joys of sweet domesticity. In a few weeks this army of two or three hundred thousand men melted back into the heart of the people from whence it came, and the great spectacle of the Grand Army of the Republic on review disappeared from sight."

JUNE

We Live Like Beggars

S heffield, Illinois, a hundred miles west of Chicago, was but one of thousands of pinpricks of habitation into which the veterans "melted back." Trainloads of Southern prisoners of war passing through the little farming community to the nearby prison camp at Rock Island, on the Mississippi, had kept the rebellion both visibly and audibly alive for the residents.

"Sheffield had its war heroes and so did every town the country over," wrote Willis Boughton, a teenage dairy and animal farmer. "As they were discharged, the soldiers returned to their homes to find their little children grown almost to manhood and womanhood . . . Efforts were made to find occupation for all who cared to work."

Some assumed their old jobs. Others went west and southwest to work on the railroads. Many were both surprised and disappointed to find that "immigrants from European shores were doing the work formerly done by oldtime pioneers . . . Often they were more willing and better workmen than the veterans." Union commissaries with seemingly limitless supplies had, as well, spoiled the soldiers: ". . . Our veteran farmhands objected to using roasted barley for coffee and johnnycake instead of white bread, as the rest of us had to. We sometimes used sorghum molasses instead of sugar, though brown sugar was more commonly used."

Wages, too, were disappointing, even though area merchants tried to create small, often part-time jobs for the soldiers. Then there was competition where none had existed before the war. Such was the case of the returning blacksmith, whose business had been preempted. He changed to farming.

Others came home ill or crippled, or both: "Uncle George W. Farnham returned with well defined tuberculosis. Cousin John Parks, a cavalryman, though maimed by a rifle ball, served until he was discharged . . . Cousin Egbert Scudders . . . at Lookout Mountain was wounded by a bayonet thrust in his right arm."

Meanwhile, on May 29, President Johnson had issued an amnesty and pardon proclamation. Its palpable effects could not quickly or easily be measured. Satisfying neither radicals nor conservatives in Congress, the edict generally restored property rights (other than the right to own slaves) to citizens of the seceded states who took an oath of loyalty. But there were exceptions, including high military officers and Confederate government officials, and those in the higher income or net worth group (arbitrarily set at $20,000).

Nonetheless, as the federal troops disappeared into "the heart of the people," there were stirrings of new life in the areas through which they had marched and fought. More than offering forgiveness, Washington through the occupation forces was providing direct assistance, such as rebuilding bridges and supplying food—bread at six and a quarter cents a loaf, free to the destitute.

"Most of the prominent citizens of Richmond have taken the oath of allegiance to the U.S. Government and there is a disposition among the mass of citizens to follow their example," wrote a reporter for the Richmond *Whig*, who went on: "Nearly all of the old established commission houses are being reopened and, so soon as the railroads are got in working order we doubt not that business and trade, cramped and hindered every possible way during the last four years, will resume its wonted channels. We are especially interested in the commission houses for to them we look to bring in the products of the country.

"The [Virginia] Central Railroad trains are now running to Bumpass Station in Caroline County, 47 miles from Richmond, and by the last of the week it is expected they will run daily to Albemarle County, 95 miles. This opens up to us a good stretch of rich country of whose products we are as much in need as are its inhabitants of the coffee, sugar . . . new bonnets and raiment . . ."

The federal cavalry had ripped up tracks and twisted them beyond belief, even into bows over burning piles of ties. The important York River line to Yorktown was badly destroyed. It had been contested during McClellan's campaign in 1862. Railroad men, with some assistance from the U.S. Army engineers, were having more luck in repairing the Richmond, Fredericksburg, and Potomac; the Richmond and Danville; and the Richmond and Petersburg rights-of-way.

The condition of the tracks notwithstanding, cars not worn out by four years of war and engines to pull them were in short supply. Still, the people of Richmond set out to visit relatives in distant places, knowing that their journey would be interrupted part way to a given destination and they would then have to find a coach, a wagon, or a mount. Horses, for that matter, were as scarce as locomotives. Those obtainable were scrawny and weary, in testament to months of bare-bones rations.

Since the railroad bridges, burned during the evacuation, were yet to be rebuilt, train trips started or ended across the James from Richmond, mostly at Manchester. John Richard Dennett, a correspondent for a new magazine, *The Nation,* wrote: "I found no depot or baggage-master. Half a dozen dilapidated cars were standing about, and a rusty looking engine was cracking and puffing up and down, shifting them from one track to another, and making up a train. Of this, two passenger carriages formed a part, both on the outside adorned with a painted representation of two Confederate flags, and splashed half way up with a yellowish-red mud of this region and, inside, both dirty and exceedingly uncomfortable.

"Long ago, I suppose, cushions had disappeared, the only vestiges of them that remained being an occasional wad of horsehair, or a shred of faded plush still clinging to the framework of the seats. In the window sashes were many broken panes, and where the glass was wholly gone, wood had been substituted. The floors were filthy. Such as they were, these two carriages were given up to the occupancy of ladies and the gentlemen accompanying them, together with a number of sick and wounded Confederate soldiers; other passengers found sitting and standing room in the freight cars. Even at that early hour the sun began to shine hotly down upon the baked and cracked soil of the railroad, and moving my trunk into the shadow cast by the leaving train, I sat and watched the crowd assembled at the station.

"There were, perhaps, a hundred and fifty people collected together. Negro drivers, liberal of the whip and vociferous in expostulation with their mules, drove loaded wagons to the baggage cars. Dirty-looking whites and dirtier Negroes were selling 'fried pies' and other uninviting edibles. A crippled Negro was retailing cider, which he poured from a jug and cornstalk stopper into a tin can that once had held preserved salmon. Newsboys were crying the New York *Daily News* and *Herald,* and the Richmond morning papers."

Canals, all-important links in Virginia's communications, had been hurt. Sheridan's cavalry had burned locks and barges on the important James River and Kanawha Canal, thirty miles from the city. Since some nine hundred buildings, including mills, factories, stores, and dwellings, had been destroyed by fire during the evacuation, much of the debris had inevitably fallen to clog the canals.

River traffic to Norfolk and thus up the coast to New York or south to Savannah was, however, resumed. Since the U.S. Navy no longer had need of the fleet of transports that had plied the rivers and harbors and helped to blockade offshore, it was satisfied to turn over some of its vessels to the South. Thus it was a happy sound the first day of June—also decreed one of mourning for the late President Lincoln—when an erstwhile Hudson River night boat let loose a blast of her whistle and pushed off from Richmond's port, Rocketts, bound down the James for Hampton Roads.

As a bonus, horse-drawn bus service from downtown Richmond to Rocketts had been reestablished. The carriages left from Brook Avenue every fifteen minutes, returning on the same schedule. Twenty blocks of tracks for horse-powered streetcars were being repaired from 8th to 28th streets. Almost all of the local transit rails had been damaged in the fire or inundated by rubble.

Governor Francis Pierpoint pleased Richmonders by reinstating eighty-year-old Joseph Mayo as mayor and most other civic officials to their jobs. It was Mayo who had driven in a carriage to meet the oncoming federals and surrender the city.

Encouraged by Pierpoint, the mayor, and the city council, a bank—the First National—was chartered and located in the custom house–post office, the only edifice in the financial district to have survived the flames. In this building Jefferson Davis and the Confederacy's Treasury and State departments had maintained offices. There, too, the wartime cabinet had met. General Lee, who had established his first headquarters in the same spacious structure, was among the bank's early depositors.

Lee was fortunate. By far the majority of his erstwhile comrades of the Army of Northern Virginia had no funds with which to open an account.

"Every few days," wrote the historian Asbury Christian, "a large number of Confederate soldiers returned to Richmond from northern prisons, and they were in abject poverty.

"They were without homes, had no food, and were in need of clothes and shoes. Many wore Confederate uniforms because they had nothing else, and it was against military orders to wear Confederate buttons, so the street guards would stop the soldiers, cut off their buttons and permit them to pass. The people of Richmond had little, yet they could not see the soldiers suffer; they therefore called a public meeting and raised funds to help these men . . . The good women worked hard to make them comfortable until they could get home."

Richmond, at that, was somewhat better off than other cities in the South, especially those along Sherman's line of march.

"I shall never forget my first impressions of Charleston," wrote Carl Schurz, lawyer and recent major general in Sherman's army. One of many from the North inspecting "secesh country," the highly educated and articulate German-born Schurz continued: "The city of Charleston lay open to our view; on the left, a row of more or less elegant dwellings, on the right such buildings as are usually seen in the neighborhood of wharves. There was no shipping in the harbor except a few quartermaster's vessels and two or three small steamers. There was not a human being visible on the wharf. The warehouses seemed to be completely deserted. There was no wall and no roof that did not bear eloquent marks of having been under the fire of siege guns.

"Nothing could be more desolate and melancholy than the appearance of the lower part of the city immediately adjoining the harbor. Although the military authorities had caused the streets to be 'policed' as well as possible, abundant grass had still grown up between the paving stones. The first living object that struck my view when making my way to the hotel was a dilapidated United States cavalry horse bearing the mark I.C.—inspected and condemned—now peaceably browsing on the grass in a Charleston street.

"A few cows were feeding in a vacant lot nearby, surrounded by buildings gashed and shattered by shell and solid shot." Entirely appropriate to the dismal scene were the buzzards perched on almost all rooftops.

The "burned district" was one "vast graveyard with broken walls and tall blackened chimneys for monuments, overtopped by the picturesque ruins of the Cathedral."

Whitelaw Reid, who had reported the war for the Cincinnati *Gazette,* arrived in the same city, accompanying Chief Justice Salmon P. Chase, now on a tour of the South. Reid saw the city in somewhat different perspective, labeling it erroneous to conclude that "any considerable number" of houses had been burned or destroyed. The shells had failed to explode in many cases, causing "scars" rather than gaping holes or ruins. Although many roofs appeared to have been "injured" and walls "weakened," the structures nevertheless were reparable.

Reid was especially appalled at the "fashionable race course" where federal prisoners had been kept "without shelter, without clothing, and with insufficient food." Over the entrance was a placard, "Martyrs of the Race Course." A nearby "elegant cemetery" with its expensive gravestones and mausoleums was the object of considerable interest on the part of the Negro occupation troops.

Reid observed "vehicles . . . bringing in black and white refugees. The country is in such confusion that many seek the safe shelter of the cities, solely from the blind instinct that where there is force there must be protection. Such wagons and such horses were surely never seen. Each rivalled the other in protuberance, shakiness, and general disposition to tumble down and dissolve. They all bring in saddening stories of destitution . . ."

Columbia, South Carolina, was devastated. It remained unresolved whether the fleeing Confederates or Sherman's forces had fired the cotton bales heaped throughout South Carolina's capital.

"Columbia," mused John T. Trowbridge, a writer from Hartford, Connecticut, commissioned to tour the South, "must have been a beautiful city, judging by its ruins. The streets were broad and well shaded. Many fine residences still remain on the outskirts, but the entire heart of the city is a wilderness of crumbling walls, naked chimneys and trees killed by flames. The fountains of the desolated gardens are dry, the basins cracked; the pillars of the houses are dismantled or overthrown; the marble steps are broken."

Miraculously, the yet unfinished State House, "one of the handsomest public edifices in the whole country," was almost unscathed. Like the Capitol in Washington, its progress had been slowed, sometimes entirely halted by the war. Trowbridge recorded that ". . . the streets of Columbia were broad, else many of the fleeing fugitives must have perished in the flames which met them on all sides. The exodus of homeless families, flying between walls of fire, was a terrible and piteous spectacle . . . Three-fifths of the city was destroyed . . . the churches were pillaged, and afterwards burned. St. Mary's College, a Catholic institution, shared their fate. The Catholic convent, to which had been confined for safety many young ladies, not nuns, and stores of treasure, was ruthlessly sacked. Soldiers drank sacramental wine, profaned with fiery draughts of vulgar whiskey the goblets of the communion service. Some went off reeling under the weight of priestly robes, holy vessels and candlesticks.

"Not much drunkenness was observed among the soldiers until after the sacking of the city had been some time in progress. Then the stores of liquors consumed exhibited their natural effect; and it is stated that many perished in fires of their own kindling . . .

"South Carolina suffered more than any other State by the sale of lands for United States taxes during the war. I heard of one estate worth $15 thousand which had been sold for $300."

Trowbridge thus scarcely laid to rest the questions concerning the ravaging of Columbia. Sherman's officers tended to place at least a portion of the blame on drunken soldiers from their army. "The citizens them-selves—like idiots, madmen—brought out large quantities of liquor as soon as our troops entered," wrote Major Henry Hitchcock, "and distrib-uted it freely among them, even to the guards . . ." Still, he and other officers agreed that Sherman himself joined his staff to work "with their own hands . . . trying to save life and property."

It was impossible to move into or out of Columbia by rail. Maintenance shops for the railroads as well as depots had been burned. Even the water tanks lay in charred debris. As another observer wrote, the iron tracks themselves were "twisted and bent into shapes utterly baffling all efforts at restoration," like those in Richmond and most of Georgia.

At nearby Camden, Mary Boykin Chesnut would lament, "a feeling of sadness hovers over me day and night, which no words of mine can express . . . When we crossed the river coming home, the ferry man at Chesnut's Ferry asked for his fee. Among us all we could not muster the small silver coin he demanded. There was poverty for you . . ."

Once at Mulberry, the Chesnut estate, she found that Old Cuffey, the head gardener, had not been idle. Green peas, asparagus, lettuce, spinach, potatoes, and strawberries were growing "in abundance." One given to philosophizing, Mary Chesnut added: "The blooming of the gardens had a funereal effect. Nature is so luxuriant here, she soon covers the ravages of the savages. No frost has occurred since the seventh of March which accounts for the wonderful advance in vegetation. This seems providential to these starving people. In this State so much that is edible can be grown in two months."

Yet farther south in Washington, Georgia, Fanny Andrews watched the disbandment of the troops in gray who had fought under the Stars and Bars: "The great armies have about all passed through, and now are coming the sick from the hospitals and prisons, poor fellows straggling towards their homes. They often stop to rest in the cool shade of our grove, and the sight of their gray coats, no matter how ragged and dirty, is refreshing to my eyes.

"Two Missourians came to the house yesterday morning for breakfast, and mother filled them up with everything good she could find, and packed them up a generous lunch besides. She is a better rebel than she thinks herself, after all. If anybody in the world does merit good usage from all Southerners, it is these brave Missourians, who sacrificed so much for our cause, to which they had so little at stake for themselves."

Fanny did not seem to be faring as well as Mary Chesnut so far as the staples of living were concerned, claiming, "We live from hand to mouth like beggars. Father has sent to Augusta for a supply of groceries, but it will probably be a week before they get here, and in the meantime, all the sugar and coffee we have is what Uncle Osborne brings in. He hires himself out by the day and takes his wages in whatever provisions we need most, and hands them to father when he comes home at night."

Yet the ink had barely dried on the pages of her diary when an unexpected cornucopia was borne by a relative and friend: "Cousin Jim Farley and Mr. Cullom arrived from Montgomery to look after the cotton father had been keeping stored for them here. They brought all manner of nice things—candy, raisins, and almonds, canned fruits, fish, sardines, cheese, and other foreign luxuries including a basket of champagne.

". . . The best of all are two beautiful new hats in the very latest fashion, that Cousin brought Mett and me. We were so delighted that we danced all over the house when not standing before the glass to admire ourselves. We dressed up in our new finery and went to the bank."

But there was not much finery, surely scant champagne in Georgia. Arriving in Savannah, Edwin Rhodes, a ship's carpenter from Maine, noted that "everything looked very desolate, for it was really a deserted city . . . Nearly all the prominent citizens had abandoned their homes and only the Negroes and whites too poor in purse to get away remained and were dependent on the U.S. Army rations for their livelihood.

"The wharves, piers and bulkheads were going to decay and grass and weeds were growing over them. Many obstructions were placed in the river to hinder the approach of vessels to the city. At one place, piling was driven all the way across the river and close together; at another place near its mouth several old hulks of vessels were sunk close together . . . It was indeed sorrowful to know of the sufferings of the Southerner at the close of the war."

From his dry accent an obvious Downeaster, Rhodes nonetheless was made to sign an oath of allegiance. Anyone walking the streets of Savannah was suspect in the eyes of the occupation forces.

"We had to parch okra or grits for coffee and we ate potato tops during the days after the war for greens," recalled Mrs. W. H. Sauls, of the same Georgia port city. She watched "Yankee soldiers throw sacks of rice from warehouses and the populace flocked to pick the rice up from the streets, and we came home to wash and eat it." She remembered her mother successfully defying a soldier who threatened to rip her mattress with his bayonet, searching "for gold."

From Atlanta, Brigadier General Edward M. McCook, of the Fourth Division, U.S. Cavalry, was writing in early June that in this onetime major arsenal and rail junction for the Confederacy some 50,000 persons were "utterly destitute of bread or any kind of food." In an official report, he added: "Some adequate steps should be taken to supply this demand for food. Women and children walk from ten to forty miles for food and then obtain only a moiety, frequently not any. Of course, the proper source of supply should be in the State government; but as there is no such authority, our Government must take the matter in hand or intense suffering will follow . . . Until the crops of this country are cultivated to maturity the people there, both black and white, will suffer for food."

Then, as an apparently unrelated aside, the general observed, "I had no collision with any of the authorities except the ecclesiastical. The pastor of the Episcopal Church in his public service omitted the customary prayer for the President of the United States. I thought it my duty to Christianize him, if possible."

Not all Southern preachers were Christianized easily, or willingly. As another example, the Reverend George F. McKay, of Columbia, South Carolina, received a terse note from the U.S. military authorities on June 12, "hoping that a like omission in the future may not oblige the General to order your place of worship to be closed."

Nor did it much impress the occupying forces when sincere and otherwise conscientious men of the cloth protested that, although they could rationalize prayers for the nation itself, this particular chief executive did not altogether inspire spiritual emotions.

Reiterating McCook's comments about the hardships of the Georgians, General Wilson, who had organized the pursuit of Jefferson Davis, added: "I have already given to the people all of the Confederate and State stores and tithes, and appointed two energetic citizens to superintend their distribution, but the help is inadequate. All of our efforts hitherto to obtain grain by the river have failed to supply us and the additional tax imposed by the destitution of the people. The Western and Atlantic Railroad is our only sure way of getting the necessary stores. That line being State property, I have taken possession of it for the United States and am working a large force in repairing it between Atlanta and Dalton, but am greatly embarrassed for want of tools. These I am willing to buy, borrow or take by issue and compensate the Government at full prices out of the earnings of the road."

There were many anomalies and seeming contradictions in the federal government's dealing with the beaten South. The federal military in its solicitude for the "destitute" people was invariably more lenient and forgiving than its counterparts in the judiciary. In response to the fulminations of a district judge, John C. Underwood, a federal grand jury in Norfolk indicted, on June 7, General Lee, Jefferson Davis, and several other high Confederates, charging them with treason.

Hearing of it in a few days, Lee soberly wrote both General Grant and President Johnson on June 13. "I had supposed," he told Grant, "that the officers and men of the Army of Northern Virginia were, by the terms of their surrender, protected by the United States Government from molestation so long as they conformed to its conditions. I am ready to meet any charges that may be preferred against me, and do not wish to avoid trial; but, if I am correct as to the protection granted by my parole, and am not to be prosecuted, I desire to comply with the provisions of the President's proclamation and, therefore, enclose the required application, which I request, in that event, may be acted on. I am with great respect, Your Obedient Servant."

And to Andrew Johnson he had a request: "Sir; being excluded from the provisions of the amnesty and pardon contained in the proclamation of the 29th ult., I hereby apply for the benefits and full restoration of all rights and privileges extended to those included in its terms. I graduated at the Military Academy at West Point in June 1829; resigned from the United States Army April 1861; was a general in the Confederate Army, and included in the surrender of the Army of Northern Virginia, April 9, 1865."

For a proud man it was not an easy letter. Four days later he was advising his former aide, Colonel Walter Taylor: "I have no wish to avoid any trial the Government may order, and cannot flee. I hope others may be unmolested, and that you at least may be undisturbed. I am sorry to hear that our returned soldiers cannot obtain employment. Tell them they must all set to work, and if they cannot do what they prefer, do what they can . . . There is much to be done which they only can do. Very truly yours, R. E. Lee."

If proud, the graying general was as well a formal man. Four years in camp and field of battle still was too fragile a basis of comradeship to chance "Walter" on the salutation, "Robert," "Bob," "Edward," or simply "Lee" as a signature.

While the president appeared to ignore Lee's appeal, Grant replied on the twentieth, affirming that paroled prisoners of war could not be tried for treason if they observed their paroles. He recommended that the chief executive order Judge Underwood to "quash all indictment found against paroled prisoners of war, and to desist from further prosecution of them."

The general also offered his "earnest recommendation" that the president approve Lee's request for amnesty and pardon. At that, Lee was far better off than Jefferson Davis, Alexander Stephens, or Postmaster John Reagan. The erstwhile chief executive of the rebellion languished in a dark, dank stone cell at Fort Monroe. Reagan's and Stephens's accommodations inside Fort Warren, on an island in Boston harbor, were hardly more luxurious.

"The overhead ceiling of my room was about on a level with the parade grounds," Reagan would write, "and the light and air we got came down between the wall of the building and the wall of the parade ground about six feet from the house. Two windows made secure by crossbars of iron faced the space between these walls. There was no ventilation except through these."

All in all, the formidable mass of stone and masonry made the cells "more like caves than rooms." Certainly one of the sturdiest and toughest of the ranking Confederates, Reagan had refused to eat his fare of "dark-looking bread and a darker looking piece of meat," which a guard brought on a tin plate. After thus dieting for several days, the former postmaster was visited by an officer inquiring if he were sick.

"I told him I was well," Reagan recalled, "and said, 'you have my money [$2,000 in gold] can I not buy something fit to eat?' He replied that he supposed not; but added that he would see the post commander. He returned in an hour or so with the message that I could order my meals by the sergeant from the post quartermaster, who furnished meals to the officers, and that every Saturday I could draw on the commissary of prisoners, who had my money, to pay for my week's board. He told me I could order any 'necessaries,' but no luxuries. I asked him to explain what were necessaries."

Reagan won the right to order his "no luxuries" meals. Although he and Stephens were both allowed half-hour escorted strolls each day, they were not permitted to indulge this ephemeral diversion and relaxation together.

"In taking my walks," Reagan continued, "I passed by the window of Mr. Stephens' room, and from hearing me talk with the officer, he learned about the time of day I went out, and placing himself at the window of his room, he hailed me as I went by.

"I made inquiry as to his health, and after a few words, passed on. A First Lieutenant Woodman was my escort. He seemed to be looking somewhere else and took no notice of our greeting. Every day after that, Mr. Stephens would draw himself up to the window to let me know that he was still alive. He was so frail that he was soon afterward removed to a dry, well-ventilated room."

For Reagan, Stephens, Davis, Lee, and still others, war's evil harvest would go on. But for one Confederate officer, Commander James Waddell, the rebellion appeared to continue in stark, sober fact. None had told him about Appomattox.

As captain of the C.S.S. *Shenandoah*, he was in the distant reaches of the Bering Sea after raiding merchant sea-lanes in the Atlantic and Pacific since the preceding autumn. In the 1,100-ton Confederate cruiser's wake were sixteen ships captured or burned or both. Waddell had sailed his powerful command out of England under continuing diplomatic protests from Washington. It was the last of such warships to be built or outfitted by the British.

". . . Five vessels were discovered near a large body of ice," Waddell logged on June 22, "and I stood for them, hoisted the American flag, and communicated with the nearest one, which was the whaleship *Milo,* of New Bedford."

The captain, when the *Milo* had been boarded by Waddell, said that the war was "over." But he possessed no "documentary evidence" to show the captain of the raider. Waddell obviously did not believe him. He said he was willing, however, to ransom the ship if the captain gave bond and agreed to take off the prisoners who were aboard the *Shenandoah*. This was agreeable to the master of the *Milo*.

And so the gruff Waddell continued to prey upon the New Bedford whaling fleet, more than two months after the surrender of the Army of Northern Virginia.

Certainly the sea captain's ignorance was not shared in the continental United States, nor throughout the civilized world. Any literate person, and many who were not, now knew who had won the war. Repercussions continued through the land.

Since early May, vengeance had been sought for the Lincoln assassination as the trial crackled—and sometimes droned on—in the old penitentiary in Washington.* Easily the most sensational in the history of the young nation, the legal proceedings were as well the most thoroughly reported, after the military commission at first had attempted to close them to the public.

Every noon and early evening, at adjournment, the correspondents tumbled down the flights of wooden stairs of the brick building. In their hands they tightly clutched wads of scribbled notes to be passed along to a telegraphist or to a messenger who would gallop to local city rooms. The old headlines proclaiming battles and other military operations had been supplanted with a strange, often frenetic potpourri:

---

*Known but to a very few was the fact that Booth's body moldered nearby in the earth beneath one of the arsenal's magazines. At Stanton's orders, it had been transferred at night from the Monitor *Montauk,* its initial resting place. Possessed of a paranoid fear that erstwhile Confederates might somehow spirit off the assassin's remains, the war secretary himself held the keys to the storage rooms.

TRIAL OF THE CONSPIRATORS
JEFFERSON DAVIS AND THE ASSASSINATION
STARTLING DEVELOPMENTS!
PLOT TO BURN NEW YORK
SAW BOOTH . . .
STARVATION OF UNION PRISONERS
THE ASSASSINS
MINING OF LIBBY PRISON!
PAPERS FROM REBEL ARCHIVES
A DASTARDLY PLOT!

Under sometimes lurid, often irrelevant, but invariably breathless head-
ings, columns and columns streaked down the front pages of the *National
Intelligencer,* the *Evening Star,* the New York *World,* the New York *Herald,*
the New York *Times,* the Philadelphia *North American,* the Chicago
Tribune, all the large dailies.

To the reporters, fresh from the war, the proceedings became an encore
to what they had been doing over the past four years. And they wrote
with mostly the same prejudices that had already sustained them and
created a readership.

(It should be noted that testimony was officially recorded solely by
Benn Pitman (or Pittman), English-born, who, with his brother Sir Isaac,
developed a well-known system of shorthand. His transcript was, however,
subject to review by the military, and he wrote with the intent of
publishing the proceedings for profit. This he did that same year.)

Noah Brooks, reviewing the day-by-day progress, found that "the
witnesses were first examined by the Judge Advocate, members of the
court putting in a question now and then, and the counsel for the
prisoners taking up the cross-examination, each counselor attending only
to the witness whose testimony affected his own client. The witnesses
were brought in without regard to any particular criminal, all being tried
at once."

This travesty of jurisprudence, which would have made Sir William
Blackstone howl in disbelief, was equally disturbing to a spectator who
was not a lawyer. Colonel Henry Kyd Douglas, formerly with the Stonewall Brigade, was rather a pampered guest in the prison, there for a minor
parole violation (wearing his old uniform). The young cavalryman looked

at the court and concluded, "It was a strange scene. There was General David Hunter in the congenial occupation of presiding over a Court of Death with evident pride and satisfaction. There were eight others.

"It was the most severely solemn tribunal I ever faced. I never saw a smile upon the face of a judge, counsel, or spectator; and with the exception of General John G. Foster, who now and then gave a semblance of fairness and justice to the proceedings by intervening on behalf of prisoner or witness, there was never any attempt on the part of the Commission to curb or question the arbitrary insolence and injustice of the Judge Advocates."

The trial progressed so swiftly that none of the gentlemen of the fourth estate nor their editors had the time to reflect on testimony and evidence that roamed far afield of the assassination, and by the opinion of a very few should not have been admitted.

Some testimony was preposterous, challenging a reasonable mind. For example, a Canadian, one Godfrey Hyams, testified that a representative of the Confederacy in Toronto had given him a suitcase of clothing "infected in Bermuda with yellow fever, smallpox and other contagious diseases" for scattering about New York, Washington, and other cities.

Although there was some corroboration that clothing, or at least a batch of clothing, did arrive in the nation's capital under mysterious circumstances, there was no proof that it was in any way contaminated. Nor was medical or laboratory expertise summoned to ascertain the plausibility or the possibility of impregnating anything deliberately with something so elusive as yellow fever. What had been diagnosed as that infection had killed thousands of Union and Confederate soldiers.

Various individuals bore witness to the sabotage of steamships, raids launched from Canada against U.S. cities, a plot to burn New York (for which one Confederate officer had been hanged), destruction of bridges, and a more defensible fact: the deplorable condition of Union prisoners in such hells as Libby, in Richmond, or Andersonville, in Georgia. But the prosecutors were scarcely concerned with showing how such allegations were relevant to the case against these defendants. They made no effort to establish motives or, surely not, common ground.

Approximately three hundred witnesses, ranging in intelligence from above average to moronic, wove not only these stories of plots and alleged plots but a meandering fabric of what might be described as the entr'actes of the rebellion and habits, impulses, and idiosyncrasies of the participants. For example, it was reiterated that the ever restless Booth had speculated in oil in the new Pennsylvania fields and that Jacob Thompson and other Confederate emissaries to Canada maintained bank accounts in Montreal totaling in excess of $649,000.

The military commission and spectators alike, however, evinced less interest in gray backdrops than in testimony aimed directly at those on trial. At such times the reporters leaned forward over their long table and the women stopped fanning against the dead summer heat. Only the witnesses could speak. The defendants were not allowed that privilege. Since Annie Surratt was a witness, rather than accused, she could tell her story: "My mother went to Surrattsville [a crossroads in southern Maryland, about twelve miles from the District of Columbia, where the Surratt family owned a farm, home, and tavern] on the Friday of the assassination . . . I think her carriage was at the door at the time Mr. Booth called. I heard someone come up the steps as the buggy was at the door, and ma was ready to start. Ma had been talking about going during the day, before Booth came, and perhaps the day before; she said she was obliged to go on some business in regard to some land. Mr. Booth only staid [*sic*] a very few minutes. He never staid long when he came.

"I never, on any occasion, heard a word breathed at my mother's house of any plot or conspiracy to assassinate the President of the United States; nor have I ever heard any remarks in reference to the assassination of any member of the Government.

"My mother's eyesight is very bad, and she has often failed to recognize her friends. She has not been able to read or sew by gaslight for some time past. I have often plagued her about getting spectacles, and told her she was too young-looking to wear spectacles just yet . . ."

Annie's whole appearance was to one spectator and sometime witness, Colonel Douglas, "a pitiable scene"; he added, "She was tall, slender, fair, handsome; for her to stand the stare of the cruel, stony eyes riveted upon her was a trying ordeal. She must have known that her testimony made no impression on that tribunal, and toward the close of it she began to show signs of a collapse. The veins and muscles of her neck seemed swollen and she gave evidence of great suffering.

"General Hartranft [Major General John F. Hartranft, provost marshal] was about to go to her, but knowing her horror of him as her mother's jailer, he, with delicate consideration, asked me to bring her from the stand. I brought her out, passing just in front of her mother, and as she reached my room she fell forward and fainted.

"The door was shut quickly, a doctor called, and at his instance, General Hartranft and I carried her below, to his room. There she had a spasm and began to tear out her beautiful hair and to rend her dress. Women arriving, she was left with them and the Doctor, who succeeded after a while in quieting and putting her to sleep."

Even as Annie Surratt was being calmed down, a former slave, Henry Hawkins, took the stand. Noting that he had lived in Surrattsville about eleven years, he asserted that his onetime owner had "always treated me kindly, and she was very good to all her servants.

"I remember the Government horses breaking away from Giesboro [a cavalry stabling area], and that seven of them came to Mrs. Surratt's stable; they were there for a fortnight or more, and then the Government sent for them. I do not know that Mrs. Surratt had a receipt for them, but I know that she bought hay and grain to feed them.

"I have never heard Mrs. Surratt talk in favor of the South; never heard any expressions, loyal or disloyal, from her while I was there. She often fed Union soldiers that passed her house, and always gave them the best she had; and I do not think she took any pay for it; she took none that I know of.

"I do not know much about Mrs. Surratt's eyesight being bad, but I heard she could not see some time back, and that she had to wear specs.*

Mary Surratt's character was also vouched for by no fewer than five Catholic priests, including the Reverend N. D. Young, pastor of St. Dominick's Church, not far from her boardinghouse.

"I became acquainted with Mrs. Mary E. Surratt," he testified, "about eight or ten years ago. My acquaintance has not been intimate. I have occasionally seen her and visited her. I had to pass her house about once a month, and generally called there—sometimes staid an hour. Her reputation, as far as I have heard, is that of a Christian lady, in every sense of the word. I have heard her spoken of with the greatest praise, and never heard anything of her but what was highly favorable to her character. She never expressed any disloyal sentiments to me."

---

*Since there was no documentation that Hawkins had been exposed to any education, even rudimentary, it has to be assumed that the stenographer, Pitman, was paraphrasing Hawkins's testimony. The words "fortnight" and "expressions," for example, would not normally be part of such an individual's vocabulary, regardless of his other abilities or virtues.

But Mary Surratt, generally considered a regular worshipper at church, did not confide to priests, much less the military or even the civil authorities, what was going on at either her boardinghouse or her tavern at Surrattsville. The latter clapboard structure was rented to one John Lloyd. He proved no friend of his landlady. Neither did a boarder at her H Street house, a twenty-three-year-old Louis J. Weichmann (also spelled Wiechmann), a War Department clerk who was the same age as Lloyd.

Compromised by his own conceivably guilty knowledge and in likelihood threatened by his superiors, Weichmann testified at length as to the comings and goings of Booth, who was a friend of Mary Surratt's son, John. The latter, now hiding in Canada, knew Weichmann in college. The witness also placed the other primary conspirators—Atzerodt, Herold, and Payne—at the boardinghouse on frequent occasions.

Yet more damaging were the allegations of John Lloyd, arrested and in mortal fear of his own life. He had been promised immunity from prosecution if he implicated Mary Surratt in the plot. And this he did wholeheartedly. He associated the woman not only with Booth but also with "shooting irons" supposedly secreted in a shed behind the Surratt tavern.

Anna Surratt herself had testified that her mother went to Surrattsville on the day of the assassination for the purpose of checking on "some acreage." Unfortunately, the daughter could not be more specific.

Mary Surratt, Lloyd asserted, wanted to have the "shooting irons" ready for unnamed "parties" who would be there for them that very night. There was also, Lloyd added, a field glass for Booth's use. But this seemed largely surmise. Indeed there were those who swore that Lloyd was too drunk that day to remember anything—blind, stumbling drunk. Furthermore, the prosecution was unable to produce even one of the "shooting irons."

In the likelihood that Lloyd was a perjurer, he was not alone. The drunkard was joined by other "special" prosecution witnesses, those with loose memories at best. A number would subsequently recant. The most adroit liar was Sanford Conover—Charles Dunham at birth—alias James Watson Wallace, sometime newspaperman but mostly con artist. He saw this as an opportunity for revenge on the Confederacy that once had imprisoned him, tenuous as the threads of the accused were to a defunct government.

Conover's accusations against Mary Surratt—linking her to her son,

John, the subject of supposedly sinister meetings in Canada—were wholly based on guilt by association. His testimony seemed the stuff of gossamer, although the commission members appeared to be satisfied. Conover, in turn, was seconded by his henchman, Henry von Steinecker, and also answered to Hans von Winkelstein, who deserted both the Union and the Confederate armies and was a convicted horse thief.

Others of the motley crew of witnesses included Captain Richard Montgomery, admitted double agent for the North and South, and a shadowy figure, Dr. James R. Merritt, about whom little was known. A few lesser pawns were briefly paraded before the commission by Judge Holt in what appeared to spectators such as Colonel Douglas as an effort to link the Confederate government, especially such members as Clay and Jacob Thompson, directly with the actual assassination. Manifestly, they were paraded before the court with Secretary Stanton's approval, just possibly in an effort to assure a guilty verdict. That each, like vintage wine, was a well-seasoned liar apparently eluded none except the judges. Truth, observed the old Chinese proverb, was too precious a gem to tarnish through overuse.

None of the defendants was allowed to testify in his or her own defense. Only one, Atzerodt, made a statement. This was read by his counsel, William E. Doster, a former provost marshal of the District of Columbia. Several witnesses had already sworn that this man Atzerodt was "remarkable for his cowardice." Denying any part in the plot, the carriage-maker from southern Maryland stated: "I met Booth and Payne at the Herndon House, in this city at 8 o'clock. He [Booth] said he himself should murder Mr. Lincoln and General Grant, Payne should take Mr. Seward, and I should take Mr. Johnson. I told him I would not do it; that I had gone into the thing to capture, but I was not going to kill. He told me I was a fool; that I would be hung anyhow, and that it was death for every man that backed out; and so we parted . . . I wandered about the street until about 2 o'clock in the morning, and then went to the Kimmell House, and from there pawned my pistol at Georgetown, and went to my cousin's house in Montgomery County [Maryland] where I was arrested the 19th following." Actually, carrying a sheathed bowie knife, Atzerodt got as far as the bar of the Kirkwood House, then lost his nerve.

Each defendant was distinct and different from the other. Observing Atzerodt, Noah Brooks wrote, "When any ludicrous incident disturbed the gravity of the court, as sometimes happened, [he] was the only man who never smiled, although the others, Payne especially, would often grin in sympathy with the auditors."

While it was conceded by the reporters present that the three male conspirators were ruffians who deserved the noose, the prosecution, in a rare deferral to fairness, sought medical testimony on their mental balance or lack of it. But as it turned out, the doctors were fascinated by the neanderthal-like Payne and devoted their attentions to him.

Surgeon General Barnes, who was at Lincoln's deathbed, admitting he was "not familiar with cases of insanity," nonetheless offered, "It is not usual for madness to escape the scrutiny of physicians on a single inter-view, or two interviews. I think there is something always in the appear-ance of a man, in his manner or in his speech, that would arouse a suspicion of a physician, or indeed of any intelligent persons, even on one interview . . .

"I do not think the conduct of the prisoner in my presence was the conduct of a madman during a lucid interval. It will be found upon scrutiny that the conduct of a madman in a lucid interval differs from the ordinary conduct of men . . . I would regard it as a very exceptional case if this man should be insane."

Yet, in concluding his vague, rambling testimony, Dr. Barnes conceded that Payne could indeed be a "monomaniac." That seemed to please the commission, unknowing as all its members were as to what the surgeon general was talking about, and he was excused.

Assistant Surgeon General George L. Porter stated unequivocally, "I have not observed any indication of insanity."

In a coming era—really on the horizon—Sigmund Freud would have studied this testimony with unabashed wonderment.

Brooks, writing later as a nonprofessional about the same conspirator, wrote of Payne's "coarse, black hair . . . brushed well off his low broad forehead . . . his brawny, muscular chest . . . covered only by a dark, close-fitting sweater . . . It was curious to see the quick flash of intelligence that involuntarily shot from his eyes when the knife with which he had done the bloody work at Seward's house was identified by the man who found it in the street near the house in the gray dawn of the morning after that dreadful night. The knife was a heavy, horn-handled implement, with a double edge at the point, and a blade ten inches long, thick at the back but evidently ground carefully to a fine point."

Other clinical questions, not involving insanity, had been asked of the unhappy defendant Dr. Mudd. But his testimony, like that of the others, had to be second or even third hand. According to Colonel H. H. Wells, who had interviewed the physician, "he was aroused by a loud knock at his door. Going to the window, he saw in his front yard a person holding two horses, on one of which a second person was sitting . . . The person on horseback had a broken leg, and desired medical attendance."

Dr. Mudd, according to the statement, then assisted the injured man onto a sofa, and let him rest "for some time." When the physician examined his right leg, he "found that the front bone was broken, nearly at right angles, about two inches above the instep. It appeared, in his judgment, to be as slight a breaking as it could possibly be."

He dressed the limb "as well as he was able to do with the limited facilities he had, and called a young man, a white servant, I think, to make a crutch." All then sat down to breakfast, after which Dr. Mudd studied his patient once more and found him "much debilitated, and pale to such an extent that he was unable to tell what his complexion might have been, light or dark."

The pair remained until "some time after dinner." Although Dr. Mudd admitted he had "been introduced to Booth at church, some time in November last, as wanting to buy some farm lands," he insisted that he had not recognized him as the one with the broken leg bone. But Mudd did think "there was something strange about these two persons from the young man coming down shortly after breakfast and asking for a razor, saying his friend wished to shave himself; and when he was upstairs shortly afterward, he saw that the wounded man had shaved off his moustache." He was sure his patient originally possessed "a long, heavy beard," although he remained uncertain that it was natural.

The country doctor asserted he had not heard of the murder until Sunday morning, or "late on Saturday evening." All in all, he was a puzzler. Even one of the defense attorneys, Thomas Ewing, who was the brother-in-law of General Sherman, had to admit that the defendant's "manner was so very extraordinary . . . I scarcely know how to describe it." Dr. Mudd, well-known Southern sympathizer, was probably unable to describe himself, remaining in a state of semishock. How could he, a medical man by training but one not engaged actively in practice, be drawn into such a compromising, if not fatal, situation?

If the court had focused its collective attention on Payne, Atzerodt, Herold, and Mrs. Surratt, the reporters found comparable fascination in the companion defendants, easily as strange a crew as the foursome who occupied center stage.

These included Arnold, "generally . . . inattentive to everything that went on," according to the perceptive Noah Brooks; Spangler, the stage carpenter whose "hands were incessantly moving along his legs from knee to thigh, his bony fingers traveling back and forth like spiders"; and Michael O'Laughlin, reported to have been at Stanton's door the fateful night, inquiring for General Grant, now nervously "scanning each new arrival at the door, watching the witnesses, but occasionally resting [his eyes] on the green trees and sunny sky seen through the grated window on his left."

Brooks continued of O'Laughlin, "He often moved his feet, and the clanking of his manacles would attract his attention; he would look down, then back and forth at the scene within the courtroom."

The trial, much in the tradition of litigation involving far more mundane issues, was periodically interrupted by discussions of jurisprudence. Sublimely ignorant as they were of these technicalities, the court officers half dozed or looked at the walls or out of the windows. Defense counsel Thomas Ewing, for example, vainly sought a clarification of the basic question of whether there were "four distinct crimes in this one charge."

To this query, Assistant Judge Advocate John Bingham replied, "that where parties are indicted for a conspiracy, and the execution thereof, it is but one crime at the common law, and upon all authority, as many overt acts in the execution of that conspiracy as they are guilty of, may be laid in the same count."

Persisting, Ewing observed, "It is then, I understand, one crime with which they are charged . . . the crime of conspiracy?"

Bingham: "It is the crime of murder as well. It is not simply conspiring, but executing the conspiracy treasonably, and in aid of the rebellion."

Still not satisfied, Ewing pursued, "I should like an answer to my question, if it is to be given: how many distinct crimes are my clients charged with and being tried for? I cannot tell."

Judge Advocate Joseph Holt then interrupted, "It may be my misfortune, but I think it is not my fault, if the gentleman has not already the answer which he seeks. I cannot give him a better one." (It somehow seemed more than coincidence that Lewis Carroll's *Alice's Adventures in Wonderland* was published this very year, 1865, bequeathing to posterity double talk and non sequiturs that illuminated such sequences as the mad tea party.)

Protesting that Holt's answers were not "intelligible," the attorney avowed that "a question of the utmost gravity" remained to be answered. Instead, Holt continued to find refuge in the catchall "the common law of war."

Reverdy Johnson, patriarchal, respected U.S. senator from Maryland, felt it his duty to come to the defense of the woman from his state who appeared to be in mortal trouble. Vainly, the legislator-lawyer endeavored to discredit the jurisdiction of the military tribunal.

"Reverdy Johnson," wrote the correspondent Townsend, "having made an excellent plea for civil tribunals, and the power of the common law, has become incensed at the cavalier bearing of the court martial officers, whose examinations of witnesses are both informal and arbitrary."

The reporter had, in effect, voiced the rationale of General Horace Porter, Grant's distinguished aide who had declined a seat on the tribunal. Then, with the month of June drawing to a close, Townsend summed: "Judging from the evidence already presented, it would appear as if Booth—[with a] mania . . . for assassination—had conceived the plan as far back as November last," with "little encouragement or assistance" from the Confederacy. Although Townsend conceded that Mary Surratt was "by no means a demon in female form," he saw her as "capable of perilous enterprise" and agreed with the prosecutors as to her "connivance and complicity." To Townsend, she was a "representative secession woman, of a type with those who spit in the faces of our soldiers."

He thought Dr. Mudd's "chief error was in suppressing part of his strange hospitality till a late moment. His previous intimacy with Booth is hardly established."

William E. Doster, counsel for Atzerodt, was less circumspect, noting that "the prosecutors had a month assisted by the whole war power of the Government, its railroads, telegraphs, detectives, and military bureau to get its evidence into shape. The prisoners did not receive their charges until the day the trial opened and then they could only communicate sitting in chains, with a soldier on each side, a great crowd surrounding them, and whisper through the bars of the dock to their counsel."

Suggesting that the defense needed "weeks" to prepare, Doster criticized the very attitude of the commission; "Surrounded by bayonets . . .

in a penitentiary . . . the judges could not be challenged," even though they were ignorant, Doster asserted, of "all the rules of evidence."

Furthermore, he would subsequently charge, "Many of the witnesses were detectives in the Government pay." He found in the casual remark of one member the mood of the entire commission: "Well, Payne seems to want to be hung, so I guess we might as well hang him."

John W. Clampitt, counsel for Surratt, denounced the "wholesale perjury" of government witnesses, only to have these and similar charges stricken from the record.

But Doster, Clampitt, and others for the defense had not demanded Booth's diary, now in the possession of Secretary Stanton. Its existence had been made known in the press as early as April 27. (It was found later that several pages had been cut out of it, covering the critical days before the assassination. It would be theorized that the contents of the missing pages would have exonerated Mary Surratt and possibly Arnold and O'Laughlin as well. But this was conjecture, as were statements about the motives for their removal.)

Henry Kyd Douglas wrote: "If justice ever sat with unbandaged blood-shot eyes, she did on this occasion.

"I suppose there is no case on record where a distinguished attorney was compelled to submit to such indignities as General Hunter and several of the court put upon the venerable Reverdy Johnson. Although the court was organized to convict, the trial need not have been such a shameless farce.

"When I stood at the door, looking in at the proceedings, I saw another scene which reminded me of the French Revolution. Ladies of position, culture and influence enough to be admitted sat about the Court, near the Judges, talked to the prosecutors, and with scowls and scorn, white teeth and scorching eyes, augmented the general horror. I never felt as wicked in my life as when, on the stand an unwilling witness, I saw the gaze of their wrathful eyes upon me; they glared at me as if they thought I had taken a hand in a murder which I thought the direst calamity that could have befallen the South."

Finally, on June 29, the commission adjourned behind closed doors. There was little deliberation or strikingly opposing viewpoints. The very next morning, the last day of the month, "after mature consideration," the judges committed the verdicts to paper. There were no surprises.

The decision: guilty, with, by its own guidelines, "two-thirds of the members of the commission concurring therein."

For George Atzerodt, David Herold, Lewis Payne, and Mary Surratt, death was the sentence. Each was to be "hanged by the neck . . . until dead, at such time and place as the President of the United States shall direct; two-thirds of the commission concurring therein." Of scant consolation to the four was the fact that on lesser conspiracy charges they were declared not guilty.

Secondary defendants Michael O'Laughlin, Samuel Arnold, and Dr. Mudd were sentenced "to be imprisoned at hard labor for life." Edward Spangler, stagehand and sometime horse groom, received a comparative slap on the wrist, hard labor for six years.

The findings remained sealed, to be approved by the president.

But the court was shaky at the prospect of sending a female to the gallows, historically reserved for male criminals such as murderers and horse thieves. Even the more thick-skinned conceded that it was not a nice way to meet one's maker. The federal government, besides, had never put a woman to death.

Although a minority of the commission professed to find no distinction between hanging Mary Surratt and the men, all entertained qualms. None would admit any desire to be present at the executions.

Stanton wanted these people hanged. There continued discussion over Surratt's fate, and then finally a compromise. Why not pass the entire responsibility—and the guilt—along to the president, while at the same time obediently condemning the boardinghouse keeper, just as Stanton had so passionately desired? But more intriguing yet was the general belief that the secretary of war, blithely flaunting all codes of legal and moral conduct, had himself suggested such a mortal caper.

A short addendum was attached, which was also to be approved by the chief executive: "The undersigned members [five in number] of the Commission detailed to try Mary E. Surratt and others for conspiracy and the murder of Abraham Lincoln, late President of the United States . . . respectfully pray that the President in consideration of the age and sex of the said Mary E. Surratt, if he can upon the facts in the case find it consistent with his sense of duty to the country, commute the sentence of death which the Court have been constrained to place upon her, to imprisonment for life. Respectfully submitted . . ."

Sniveling, weasel cowardice had plummeted to new depths.

JULY

The Woman on Their Conscience

The month of July arrived in the nation's capital, hot, sultry, and stifling. It was typical of summer in the city beside the miasma of the filth-ridden Potomac.

The wounded and sick soldiers lingering in the steamy and pestilential wards of the frame and tent hospitals on the Mall and elsewhere around the city's perimeters sweated, groaned, and, even as during the long hostilities, expired. From a surgeon's perspective, the ratio of those cured to those who succumbed remained, at the very least, "undesirable."

In Washington Penitentiary, the cells were as oppressive as the clinical purlieus of life—and death. There the convicted waited as the sands ran low—July 1, July 2, July 3, then Independence Day, July 4. The city was rocked and illuminated by fireworks this first peacetime observance of independence in four years. And all this while none had told any one of the hapless eight under trial that the commission had already reached a verdict.

Officially, the president was sick. Gideon Welles, in his diary, would attest to that: "The President is indisposed . . . He has been threatened with apoplexy . . . pale and languid. It is a month since he came to the Executive Mansion and he has never yet gone outside the doors."

For two months Andrew Johnson had lodged in the modest comfort of the Kirkwood while the distraught Mary Todd Lincoln packed up her family to leave. Yet this apparent act of charity did not impress a former

79

slave and modiste for Mrs. Lincoln, Elizabeth Keckley. The president, she remembered, "never called on the widow, or even so much as wrote a line, expressing sympathy for her grief and the loss of her husband." Then she added, "Mrs. Lincoln firmly believes that Mr. Johnson was concerned in the assassination plot."

The executive remained an enigma, in health, in personality, and certainly in national considerations. His emotions were proving to be a cauldron of contradictions: punishing some whom he labeled prime instigators of the rebellion, while being so forgiving to masses of others as to alienate, early, the radicals of Congress.

"If it is the last act of my life I'd hang Jeff Davis as an example . . . and a few others of the arch-conspirators and traitors," he confided to one of his secretaries, Benjamin Truman.

This did not much impress the Radical Republicans since they assumed that any right-thinking American would inevitably arrive at the same conclusion. In addition to the ever powerful Senator Sumner, of Massachusetts, their number included Congressman Thaddeus Stevens, of Pennsylvania, and Benjamin F. "Ben" Wade, of Ohio. Stevens, with his club foot, big black wig, overriding ugliness, profanity, and sarcasm, was all too familiar a sight, limping about the halls of Congress.

"The whole fabric of southern society *must* be changed . . . The southern States have been despotisms, not governments of the people . . . If they (the so-called southern 'nobility') go, all the better!" Stevens shouted in Congress. And he was seconded as well by those outside the august chambers, especially the fire-breathing abolitionist Horace Greeley, editor of the New York *Tribune*, and Wendell Phillips, an orator and author of the same mind.

Wade had been anathema to all Union generals, not excepting Grant, Sherman, and Sheridan. They all moved too slowly, he stormed. Why had not the Southern foe been annihilated at once! Perhaps only an Attila or a Genghis Khan would have satisfied him, complete with rape, pillage, and mayhem. Now, so far as Ben Wade was concerned, the South need never rise again.

In the face of this congressional storm and bombast on Reconstruction, President Johnson withdrew more and more into himself. His only communication with the outside world lay in formal pronouncements, including the reward for the arrest of Jefferson Davis and others, and the proclamation of amnesty.

Certainly he was the poorer for the lack of a first lady. Because of the chronic illness of his wife, Eliza, a sturdy daughter (one of five children, including two daughters), Martha Patterson, filled in with dignity and grace. She disarmed guests with the aside "We are just plain people from Tennessee."

But what, if anything, was wrong with the chief executive? Apoplexy was a catchall, and likely an overstatement. Others believed he suffered from gallstones, a severe cold, a cough, "bilious fever," perhaps only a hangover, although his alleged predilection for alcohol remained much in dispute.

"He did take two or three or four glasses of Robertson County whiskey some days," recalled Ben Truman of Johnson's Nashville military governorship, "some days less, and some days and weeks no liquor at all. So as drinking went in Tennessee, Johnson would have been termed a strictly temperate man." Later, his sometime secretary added, Johnson switched to sherry.

Foes made much of the Tennessean's reeling behavior and rambling speech at Lincoln's second inaugural on March 4, so much so that the latter was forced to defend his vice president as "not a drunkard." Cronies declared that Johnson had imbibed too much brandy earlier in the day since he had not felt well.

A more or less impartial observer, however, General Charles Hamlin, was certain he saw Johnson toss off three glasses of raw whiskey. Hamlin was the son of Hannibal Hamlin, the retiring vice president.

But it was hard to convince the radicals and a slowly accumulating battalion of assorted foes that the president was not in his cups more of the time than he was sober. Those who supported him believed that Johnson was for the most part moderate in his drinking habits, certainly measured against his contemporaries who regarded whiskey as a soft drink, a form of health insurance in an era of unchecked bacterial assaults. Even sober, Johnson, of a volatile nature, could effortlessly launch into a tirade that listeners would ever remember.

The waiting continued, until Wednesday morning, the fifth. Those surrounding the president knew that Judge Holt wanted to see him. Finally, Preston King, former senator from New York and now a White House guest, advised Holt early Wednesday that Johnson was "better" and "he is sitting up."

Immensely overweight and a onetime mental patient, King, a lawyer, had served in both houses of Congress, and was considered a power on the legislative floors. In 1864, he had been instrumental in securing Johnson's nomination for vice president.

Almost immediately, Preston King sent another messenger racing to Holt's office, bidding him to come to the executive mansion. But from then on there was to be no full account of what transpired. The two men met, with no third party present.

According to Andrew Johnson, Judge Holt arrived by a "private or family" entrance, in the afternoon. "The examination of the papers took place in the library and he and I alone were present . . . In acting upon her [Mary Surratt's] case, no recommendation for a commutation of her punishment was mentioned, or submitted to me." The president would later acknowledge that the question of sex did arise, at which time Holt "with peculiar force and solemnity . . . urged that the fact that the criminal was a woman was in itself no excuse or palliation," that she had "unsexed" herself by entering "the arena of crime."

In a diametrically opposing version, Judge Holt would declare that he entered through the main portals of the White House, in the morning, not afternoon, and certainly "the forenoon."

The jurist added, "I drew the President's attention specially to the recommendation in favor of Mrs. Surratt which he read and freely commented on . . . He could not . . . accede or grant the petition for the reason that there was no class in the South more violent in the expression and practice of treasonable sentiments than the rebel women."

But what was the truth?

Colonel Reuben D. Mussey, a presidential secretary, would declare, but not under oath, "I am certain he [Johnson] did so inform me" about the petition for clemency. Mussey, who had fought in Tennessee before he joined the staff of Andrew Johnson's military governorship, expanded on what he recalled was Johnson's philosophy: "If she was guilty, her sex did not make her any less guilty."

The fact that Johnson told him that "he didn't desire to see anyone who came on such errands" (asking for commutation of Mrs. Surratt's sentence) tended to substantiate what Mussey thought was the chief executive's unyielding position.

Whether or not he knew about the disputed document, President Johnson did sign the death warrants of four humans this hot Wednesday,

July 5, 1865. But he did not put a time on it, morning or afternoon. Datelined the executive mansion, the document read:

The foregoing sentences in the cases of David E. Herold, G. A. Atzerodt, Lewis Payne, Michael O'Laughlin, Edward Spangler, Samuel Arnold, Mary E. Surratt, and Samuel A. Mudd, are hereby approved, and it is ordered that the sentences of said David E. Herold, G. A. Atzerodt, Lewis Payne, and Mary E. Surratt be carried into execution by the proper military authority, under the direction of the Secretary of War, on the 7th day of July, 1865, between the hours of 10 o'clock A.M. and 2 o'clock P.M., of that day. It is further ordered that the prisoners, Samuel Arnold, Samuel A. Mudd, Edward Spangler, and Michael O'Laughlin be confined at hard labor in the Penitentiary at Albany, New York, during the period designated in their respective sentences.

Andrew Johnson,
President

(Scholars would later assert that the text appeared to match the handwriting of none other than Judge Holt, and "Andrew Johnson" had been signed in rather "wiggly" fashion, although none went so far as to charge the president's signature was a forgery.)

There could be no appeal through the federal courts to the Supreme Court since this was a military, not a civilian judgment. The president of the United States alone held the power of commutation—of life and death.

About midday this Wednesday, another prisoner at the Washington Penitentiary, Burton Harrison, not quite as pampered as Colonel Douglas, was surprised when his guards failed to appear to escort him on his regular walk. The former secretary to Jefferson Davis had been fortunate to escape the direct attention of Edwin Stanton. Nonetheless, the curse of the Confederate cabinet rested heavily upon young Burton's shoulders.

His fiancée in Richmond, Connie Cary, would paraphrase his letters to her: "From the yard below arose a greater clamor of saws and hammering . . . He surmised what was to be."

Military carpenters had just forty-eight hours to erect a gallows. They must work fast. In the northeast corner of the high brick-walled arsenal grounds, near the shoe shop and next to the prison, the structure was "very strong, with heavy timbers," the reporter for the *Constitutional Union* related. It must effect the simultaneous hanging of all four condemned. This gruesome bit, defense counsels would speculate, must somehow be attributed to the vengefulness of Judge Holt and Secretary Stanton. Three quarters of an inch hemp was procured from the Navy Yard.

The army's official hangman, Captain Christian Rath, had a very difficult time recruiting soldiers or ⸗nyone else to perform the most gruesome parts of the execution: digging graves, setting the traps, binding the hands and feet of the condemned, and, finally, placing the bodies in plain pine coffins. They didn't waste much sympathy on the three convicted men. They wanted no part in hanging a woman.

But Rath was equal to his gory challenge. He offered copious servings of whiskey to those of the provost's military guard who would volunteer. The entire regiment came forward.

The shadows of Wednesday grew long. Connie Cary continued: "Every night before he [Burton] had heard coming through the ventilating tube the melancholy whistling of an occupant of the cell beneath his, evidently absent in the day; for which sound he had learned to listen with an odd sense of companionship. That evening the whistle began—but was halted suddenly and the listener thought the effort was beyond the power of a condemned man probably on the eve of execution.

"That night also he heard a new sound—a ship's bell striking the watches close by.

" 'Some of them are to be transported, and that boat is here to take them off,' flashed through his mind." Although the arsenal complex lay on a landspit between the Eastern Branch River and a channel of the Potomac, no boat had moored to remove any of the unfortunates. It was a prisoner's blind speculation.

And, still, as Thursday, July 6, neared, the condemned had not been advised of their fate. On Wednesday, the Reverend Jacob A. Walter, pastor of Mary Surratt's parish, St. Patrick's Church, at 10th and F streets (a block from Ford's Theatre), had "learned that the trial was over." Although he had received one letter from this "quiet, amiable lady," in late April, he had not yet met her. Nor had he closely followed the proceedings. The whole tragedy had bothered this holy man immensely as an affront to his sense of reason: "If the parties had reflected on what they proposed doing, the act would never have been consummated," he would later observe.

Not having any idea of the verdict, about 10:00 A.M. Thursday Father

Walter decided he would attempt to procure a pass to call on Mrs. Surratt. Accordingly, he walked the several blocks to the War Department and made his request to Brigadier General James A. Hardie, then the inspector general. The officer, who apparently himself did not know about the verdict, said that Secretary Stanton, who, like Johnson, had been ailing, was not in. However, he assured the priest he would have a pass for him "in a few hours."

Satisfied, Jacob Walter returned to the rectory for his customary noontime dinner.

Even as the priest commenced his meal, Major General Winfield Scott Hancock, named by an uneasy President Johnson after the assassination to command the capital area—the Middle Military District—was galloping his horse into the penitentiary grounds. There he handed General Hartranft, his provost, the four death warrants, burdening him at the same time with the unpleasant duty of personally reading them to the condemned, one by one.

Payne, as the *Evening Star* would report, showed no surprise, big, stolid, and inscrutable as always. Atzerodt tried manfully to assume indifference, but "the telltale tremor of his extremities and the ashy pallor upon his face" gave his emotions away. Herold, who had expected a light sentence, was numbed as if struck by "a thunderbolt." He could not speak, much less move his lips.

The last to learn, Mary Surratt, was "completely unstrung," the same daily paper wrote. Like Herold, she had anticipated a minor rebuke, if not exoneration. Magnifying her shock and disbelief was the fact that she had been ill throughout almost the entire trial—change of life, perhaps, some disorder that prison physicians either could not properly diagnose or were insufficiently interested in so doing. When the hearings adjourned in the evening, she would lie on her straw mattress upon the bare brick floor of her cell, number 153, refusing all but the most meager sustenance. (Confederate prisoners at the notorious Elmira, New York, camp had been accorded relatively more compassionate treatment.)

Shortly after noon, General Hartranft could report to General Hancock that he had carried out his orders.

Father Walter was finishing his meal and enjoying a cup of coffee when two visitors knocked on the rectory door. One was John F. Callan, the other a Mr. Holohan, both boarders at Mrs. Surratt's. Only then was the priest informed of the verdict.

"To act so hastily in a matter of this kind . . . certainly strange on the part of the Government!" he gasped in understatement.

Immediately, an orderly arrived with Colonel Hardie's pass. Before sending the young soldier on his way, the priest delivered a short sermon on capital punishment: ". . . I had read all the evidence of this trial and, as regards Mrs. Surratt, there was not evidence enough to hang a cat; besides, you cannot make me believe that a Catholic woman would go to communion on Holy Thursday and be guilty of murder on Good Friday!"

Within the hour, a fourth visitor arrived: Hardie himself, red-faced, puffing. The orderly reported to the officer on "the violent and excited language" of the priest, "so inflammatory . . . at this, a time of great public excitement."

Walter led Hardie into the parlor. The officer explained that he had brought a pass from Secretary Stanton, fearing the one he had signed earlier would be insufficient.

"I asked him," General Hardie would report, "in a friendly and kindly way to promise me that he would desist from talking about the matter . . . Since it appeared that Mr. Walter could not approach the subject with temper and discretion, it was better he should let it alone."

This, according to the inspector general, infuriated the man of the cloth, who became "denunciatory . . . He harangued upon the Administration and rebellion, and dwelt with bitterness on what he called military tyranny." The priest would recall, however, that he replied "coolly and deliberately." His remarks on the subject: "You wish me to promise that I shall say nothing in regard to the innocence of Mrs. Surratt. Do you know the relation existing between a pastor and his flock? I will defend the character of the poorest woman in my parish at the risk of my life. Thank God I do not know what fear is, I fear neither man nor the devil, but God alone. You wish to seal my lips; I wish you to understand that I was born a freeman and will die one."

Now raging, the priest turned his wrath on Edwin Stanton: "I know where all this comes from . . . your Secretary of War, whom a Congressman in my breakfast room two weeks ago called a brute!"

Then, once more objective, he admitted he could not allow Mrs. Surratt to die "without the Sacraments." He shrugged, "If I must say yes, I must say yes."

Hardie, feeling that he had prevailed, gave him the pass. It was now past mid-afternoon. The Reverend Mr. Walter set out for the penitentiary.

At this time, John W. Clampitt, Mary Surratt's attorney, sitting in his office and still speculating on the findings of the commission, was startled by the cry of newsboys: "The Execution of Mrs. Surratt!"

Expecting an acquittal or at most "a temporary confinement of our client," Clampitt "hardly knew how to proceed." For want of a better course, he hurried to the White House. There he was met by Preston King, who had summoned Judge Holt the previous day.

Pointing to soldiers with fixed bayonets, King informed Clampitt that it was "useless to attempt an issue of that character." He was alluding, presumably, to any efforts to save the condemned woman.

Clampitt, dread mounting in his heart, next "collected" Annie Surratt, probably at the boardinghouse, and called on Judge Holt. But, as the lawyer would record, "our plea was in vain. His heart was chilled, his soul impassive as marble." Annie herself, "the forlorn girl," went down on her knees, her face "bathed in tears," to plead with the judge advocate for a three-day extension of execution. Certainly, there must be further legal avenues to explore . . . ?

The best Holt would do was to agree to meet the pair in an hour at the White House. Clampitt left without the judge ever volunteering a word about the clemency addendum.

Meanwhile, Father Walter was finishing his prison visit with Mary Surratt. Before he left, he assured her he would be back in the morning to give her communion. The priest hurried along to the White House, where he met Annie Surratt and Clampitt. Also present was a Pennsylvania congressman, Thomas Florence, who remarked: "Father Walter, you and I are on the same errand of mercy. The President must not allow this woman to be hanged!"

Inside, the priest and the congressman encountered a formidable trio: King, Colonel Mussey, and another legislator, Senator James H. Lane, of Kansas. The priest requested the secretary, Mussey, to ask Johnson for an interview. Clampitt entered just as Judge Holt was leaving.

"I can do nothing," asserted the judge advocate. "The President is immovable. He has carefully examined the findings of the commission and has no reason to change the date of execution."

Mussey conveyed much the same answer, but patiently returned twice at the priest's insistence, the third time to explain that Father Walter was not asking for a pardon but only "ten days . . . to prepare Mrs. Surratt for eternity." And each time the chief executive refused to see any of the callers.

"Come, Annie," the priest said to the young woman, leading her from the White House, and would later write, "The poor child, with eyes streaming with tears, was left without any sympathy from this cold, heartless man."

Doubtless, he referred to Johnson and Holt. Being shunted back and forth between the two he likened to a game of "battledoor and shuttle-cock."

There was nothing for the priest to do but return to his rectory until morning. It was late. The gas lamps had already come on to shed their glow over the still hot streets.

As the night wore on, Clampitt was frantic, "in despair." He could not rest. Discovering a light still burning in the telegraph office, he opened the door and sent a telegram to Reverdy Johnson in Baltimore, requesting his "immediate presence."

At midnight, the reply: "It is very late. There are no trains to carry me to Washington City. Apply for a writ of *habeas corpus*, and take her body from the custody of the military authorities. We are now in a state of peace—not war."

But what judge, Clampitt pondered, was "bold enough" to issue such a writ "in the face of public clamor"? Of all jurists, Clampitt hit on a friend of Stanton's, Judge Alexander Wylie, of the Supreme Court of the District of Columbia.

"Just as the clock tolled the hour of two in the morning," Clampitt rang the justice's door bell. Wylie resided at 12th Street and Vermont Avenue, a brisk ten minutes' walk from the White House.

A window was raised, and "the well-known voice of the judge greeted us . . . 'What do you want?' " Clampitt explained it was a mission of life and death. The urgency in his voice impelled the judge to shuffle down-stairs, "clad only in his dressing gown," and led Clampitt into his study, where, "sitting like a statue in the glimmer of the gaslight," he listened without interruption to the reading of the petition. At the conclusion he took the papers, politely declared, "Please excuse me, gentlemen," and retired to his bedroom.

Although "our hearts fell within us" (Clampitt's companion presumably being his associate Frederick Aiken), the judge soon returned, explaining that he had always "endeavored to perform my duty fearlessly . . . I am about to perform an act which before tomorrow's sun goes down may consign *me* to the Old Capitol Prison."

He issued the writ, demanding that Mrs. Surratt be turned over to the civil authorities. Before 4:00 A.M., U.S. Marshal David Gooding had served it on General Hancock at the Metropolitan Hotel, his headquarters.

At the penitentiary, there had also been nightlong activity. None— visitor or condemned—had slept. There had been a host of ministers including the Reverend J. George Butler, a hospital chaplain, and the Reverend W. W. Winchester, attending Atzerodt, described as the most nervous of all the prisoners; Dr. M. L. Olds, of Christ Episcopal Church, Capitol Hill, one of Washington's original churches, praying with Herold; Dr. A. D. Gillette, of the First Baptist Church, and as well the Reverend A. P. Stryhan, with Payne; and a second priest, the Reverend B. F. Wiget, attempting to comfort Mary Surratt. She had been ill all the night with cramps, headaches, and generalized pains.

At 5:00 A.M., with the sun just up, Mrs. Surratt was moved to a solitary cell on the first floor. About half an hour later, Payne, as the least nervous of the four, requested to talk with Hartranft. The provost honored the doomed man in prompt, soldierly fashion. Seated in Payne's cell, the officer listened to his words. When he returned to his office, the general wrote rapidly: "The prisoner Payne has just told me that Mrs. Surratt is entirely innocent of the assassination of President Lincoln, or of any knowledge thereof. He also states that she had no knowledge whatever of the abduction plot, that nothing was ever said to her about it, and that her name was never mentioned by the parties connected therewith." Hartranft paused, then added, "I believe that Payne has told the truth in this matter."

The provost then put the declaration in an envelope and asked an aide to get it to the White House.

Someone else was up and writing feverishly at this early hour, John P. Brophy, a friend of the Surratt family. His acquaintance, Louis Weichmann, had been stricken with an attack of conscience in the past twenty-four hours. After all, the testimony of this former occupant of the Surratt boardinghouse had borne deadly weight in her conviction.

Weichmann had babbled many things to Brophy, including the fact that in early March, before the second inaugural, he had warned the War Department of a plot to kidnap Lincoln. But there had been so many such tips that the authorities paid him little heed.

Now, however, Weichmann was allegedly confessing to Brophy that "he swore to a falsehood on the witness stand." Brophy, who believed Weichmann "is and always was a coward," was preparing what he called an "affidavit," elaborating on the boarder's remarks. Weichmann, "an avowed secessionist," told Brophy he would present a full confession for President Johnson's eyes if the latter "would keep it a profound secret." He would not give it to Holt "because I have no confidence in him."

The trouble was, Brophy did not know whether to believe all or none of this "coward's" confession—and if he did, if he presented it to Johnson or Holt, whether either of them could place any credence in it. Had Louis Weichmann perjured himself or not?

At a little after 7:00 A.M. Father Walter arrived to give Mary Surratt communion: "Poor Mrs. Surratt had been sick for several weeks and was quite feeble. She was lying on a mattress laid on the bare brick floor of her cell. Certainly, this was not the way in which to treat the vilest convict just before execution . . . ," the priest recalled.

Most of the other men of the cloth had continued their vigil into the morning hours. Payne, satisfied that he had presumably absolved Mrs. Surratt in his statement to Hartranft, sat and listened "attentively" to the Reverend Mr. Gillette, himself sweating and verging on exhaustion. With little ventilation in the dank brick structure, sweat ran from the minister's brow and arms and onto the Bible from which he read almost ceaselessly, hardly pausing for breath.

Herold, now joined by five of his seven sisters, lay back on his cot, semiconscious. Atzerodt was with his wife, a small, shy, quiet woman who had kept away from the trial. She sat there, staring, wide-eyed.

About 8:30 A.M. Annie Surratt, accompanied by John Brophy and the other two sisters of Herold, returned to the White House. Increasingly desperate, she tried to run up the stairs to the second floor, only to be confronted once more by the corpulent figure of Preston King and by the gaunt, vulturelike person of Senator Lane. She flung herself down on the stairs' carpet and cried and screamed until the president's daughter, Martha Patterson, appeared and at once introduced a White House guest, the former Adele Cutts. She was the widow of Stephen A. Douglas, the Little Giant who had opposed Lincoln for the first term and unexpectedly died in 1861.

"My poor dear," Mrs. Douglas soothed, putting an arm around the shoulders of the young lady. "You break my heart, but there is nothing I can do." She then led Annie to the East Room as guards, with curious expressions, watched. Could they possibly have been touched by the scene?

Annie's sobs became more stifled. Nonetheless, she started each time a door opened. But never was it the president who emerged.

About mid-morning, the cabinet met in the president's office. The attendance was sparse. Present were Stanton; Seward, only partly recovered from his wounds; Attorney General Joseph Speed, former Democrat and now a South-hating Black Republican; and James Harlan, former judge, onetime senator from Iowa, who had just assumed the secretaryship of the interior.

Judge Harlan, in a letter that was to be quoted by Colonel Henry Burnett, who had assisted Judge Holt at the trial, recalled that he had entered the room while the others were engaged in "earnest conversation on the question of whether the sentence ought to be modified on account of the sex of the condemned."

Harlan then singled out one speaker whom he identified only as an "eminent statesman," but in likelihood was none other than Secretary Stanton.

" 'Surely not, Mr. President,' " the statesman was quoted as saying, " 'for if the death penalty should be commuted in so grave a case as the assassination of the head of a great nation, on account of the sex of the criminal, it would amount to an invitation to assassins hereafter to employ women as their instruments under the belief that if arrested and condemned they would be punished less severely than men.' "

The speaker then concluded with the sweeping assumption that "every" civilized nation on earth would surely "reject such a plea." This seemed to satisfy all present, and the conversation turned to other matters. (Johnson would later rationalize to the Reverend Mr. Butler, one of Atzerodt's spiritual advisers, that he "could not be moved," since "Mrs. Surratt kept the nest that hatched the eggs." It was an old Tennessee saying.)

The commission's own clemency addendum was not treated at the cabinet meeting. At least two of those present must have known about it: Speed and Stanton. Colonel Burnett himself would affirm that he had shown it to his superior, the secretary of war. There was no indication that the chief executive had read Hartranft's urgent communication, much less that Brophy had actually delivered his own affidavit.

Attorney General Speed excused himself before the meeting adjourned.

There was ample reason, although secrecy as well surrounded this gambit. President Johnson, having been advised of the writ of habeas corpus, thereupon himself signed, at Speed's insistence, an order to General Hancock that such a writ "has been heretofore suspended in such cases as this . . . and I do hereby especially suspend this writ . . . and direct that you proceed to execute the order heretofore given."

At 11:00 A.M. the attorney general, Hancock, and Clampitt appeared before Judge Wylie at City Hall. Senator Orville Browning, of Illinois, certainly no friend of Andrew Johnson as he had been of Abraham Lincoln, was present. According to the attorney for Mrs. Surratt, the justice quickly "acquiesced" to the executive order and "all hope faded."

Hancock was shaken. He remarked to Clampitt, "I have been in many a battle and have seen death and mixed with it in disaster and in victory. I've been in a living hell of fire and shell and grapeshot and, by God, I'd sooner be there ten thousand times over than to give the order this day for the execution of that poor woman."

Then the general left.

Senator Browning was equally upset. He observed, "The Commission was without authority and its proceedings void. The execution of these persons will be murders. I trust the day will come when the country will be vindicated."

Thus the president and Speed had prevailed. Mrs. Surratt would not be delivered to the civilian authorities as Reverdy Johnson had hoped. Browning wished that the judge could have been a whit more courageous, ignoring the White House and arresting General Hancock "for contempt" in not obeying the court's order. Then let the Supreme Court decide the case.

While John Brophy hastened to the executive mansion to meet Annie Surratt and take her to the penitentiary, high noon came to a city solemn with the presentiment of doom. Bells tolled and soldiers tramped over the hot roadways. Wrote the correspondent for the *Constitutional Union*: "A great quiet prevailed, and it seemed as though the very elements partook of the awful scene soon to take place . . . A death-like calm was the predominating feature."

George Alfred Townsend, commencing for the New York *World* one of his longest and most flowery reports of the war or its aftermath, depicted the broad setting for the execution: "It was a long and dusty avenue along which rambled soldiers in bluishly white coats, cattle with their tongues out, straying from the herd and a few Negroes making for their cabins which dotted . . . the vacant lots of the suburbs. At the foot of this avenue where a lukewarm river holds between the dividing arms a dreary edifice of brick, the day was filled with collections . . . of people . . . The low, flat dusty white fields to the far left were lined with patrols of soldiers lying on the grounds in squads beside their stacked muskets."

There were, in fact, "monotonous" lines within lines of soldiers, even posted on the high, grim brick walls of the arsenal-penitentiary. No one professed to know why such legions were necessary.

Burton Harrison had been watching all morning the gathering of the guard, having been awakened early by the noise of renewed hammering. His fiancée, Connie Cary, wrote, "He could see [from his window] many troops massing in Pennsylvania Avenue, and amid them, riding alone, the Catholic priest Father Walter, the intrepid soldier of Christ . . .

"The officer detailed as usual to watch him at his breakfast, generally so genial, today avoided meeting the prisoner's eye, as did the soldier always holding a musket before his door. He asked no questions, ate his food, and sat afterward for hours without stirring from his chair.

"Thenceforward, every sound in the prison came unnaturally distinct. On all sides he heard the incessant tramp of gathering soldiers. On the roof facing the arsenal he saw gazers assembled, and could not look at them."

As Brophy with Annie Surratt returned to the prison, he noticed "cavalrymen stationed at points along the line from the White House to the Arsenal. These were couriers stationed by order of General Hancock to speed the tidings, should the President at the last moment relent, and grant a pardon or reprieve."

Annie found both Father Walter and Father Wiget with her mother. "Mother, are you resigned?" Walter quoted Annie as asking, to which she replied, "Yes, my child."

Her mother then said, "Annie, my child, this is no place for you, go to your room." And her daughter departed. At this point Mary Surratt was led from her cell and seated upon a small chair at the doorway. She whispered to the Reverend Mr. Walter, "Father, I wish to say something . . . that I am innocent."

At 12:20 General Hancock arrived for a final inspection. Ten minutes later, Herold's sisters, "weeping bitterly," Atzerodt's wife, and all other visitors except the ministers left the cells.

Alexander Gardner, a photographer who had studied under the better-known Matthew Brady, was busily setting up his camera at the window of one of the buildings, overlooking the gallows. His was a particular challenge. He would have to change the glass plates rapidly. He also was well aware that the emulsion would remain sensitive to light only fifteen minutes before developing.

"At ten minutes to one," wrote the *Constitutional Union*'s reporter, "the chairs for the condemned to rest upon while on the scaffold were carried out of the prison. General Hancock, deeply impressed, was overlooking all the arrangements through a grated window opposite the west side of the gallows."

Burton Harrison listened to "cell doors opening below, and their occupants led out into the corridor," heard "the sobbing of anguished women whose feet kept hurried pace a little with the others, then turned back heavily.

"And lastly a hush, an awful calm . . ."

Among the spectators near the gallows, the sole woman was Dr. Mary Walker, the army's only female surgeon. She sat impassively, a small figure on her horse, full saddle "as a man."

It was 1:00 P.M. July 7, 1865.

Then, "suddenly the wicket opens," wrote Townsend, "the troops spring to their feet, and stand at order arms, the flags go up . . . spectators huddle a little nearer to the scaffold, all the writers for the press produce their pencils and notebooks."

First came Mary Surratt, heavily veiled, wearing a long black dress that dragged on the ground and a black bonnet. Fathers Walter and Wiget preceded her, the former holding a crucifix against his breast. An officer and a sergeant supported her on either side, since both her arms and ankles were bound—a final indignity which seemed wholly unnecessary to all witnessing, since how was this sickly woman to escape?

Then Atzerodt, "in a shabby suit of gray mixed goods" and shod in blue cloth slippers. Townsend thought the condemned's manacles clanked audibly as he moved. His spiritual advisers, the ministers Winchester and Butler, read from their Bibles as he progressed. He was followed closely by Herold, the "half-witted youth of nineteen," as attorney Clampitt described him, his limbs tottering from fright.

Payne brought up the rear of this somber procession, firmly erect, staring straight ahead, seemingly unafraid. He "looked like a sailor man," wrote the *Constitutional Union*'s representative, "being contained in a blue suit and straw hat." He lent an almost incongruous air of gaiety to the morbid occasion, "acting more like a quiet spectator."

"Few who looked at him . . . did not respect him," wrote Townsend.

About 1:05 the condemned were seated on the scaffold's chairs as if at some board meeting. General Hartranft "in a clear voice" read the death sentences. Herold and Atzerodt, wrote the *National Intelligencer*'s correspondent, began to cry. Payne "gazed toward . . . heavens." Mrs. Surratt "groaned audibly" then whispered either to the priests or to one of the guards, "Please don't let me fall."

The four stood as white "death caps" were placed over their heads, muffling Atzerodt's attempt to finish, "Gentlemen, take warn . . . goodbye . . . may we all meet . . ." Manacles were replaced with strips of white muslin.

Scribbled Townsend, "So they stood, while nearly a thousand faces from window, roof, wall, yard and housetop, gazed, the scaffold behind them and densely packed with the assistants . . . The priests continued to murmur prayers. The people were dumb as if each witness stood alone with none near by to talk to him."

At 1:17, the nooses, with their grotesquely large knots, were adjusted. Payne "stood like a statue . . . to receive his," as if it were some medal of merit.

At 1:21, a Captain Smith of the Seventeenth Michigan Infantry waved the crowd back, then clapped his hands three times. It was a signal for the four soldiers under the scaffold to knock away the heavy support beams. "The two traps," wrote Townsend, "fell with a slam!"

It was all over.

Just four days later, at nine o'clock Tuesday morning, the eleventh of July, a reporter for the New York *Tribune*, signing himself "WRH," took paper and pencil and set out on quite a different, happier assignment. He would ride the first train to resume service toward Richmond, which had been interrupted since April 1861. With a mixed group of passengers including blacks going to visit newly freed relatives, soldiers guarding rebel prisoners, salesmen, other businessmen, and farmers, the correspondent started out over Long Bridge, aboard the Orange and Alexandria Line. As the wheels creaked and the old locomotive spewed wood sparks and wheezed, he wrote: "Much of the lining of the cars is torn, all is dirty while every broken pane of glass is replaced by a wooden one . . . The rails are thin and worn.

"Tall grass had grown up . . . and rust covered the iron bars. Still we slowly worked our way along till we arrived at Marsh Creek where a missing bridge invited us to stop and rest."

But "a strong gang of laborers" miraculously appeared and hoisted the span back into place. The train proceeded after but an hour's delay to the Rappahannock River, "swollen and angry with rain," where the travelers took a boat to connect with a waiting Virginia Central train. All afternoon and all night the Central wailed and rattled along, and the reporter wrote that it was "depressing to travel 100 miles over a country that nature created for a garden and to witness the ravages of a civil war.

"In no other part of our whole country can so much of the desolating effects of war be seen as on this trip . . . The country is a desert. Between Alexandria and Gordonsville, 87 miles, but one church remains standing, the Catholic Church at Fairfax. At Manassas, where 40 or 50 houses stood before, now 40 or 50 chimneys, and cellars tell where the village once stood; not a house remains. There were no signs of cultivation . . . The land had all returned to its original state of meadows and pasturage."

He saw but one mowing machine the entire distance, although such horse or mule-drawn or even steam-propelled implements were in widespread use. From plowing through harvesting, old-fashioned hand tools were disappearing from America's farms.

Laborers, such as those who repaired the fallen bridge, moved in sparse, scattered groups. They appeared to live by the right-of-way in tents, and some obviously were Confederate soldiers simply trying to exist.

The correspondent's journey was exhausting as well as grimy. The passengers arrived at their destination at 5:00 A.M. Wednesday, twenty hours after departing Washington. Thus the average speed was six miles an hour. It was a rate Southerners who could find a train at all had to live with.

WRH apparently expected too much of the fallen capital, expressing surprise that "only a few one and two-story buildings have been built, but the great bulk of the ruined district is still a mass of bricks and ashes . . . The country has nothing to send in to sell, and therefore nothing is sold. The South has no money with which to buy foreign importations."

There, too, he learned that newspapers were experiencing their own challenges. One writer, A. M. Kelley, was clapped into the old "Yankee prison," Castle Thunder, for an editorial displeasing to the U.S. military. Robert Ridgeway, editor of the *Whig*, was suspended from his editing for two weeks for a similar transgression.

But it was all a matter of perspective. Many of the occupation forces appeared to enjoy their once-in-a-lifetime experience.

"Life passed quickly in Richmond," wrote young Captain Albert Maxfield, from Windham, Maine, a member of that state's Eleventh Infantry Regiment. "Our camp was a pleasant and healthy one. Our duties were light, our provisions were good and plentiful and short leaves of absence could be had for the asking. Every officer became a horseman. Quartermaster Andrews had plenty of horses in his stables, and any officer that would use a horse well had but to request one of our whole-souled friend to get it. We made up parties and rode into the interior, visited old camp grounds and battlefields, studied the fortifications around Richmond, and in a way fought some of our battles over again.

"Both officers and men were inclined to fraternize with ex-Confederates, and while, as a matter of course, the invaders were not admitted to Southern social circles, in hotels, cafes, and theaters, there was much hobnobbing among the old soldiers and many warm friendships were formed."

Far from fraternizing, on the other hand, three young Richmond ladies at this relatively late stage of the occupation actually hissed Major General Alfred H. Terry, Virginia's military commander, as he rode with his wife down Broad Street. The former corps commander in Sherman's army was manifestly more lenient than Major General Benjamin "Beast" Butler when he ruled New Orleans with a mailed fist. That citizens of Richmond would actually feel privileged to manifest such disrespect brought immediate criticism from the Northern press.

Editorial anger was salved, however, when the military governorship invalidated the municipal election that brought back to office the original cast of city fathers led by Mayor Mayo. Governor Pierpoint, against his own emotions and sympathies, then issued an order that none could hold office in Virginia who had served in the Confederate government. This eliminated quite a few persons with administrative abilities.

With its hissing females and electoral problems, Richmond at least appeared to be avoiding the excesses of the historically rough, rowdy port city of Norfolk, where racism had flared in recent weeks. According to the

Boston *Commonwealth*, at least three blacks had been lynched since late June, one of whom was found hanging from a lamp post.

Noting that "day and night, men, boys and soldiers cry 'Nig!' at the sight of a colored man and hasten to molest him," the reporter cited several instances of what he labeled "race riots," including one when newly freed slaves had been beaten as they tried to enter a circus performance. On a Sunday a middle-aged black man was "quietly passing to his house when three soldiers ran after him and fired three shots, none of which took effect. They cried 'halt!' but as the man knew their order was not to be respected he walked on. Another shot was fired and the ball passed through his mouth.

" 'Finish him!' " another in uniform cried, the reporter continued. Bleeding, the man was taken to a guardhouse. It was not said whether he recovered.

From Lynchburg and Raleigh emanated other stories of violence, including the rape and subsequent death of a black woman in the North Carolina capital. At the same time, editors of papers, especially in the middle and Southern states, pointed out, with a certain justification, that New England had sent quite a few abolitionist correspondents southward. Objectivity could be clouded by their zeal.

The South carried no patent on mayhem. This month, on the twenty-first, the Ninth Iowa Infantry Regiment rioted in Chicago while waiting for a train home. The troops tore up a bar and attempted to lynch the owner who had, in self-defense, shot and killed one of their number.

Yet the overwhelming motif and desire of the people was for quiet. They had had enough of fighting. They wanted peace. They were weary of anger, hatred, strife.

Nineteen-year-old Randolph Shotwell, from Rutherford, in the western part of North Carolina, was released in June from Fort Delaware and slowly made his way homeward, finally arriving in Petersburg, Virginia, at the end of the month.

There he found "wretchedness on all sides . . . The place still resembled a sacked village. The once fashionable old Bolingbroke Hotel was 'open,' just as a sawmill, or barn door is open in summer time. But not a mouthful of food could be had for love or money, and the crusty keeper grudgingly granted us a room on the fourth floor, without furniture save an old mattress minus covering or pillows, for the modest sum of one dollar per head, per night!"

The most hazardous part of his journey was at the end, when he had to cross the swollen Catawba River in a dugout canoe, the railroad bridge having been destroyed by federal cavalry: "We shot down with fearful velocity . . . and gradually obliqued towards the opposite shore. Our greatest peril came at the moment of landing, as we attempted to glide in above a tree, where the pendant branches formed a slight slackwater. Unable to manage our narrow craft, we struck the tree itself with a tremendous crash, and swung around like a boom.

"Unable to swim a stroke even in placid water" and with "a constitutional terror of the deep," Shotwell clutched at willow branches and thus saved himself. At least one of the other former soldiers with him was not so lucky. He was swept to his death.

"Wearily and dispirited," Randolph Shotwell at last neared Rutherford, reflecting, "the four years of the war rolled up like a black scroll behind me. A thousand memories of my childhood rushed over me. Six years of absence had ended. I had reached home."

James Huffman wrote from Page County in the Shenandoah that he was "now twenty-five years of age." A member of the Tenth Virginia Infantry, he had just been released from Elmira Prison. "I reached home to find destruction, waste and poverty. Nothing, and nothing to do with. The whole estate practically lost . . . The country was stripped and bread must be dug from the soil.

"Almost all the families on the creek had lost some of their members during the war, either killed or dead of disease, and they had lost interest in everything except the necessities of life.

"Everybody was living short. Hardly any livestock of any kind was to be had. There was no money; the start must be made from the bottom. No store clothes were worn, there were none to be had and no money nor trade to buy with when stores were established. Rye coffee was the best we could afford. One could not help another. I went to work with a will. The start was slow and I tugged along the best I could.

"Even preaching and Sunday school had gone down at our church . . . Many of the church members had become cold and careless and do-less, with shadows of gloom resting upon them."

At once the plight of the little log church and schoolhouse became a challenge to Jim Huffman. "I determined to revive a deeper interest spiritually . . ." He persuaded the minister, who had been visiting only once a month, to preach every Sunday, and he also organized a Sunday school. Huffman became the teacher.

Surprisingly soon, there was a "great revival . . . All the old, cold and lukewarm and backsliding members were happily reinstated and new life and former happiness restored, and the cloud of darkness and gloom was rolled away."

Not far away, in Warrenton, Virginia Mosby, wife of the cavalry general John Singleton Mosby, was welcoming other returned prisoners.

"Mr. Mosby, Flossie, Mattee and myself walked to the depot, saw a good many persons, expected Vic and Ada from town but they did not come," she wrote in a spasmodically kept diary, which was always subjective, often emotional. "Mr. Sam McKenney returned home, he was severely wounded the last day of the battle, but he is rapidly recovering, how it pains me to see our soldiers returning home, wounded or broken down from cruel treatment in the northern prisons and we left to the tender mercies of a cruel foe without means or men to help ourselves—how long oh Lord! shall we be left thus afflicted? Shorten the days of our trials if consistent with Thy holy will . . ."

Then, before returning to her household chores, she added, "Raining again . . ."

At July's end, the government, which had arbitrarily seized Ford's Theatre, offered to rent the dark and guarded precincts for the princely sum of $1,500 a month. The wishes or legal claims of John T. Ford, the owner, had been airily brushed aside. No one had suggested any future use for the ill-starred house. Ford was lucky at that. He was freed after thirty-nine days in Old Capitol for want of any incriminating evidence. (Eventually, the government paid him $100,000 for his playhouse.)

Secretary Stanton's original desire had been to demolish the place like Carthage, so that future generations of scholars could solemnly pronounce, "Ford's delenda est!"

Beset with phobias, the war secretary, whose powers manifestly persisted unassailed by the Constitution, had worried that reopening the tawdry playhouse would somehow hallow it. Any smouldering remnants of the Confederate mystique might thereby be fueled. As just one other example, Stanton also was not convinced that the continuing use of Jefferson Davis's handsome Richmond mansion by federal officers had fully cleansed it and exorcised the secessionist demons. Perhaps that, too, should be razed or burned to the ground.

Yet the introverted cabinet member with the violent emotions was not the only one to be haunted by the murder of Lincoln and the demons of vengeance, like evil genii, it had unleashed. Colonel Henry Kyd Douglas, now released from his nominal confinement, put it this way: ". . . There has been a struggle for forgetfulness."

He added that the death of Mary Surratt had already become for the commission members "a skeleton in each one's closet."

The women of the South were especially stunned at Mary Surratt's "military murder." Ever since her hanging, some of them had worn long, dark dresses, a few also heavy black chains, as a dual symbol of mourning for her and protest over the imprisonment of Jefferson Davis.

The gallows had been hastily dismantled, as if by some casuistry of the military mind this excising and elimination would remove moral stigma and personal involvement. Only four mounds of earth—over shallow graves—bore witness to the stark events of three short weeks past. Efforts to recover Mary Surratt's remains were rebuffed. Next of kin of the other three did not possess sufficient funds even to ask.

Still, with the execution and its physical reminders retreating into history, many could not or would not forget.

Already, Judge Holt was offering what he considered justifications for the lady's death sentence. These were nonetheless unsolicited. Attorney General Speed, who had so effectively quashed the writ of habeas corpus, left on July 27 for Cape May, New Jersey. His stay would be "indefinite" while "recuperating his health."

Stanton's own condition was not a great deal better. His recurrent asthma spasms had become progressively worse. He talked of a vacation in New England. It might help his own struggle for forgetfulness.

Louis Weichmann and John Lloyd, whose testimonies had been so valuable to the prosecution, were blaming the government. They had been coerced, they indicated. They had had no choice, they insisted, but to say what they had, out of fear lest they follow the others to the gallows.

The sixty-year-old Preston King, who had barred Annie Surratt's access to the president, had become morose, as if relapsing into his mental disorders. Thinking perhaps to cheer his friend and staunch supporter, the president appointed the former senator to the post of collector of customs of New York.

Andrew Johnson himself remained plagued by headaches of unusual intensity. Refusing to discuss the trial or the executions, he renewed orders to his aide and secretary, Mussey, to continue to send away all who might yet bear such inquiries. At the same time, Johnson was formulating a sort of personal exoneration that would transfer the whole onus to Edwin Stanton.

He had come to regard Lincoln's war secretary at best with disdain. At worst, Johnson considered him a "traitor." Such harsh estimation was scarcely original with the president, or even unshared.

Senator Ben Wade, the Radical Republican from Ohio, branded the trial "a damned outrage! An everlasting disgrace!" A former judge, he was assumed to know something about criminal law and procedure.

Even General Butler, whose name was rarely associated with compassion and who was an outspoken advocate of hanging Jefferson Davis and possibly the full Confederate cabinet, decided the proceedings had been too much for him, if only on political grounds.

"An innocent woman hung upon the scaffold!" he would fling at Judge Advocate Bingham.

And so, in a matter of days, Mary Surratt was becoming a woman on the conscience of men. She could not be forgotten.

AUGUST

A Heap of Rubbish and Ruins

It was now almost four months since Appomattox. But the war would not go away, in memory or in fact. There were even a few who still could not convince themselves that the great rebellion was over, much less that the South had lost.

Such was the case of the C.S.S. *Shenandoah*.

On August 2, Captain James Waddell was sailing away from his depredations on the whaling fleet in the Bering Strait, on a course for San Francisco. In a new theater of operations he could prey on the lush trade to Australia and to Asia. Or perhaps he could even threaten the City by the Bay itself and collect ransom?

Whatever, Waddell needed refueling, reprovisioning, possibly even some shore time for his weary crew, if that proved feasible.

Then, through the morning mists, a distant sail. With her own billowing amplitude of canvas, the fleet *Shenandoah* easily overhauled the stranger: the English bark *Baracouta*, of Liverpool, thirteen days out of San Francisco. A boarding party, led by the *Shenandoah*'s master, Irvine Bulloch, soon returned. Master Bulloch, a man not prone to verbosity, had a piece of news.

The war, he announced in a fair example of understatement, was "a thing of the past." And having thus unburdened himself, Bulloch clomped off to his morning's salty routine.

What Waddell had refused to believe in late June from the New Bedford whaler *Milo* he now accepted from a British captain: Lee had surrendered in early April. True, also in June, newspapers on another New England vessel had told of the fall of Charleston, Petersburg, and even Richmond. But that General Lee had capitulated?

"It cast a gloom over the whole ship," Waddell would write, "and did occupy my thoughts. I had, however, a responsibility of the highest nature resting upon me in deciding the course we should pursue, which involved not only our personal honor, but the honor of the flag entrusted to us which had walked the waters fearlessly and in triumph.

"At the blush of surrender of the *Shenandoah* I saw the propriety of running her for a European port which, though it involved a voyage of 17 thousand miles, it was the right thing to do. A long gauntlet to run, to be sure, but why not succeed in baffling observation or pursuit. The enemy had gloated over [his] success and, like a gorged serpent, would lie down to rest.

"The *Shenandoah* up to that time had made more than 40 thousand miles without an accident. I felt sure a search would be made for her in the North Pacific and that to run the ship south was important to all concerned."

The ship's surgeon, Dr. Charles Lining, of South Carolina, reported that after all the guns were dismounted and stowed in the holds, a petition was sent to Waddell asking that the vessel be sailed to the nearest English port. The captain assembled "all hands aft and made a very pretty little speech." Although he sounded as though he were acquiescing to the men's wishes, he did not mention that, at the moment, Liverpool appeared to him "the nearest English port."

The war had interrupted varied endeavors in addition to the livelihood of many New England whalers. For another, the brave venture to stretch a transatlantic cable was tabled for more peaceful times. It had been seven years since Cyrus Field's first and unsuccessful attempt.

Now, also on August 2, the *Great Eastern*, at 27,000 tons the world's largest steamship, was 606 miles from Heart's Content, Newfoundland, or 1,062 miles west of Valentia, Ireland. Field, the wealthy Massachusetts merchant, believed that he *would* make it this time.

Submarine cables had long teased the public imagination. Messages were flashed routinely under such lesser bodies of water as the Irish Sea, the English Channel, the North Sea (to Holland), and the Mediterranean. Ambitious international efforts were currently at work to link Canada and

Russia by way of the Bering Strait. Waddell himself had taken note of this in June.

The *Great Eastern*, carrying 5,000 tons of gutta-percha–insulated seven-strand cable (also 114 sheep and 500 chickens in a vast larder) had put the Irish coast astern on July 25. Aside from some routine electrical problems, the cable, one and an eighth inches in diameter, had been unrolling from the drums into the ocean "as easily as the thread flies from the reel in a lady's workbasket." So wrote William Howard Russell, a correspondent during the Crimean War. He was also known as "Bull Run" Russell from his coverage of the first, ill-starred battle at Manassas. He was abroad to tell readers of the London *Times* about the $3 million expedition. If shamelessly pro-South in his wartime reporting, Russell now covered a story about which he could be easily objective: "Light grey sheets of drizzling cloud flew over the surface of the sea, and set men talking of icebergs and Arctic storms; but towards evening the wind fell, and a cold clammy vapour settled down on ship and sea, bringing with it a leaden calm; so that the waves lost their tumbled crests, and slept at last in almost unmurmuring slumber. But the big ship slept not. The clank and beat of machinery ceased never, and the dull mill-like clatter of cable apparatus seemed to become more active as the night wore on.

"The forge fires glared on her decks and there, out in the midst of the Atlantic, anvils rang and sparks flew; and the spectator thought of some village far away, where the blacksmith worked, unvexed by the cable anxieties and greed of speedy news. As the blaze shot up, ruddy, mellow, and strong, and flung arms of light aloft and along the glistening decks, and then died into a red centre, masts, spars and ropes were for the instant touched with a golden gleaming, and strange figures were called out from the darkness . . . Outside us all was obscurity; but now and then vast shadows, which moved across the arc of lighted fogbank, were projected far away by the flare."

The fog thickened, "it was a dead calm, and the *Great Eastern* seemed to float on a grey and polished surface of a cloud." Communications with Ireland continued until the galvanometer abruptly indicated that the electric signal had ceased. More than a thousand miles of cable had gone dead, with three quarters of the job done. The end was in sight. There was nothing to do except start hauling the cable in and attempt to find the flaw. This proceeded for several hours until suddenly the restraining gears, the "stoppers," let go and the cable, snapping, "with one bound leaped over intervening space and flashed into the sea.

"The shock of the instant was as sharp as the snapping of the cable itself. No words could describe the bitterness of the disappointment. The cable gone!"

From then on, for the next several days as the crew grappled for the lost strands, "all life died out in the vessel," Russell continued. "The time passed heavily . . . the drums beat no more, their long reveille ended in the muffled roll of death; that which had been broken could give no trouble to break . . . No noise was heard except the dull droning grating of the wire rope over the wheels at the bows."

On August 8, following a moonlit night "of great brightness," it appeared that the "picking up" line, with its grapnel hooks (mounting huge flukes and weighing three hundred pounds each) was about to reel the lost cable back on board. Slowly, it was retrieved and success appeared imminent, then "the end of the rope flourished its iron fist in the air and struck out with it right and left, as though it were animated by a desire to destroy those who might arrest its progress . . ."

Three days later, another try. At 9:40 P.M. in deep blackness the line went again, "whistling through the air like a round shot." From the decks a chorus, "It's gone!"

Russell concluded, "The battle was over!"

H.M.S. *Terrible*, the escort, putting out for St. John's to take on coal, came alongside the *Great Eastern* to pick up mail for North America. The wind and sea were rising. "It was wild and dark . . . The flash of a gun from the *Terrible* to recall her cutter lighted up the gloom, and the glare of an answering blue light, burned by the boat, revealed for an instant the hull of the man-of-war on the horizon waters. There was a profound silence abroad the big ship.

"She struggled against the helm for a moment as though she still yearned to pursue her course to the west, then bowed her head to the angry sea in admission of defeat, and moved slowly . . . The signal lanterns flashed from the *Terrible*, 'farewell!' The lights from our paddlebox pierced the night, 'goodbye! thank you!' in sad ackowledgment.

"Then each sped on her way in solitude and darkness."

Once again, news between the Old World and the New would consume some two weeks in transit. The fall of Richmond—occupied on April 3— had not been announced in London until April 17. On that date the steamship *Australasian,* bearing New York newspapers, docked in Liverpool. On April 24, the S.S. *Asia* told a saddened Great Britain of General Lee's capitulation on the ninth.

The waters off the eastern United States this summer were also playing a role in the escape of Confederate leaders. Former Secretary of War John C. Breckinridge had slipped southward after the surrender of General Johnston's army, heeding Sherman's advice that he had "better get away." He had not a whit of faith that if paroled the terms would be honored. Having served in Washington with Buchanan, he was somewhat familiar with the workings of government and, more lately, with officials such as Edwin Stanton and Judge Holt.

Now in Havana, awaiting passage to England, General Breckinridge had escaped from Florida in wild buccaneer mode. One of the party of six, which included his aide, Colonel John Taylor Wood, Breckinridge had started out in a small four-oared gig but soon exchanged that for a sloop captured at gun and sword point. The latter had been manned by sailors who seemed to be deserters from either the federal navy or what had been left of the Confederate sea forces.

Off Green Turtle Key, at the mouth of the Miami River, the party was pursued by a motley band of pirates, some thirty, paddling out in canoes and dugouts: whites, blacks, Cubans or other Latins, and possibly even some Indians.

"Though outnumbered three to one," Taylor Wood wrote, "still we were well under cover in our boat, and could rake each canoe as it came up. We determined to take all the chances, and to open fire as soon as they came within range."

Breckinridge's little group did just that, shooting and swinging wildly with the paddles, even breaking two of them. One of the attackers was knocked overboard, then the Confederates were surprised to hear the aggrieved question, "What did you fire on us for? We are friends."

The incident ended with the fleeing Confederates going ashore to an old fort and exchanging gold for rum, a ham, and other food. The little band that had pursued Breckinridge's sloop was led by a man wearing a tattered uniform who claimed to be Major Valdes, a federal officer. None believed him.

Greater peril was encountered in a few days when a fast schooner, believed to be a federal patrol, took after the fleeing Confederates. This time the general felt he had lost his gamble. The sloop, however, was sailing in shoal water. It could traverse channels far too shallow for a larger craft.

"I ordered the ballast to be thrown overboard," Wood recalled. "We watched the bottom anxiously . . . the grating of the keel over the coral . . . Together we went overboard, and sank to our waists in the black, pasty mud . . . Relieved of a half-ton of our weight, our sloop forged ahead three or four lengths and then brought up again . . .

"Looking astern, we saw the schooner coming up wing and wing." Now they jettisoned their provisions, except for some biscuits, but saved the water beaker by carrying it. The men also lightened the sloop still further by throwing heavy items like the anchor, its chain, and spare rope alongside and dragging them.

". . . Then, three on each side, our shoulders under the boat's bilges, at the word we lifted together, and foot by foot moved her forward . . . Between the coral branches we would sink at times to our necks in slime and water. Fortunately, the wind helped us; keeping all sail on, thus for more than a hundred yards we toiled, until the water deepened and the reef was passed." Bleeding, filthy, weak, the crew tumbled back aboard. "The schooner hauled by the wind and opened fire from a 9 or 12 pounder; but we were at long range, the firing was wild."

The pursuer, however, closed to rifle range. Bullets, better known to soldiers of North and South alike as Minie balls, rattled off the sides of the sloop. These were heavy slugs, which could—and did—tear arms off when shot from muskets or rifles. The wooden hull proved far tougher than muscle and bone. The balls did not penetrate.

The fugitive happened upon another reef and a shallow passage through it. The tiller was put hard over, and the little craft surged through. Now the schooner could not follow without grounding. The sharp cracks from the guns faded.

Danger had passed. Within the week, Breckinridge was in Cuba, welcomed with all the honors attending a foreign dignitary, rather than a refugee from a nonexistent government. The swashbuckling general would book on the next steamer to London, at last beyond the reach of Edwin M. Stanton. He was one of only two of the Richmond cabinet to escape.

The other was Judah P. Benjamin, who had served as secretary of state and, earlier, of war. In his mid-fifties, small, corpulent, he was as certain as Breckinridge that he would be shot or hanged if caught. Indeed, even after fellow cabinet officers and the generals had advised otherwise, the peppery Benjamin had urged Jefferson Davis somehow to fight on.

Benjamin, quite alone, was following the familiar Florida-Caribbean route. "I got a farmer's wife to make me some homespun clothes," he would write a sister, Penina Kruttschnitt, in La Grange, Georgia. "I got for my horse the commonest and roughest equipment . . . and I journeyed as far as possible on byroads, always passing around towns and keeping in the least inhabited districts."

Somewhere in the Carolinas, or Georgia, he changed his old swayback horse for a mule. His progress was a feat in itself since Benjamin had never been known as an outdoorsman, much less an athlete. Half asleep as his steed ambled down a path along the Georgia pinewoods, the rider was startled by a parrot squawking, "Oh Jeff! Oh Jeff!" The bird flapped from his perch to lead Benjamin to a farmhouse and, as it turned out, a night's lodging. The farmer admitted to having taught the bird thus to acknowledge the president of rebellion in more promising days.

When he learned that a reward had been offered for President Davis, "who was most outrageously accused of having committed the assassination of President Lincoln," Benjamin was impelled to yet greater efforts, though at the fastest he could progress no more than thirty miles a day. "I preferred death in attempting to escape to such captivity as awaited me if I became their prisoner."

He was a month on the west coast of Florida, seeking transport to one of the crown colonies in the Caribbean or to Cuba. Three times, federal ships almost sniffed him out. The first, a gunboat pushed up the Manatee River from Tampa Bay, disgorged bluejackets who sloshed toward the plantation where he was harbored. The erstwhile secretary of state and bon vivant of Richmond society hid in steamy mud and eel grass as the searchers clomped after him. He was lucky: there were no dogs.

The second time he was en route farther down the coast in a small, flat-bottomed boat. It was, however, large enough to possess a galley. Benjamin donned the cook's apron and hat, then smoked the area with a dumping of bacon grease on the hot stove. When the patrol came alongside, it could see only a white-aproned figure coughing amid the galley's noxious clouds. The third time he went overboard to hide in the rushes, after his craft had been ordered to heave to.

A man impatient for explanations, Benjamin thought hard on the reasons he was being followed. He was on no major thoroughfare. His only conclusion: enemies in his own administration or spies in Stanton's far-reaching secret service betrayed his progress.

Near-disasters dogged him: a waterspout, while sailing to Bimini in an open yawl; the sinking of a sponge sloop in which he was en route from Bimini to Nassau; and a fire aboard a vessel carrying him from New Providence Island to Havana.

But at long last Benjamin reached London, a free man. There he would pursue his career as a lawyer, although now he had to hang out a new shingle, that of barrister. England granted a home to this new lot of refugees, although little by little she must make amends to the winning side. How could an empire remain great without a liberal salting of pragmatism? (Ultimately, Benjamin rose to the eminence of queen's counsel. Bedecked with full, flowing wig, he could now practice before the House of Lords.)

Other leaders of the shattered Confederacy languished in their scattered places of incarceration: George Alfred Trenholm, secretary of the treasury, was locked up in Fort Pulaski, Georgia, a large, grim stone bastion at the mouth of the Savannah River; Stephen Mallory, secretary of the navy, was in Fort Lafayette, in New York harbor; Postmaster Reagan and Alexander Stephens called Fort Warren home, farther up the coast, in Boston harbor.

If these men, diverse in background, mental capacity, and philosophy, shared a common wonderment it was simply this: What had they done wrong? Why was the U.S. government cross with them? If there was possibly one exception to this binding trait, or mystique, it was Alexander Stephens, frail, almost emaciated, but an objective thinker. He knew the rebellion had been a mistake.

With surprising celerity, most of these names had already faded from everyday parlance, if not altogether from memory, in the South. One and only one remained: Jefferson Davis. None could forget old Jeff, the tall, aloof intellectual. He had, at least, shattered the historic, popular image of what a leader should be.

Some loathed, some hated him now, since he personified the defeat and despair of their land. Some found it in their hearts to pity him. None would admit to love, assuming that emotion ever had existed. Nonetheless, Jeff Davis was a name that lived, sharply etched, a workaday word in Southern vocabularies.

Old Jeff was no hero to North or South for the most part. But he was a curiosity to his keepers at Fort Monroe, who developed a compulsion "to secure trophies of anything Mr. Davis had touched." So wrote Varina, who, with her children, had been provided lodging in the sprawling fort complex. Later, she would be allowed to travel southward to more familiar surroundings.

"They had carried away his brierwood pipe," she wrote, "and from time to time taken five of the spoons sent over with his meals from my quarters. The meals were sent over by a bright little mulatto boy named Joe, who handed them to the sergeant of the guard outside the casemate, who passed them through the window to the lieutenant of the guard in the outer cell, by whom they were handed the prisoner through the grated doors of the inside room, the keys of which were held by the Officer of the Day. No knife and fork being allowed the prisoner, 'lest he should commit suicide,' his food had to be cut up before being sent over."

The celebrated prisoner's health was by now up to question. On August 3, for example, the Richmond *Times* revealed that he "was again on the ramparts of the Fort yesterday afternoon from 4–5 o'clock . . . The reports of failing health of Davis promulgated by certain misinformed daily papers caused an enquiry from the War Department as to the real state of the prisoner's health. The report made sets forth that the prisoner . . . is in the enjoyment of excellent health; and, moreover, that his physical condition has visibly improved since his incarceration at Fortress Monroe all of which has already been stated."

Unlike Mary Surratt, this prisoner was thus allowed regular daily exercise and fresh air, if not freedom. He was seen by the same correspondent actually talking to a fellow captive, Clement Clay, who had so readily surrendered to federal authorities. But a fine line was drawn: the two were not permitted to shake hands.

The former Confederate chief of state also conversed, sometimes at length, with his physician, Lieutenant Colonel John J. Craven. Davis harbored continuing regrets over the assassination of Lincoln, not "in affected terms of regard or admiration, but paying a simple and sincere tribute to his goodness of character, honesty of purpose and Christian desire to be faithful to his duties," according to Craven.

Andrew Johnson he characterized as "infinitely more objectionable and less scrupulous . . . Mr. Lincoln was kind of heart, naturally longing for the glory and repose of a second term to be spent in peace. Mr. Johnson, being from the South, dare not offer such liberal treatment . . ."

But not many days after the Richmond paper's rather ebullient reports of Davis's health, Dr. Craven began to detect signs of erysipelas: "high fever . . . swelling of his face . . . usual prostration . . . no appetite for ordinary food, but found the coolness and moisture of fruits agreeable . . . spirits exceedingly dejected, evinced by anxiety for his wife and children."

Davis himself thought he was afflicted with "malarial poison . . . caused by the rising and falling of the tide in the ditch outside." His malaise only strengthened the conviction that his captors were trying to do away with him, and he expressed the wish to the army surgeon that "the Washington people would take quicker means of dispatching him." Then he mused he might feel better if only "his faithful servant Robert" were at his side.

But Dr. Craven would learn shortly Davis's capacity for bouncing back. Soon he was holding forth lustily on many subjects, in particular the Southern press, which, he claimed, had given him "more trouble" than Northern newspapers. He also vented his feelings to Varina, who now had moved to Savannah and was ensconced comfortably in the Pulaski House, on the waterfront.

In his first permitted letter, he urged her not to be "alarmed by speculative reports concerning my condition. You can rely on my fortitude, and God has given me much of resignation to His blessed will."

On August 23, the ladies of Abbeville, South Carolina, interceded in behalf of the famous captive. "It will be grateful to us," they wrote Andrew Johnson, "to have thus testified our feelings for one whose faults, in our judgment at least, have not been past forgiving. Called from the retirement of his home to a position which he did not solicit, but which his manhood forbade him to decline . . . we see in his conduct everything to evoke sympathy, and nothing to merit the extreme punishment with which he is threatened. We hope there will be a merciful remembrance of his poor wife, plundered and insulted after being torn away from his prison, and of his young children, whose prospects in life have been so terribly blighted."

Yet the selective venom President Johnson, Secretary Stanton, and Judge Holt spewed at the stricken leaders of the Confederacy proved to be unpredictable, almost like the rolling of dice. Long-bearded, patrician Joseph E. Brown, governor of Georgia since 1857, became an example of the administration's whims. The lawyer by profession, a Democrat, was an extreme advocate of states' rights. As early as 1858 he had thumped for volunteer military companies.

Arrested a month after the fall of Richmond for attempting to call up the defunct Georgia legislature, Brown traveled to Washington in the most comfortable railway coaches available. And there were very few. Under "open arrest," spared the ignominy and the vermin of Old Capitol, certainly the penitentiary, he moved freely about the streets of Washington. Even White House doors were opened to Brown.

Paroled less than a month later, Brown returned to Milledgeville, which had been the provisional state capital. He resigned the governorship and thereupon commenced an "intimate correspondence" with the president of the United States. The onetime secessionist firebrand appealed to Washington for many desiderata, from cotton to the oath of allegiance.

Somewhat apologizing that "we have no mails," he noted that he was sending his first communications "by express." He explained that he traveled from Savannah to Macon by buggy, "with a view to see and converse with as many as possible of the people of the section of the country." However, "exposure to the sun and rain brought upon me an attack of bilious fever which has confined me to my bed." As another challenge, his wife, Elizabeth, was pregnant again.

Concerned over the upcoming convention for a new Georgia constitution, Brown predicted it would abolish slavery but only after "an element of opposition . . . It is hard for our slaveholders to realize the facts as they exist, and to accept them."

James Johnson, the provisional governor of Georgia, had arrived in Milledgeville as Brown's boarder. "We shall act harmoniously and I shall do all I can to sustain him in carrying out your policy." There remained a problem, however, in effecting the oath of allegiance: "The Governor holds that only the military officers have power to administer it and that he can appoint no one . . . There are 132 counties in the State, many of them remote from a R.R. or military post." By the same token, the former governor believed the citizenry of "these backwoods counties . . . are well disposed towards the government . . . They will from all these counties send delegates for immediate abolition."

Writing again, Brown reassured the president that Georgians would vote to abolish slavery "and place the State back in the Union as a loyal State . . . They are well disposed and generally ready in good faith to take the oath." At the same time, he reported that he had not encountered anyone authorized to administer the oath. He also wrote of his own difficulties with parole papers, which he had foolishly given to Secretary

Stanton. In fact, he had almost been arrested for not being able to produce them.

Then, from the clutter of his rarely clear desk, Brown turned to other matters: barter. To his boarder, Governor Johnson, he scribbled a memo concerning the South's staple and lifeblood: "The cotton is to be carried down by the State on her steamers and sold to persons who have authority from the U.S. Government to purchase and sell us in exchange necessaries which we cannot do without."

With its debt increased by $18 million, Georgia shared the economic distress of its sister states that had had the folly to secede. The major cities were dead.

"In the suburbs of Atlanta," reported the Atlanta *Intelligencer,* "a promiscuous assemblage of houseless and homeless creatures . . . living in booths, arbors, tent-flies, and rude temporary structures of old cast-off plank . . . Who these people are no one knows, and how they manage to subsist is equally mysterious . . . There are many old and decrepit females and young children . . . utterly helpless. Poverty in its direct form reigns supreme among them . . . Freedmen and freedwomen, who have left their homes in pursuit of something they do not exactly know what, comprise the greater part of the unfortunate mass.

". . . families who have been stripped of everything, and whose male members went into the war and have never returned. On the blackened ruins of their once happy homes, under sheds and tents that furnish but little protection from the storm, they simply exist, and such an existence. With barely food sufficient to keep soul and body together, and no assurance that even so small a pittance as that may long be reckoned upon, they live from day to day in an almost hopeless state of destitution. We have heard recounted from the lips of many, of these stories of their wants and sufferings . . ."

The correspondent for the New York *Tribune* who signed himself Lewellyn wrote, "Atlanta is a heap of ruins. The Court House and churches, the Masonic Hall, and the buildings belonging to the medical faculty and one block used as a hospital are all that is left standing. Everything else is a heap of rubbish and ruins. Factories, stores, banks, rolling mills, hotels, everything is gone. No one is doing anything toward rebuilding. The people are sullen . . . Said one, 'hell has laid her egg, and right here it hatched!' "

Around the Court House "at least 1,000 women were pushing and fighting" to obtain ration tickets. An old farmer from the country "had a low cart, drawn by one ox, with a few corn leaves for the ox, but nothing for himself except a few wild plums." He said he and his wife had subsisted on wheat bread and nothing else for five days, and 'God help us or we shall die!' "

Not quite everything was "a heap of rubbish." Some stores survived, as well as hotels, such as the Atlanta. The city was too large to be totally razed, although what remained surely was shabby and war-worn.

Macon, where destruction was negligible, nonetheless presented a drab and threadbare mien. The carpet in one of the two operating hotels was "all in tatters," observed the same newspaperman. And as for food, "the table . . . [was] the poorest I have ever sat down to where it was called a hotel."

He found the feeling "very bitter" against the federal government. While the citizenry did not deny the South had been "whipped," all vowed they would "never be ruled by Yankees!"

Attitudes toward the victorious government and its leader varied. For example, N. J. Crawford was writing to Mary Ann Cobb, his friend and wife of Howell Cobb, former U.S. congressman and onetime governor of Georgia: "I do not think that President Johnson intends to punish or impoverish our people any more than that we have already suffered provided he can help it. But he is doubtless afraid of impeachment and I think him in very great danger . . . The majority [in Congress] is there to do it, if he moves too fast in the matter of pardons. I think now that our greatest danger is in his death which is likely to occur any day if the rumors of his drinking are half true."

Crawford then concluded, "I was robbed last night of two mules at my plantation."

But many from the Deep South had lost little time in hurrying northward, indifferent as dependable transportation was. Washington was the prime mecca.

"All summer long," wrote Whitelaw Reid, "the capital was filled with the late leaders in Rebel councils, or on Rebel battlefields. They filled all avenues of approach to the White House. They kept the Southern President surrounded by an atmosphere of Southern geniality, Southern prejudices, Southern aspirations. Mr. Johnson declared that treason must be humbled—they convinced him that they were humble . . .

"Such were the voices, day by day and week by week, sounding [in] the President's ears. He heard little else, was given time to think little else.

"Every day the White House presented the same scene. Passing through the anteroom to the staircase one always encountered a throng of coarsely dressed Southerners, carrying heavy canes, tobacco-ruminant, and full of political talk. The unfurnished, desolate-looking room in which visitors gather, while waiting turns for interviews with the President, was always crowded. One day I saw there two or three Rebel generals, as many members of the Rebel Congress, and at least a score of less noted leaders . . .

"From nine o'clock until three the President sat in the room adjacent, conversing with one or another as the doorkeeper admitted them. Pardons were discussed, policies of reorganization were canvassed. The pardon-seekers were the counsellors on reorganization—there were none others there with whom to consult. Thus the weary day passed, with a steady stream of Rebel callers."

Then, at 3:00 P.M. the doorkeeper's hands "were full of cards not yet presented to the President, and the anteroom was thronged . . . the door was thrown open, and the crowd rushed in as if scrambling for seats in a railroad car. The President stood by his desk; to his left, at another table stood Colonel [William A.] Browning, his two private secretaries. On the table in the center of the room lay a pile of pardons, a foot high, watched by a young major in uniform."

Lieutenant General Richard Taylor, who had surrendered one of the last Confederate forces (that of the Department of Alabama, Mississippi, and East Louisiana) on May 8, was among those higher-ranking callers. He found the president "a saturnine man, who made no return to my bow, but after looking at me, asked me to take a seat . . . He had now somewhat abated his wolfish desire for vengeance, and asked many questions about the condition of the South, temper of the people, etc." But the general did not at once accomplish the purpose of his mission: to obtain a pass to visit Jefferson Davis.

A number of Union soldiers, too, sought the executive's indulgence on various matters. High on the list were pardons for desertion or lesser military infractions, and pleas for the restoration of bounties. It seemed to Whitelaw Reid that Johnson was not only patient but "kindly" in handling the remarkable number of applications himself. Some had called merely to say thank you for already signing a pardon.

". . . So the crowd thinned out, one by one. By half-past five, Mr. Johnson was alone with his secretaries—only a few idlers still passing before the open door for a stolen look at the Chief Magistrate of the Republic."

Andrew Johnson was also alone with his thoughts. To the side of his desk, behind his diminished pile of pardon forms, lay a communication from Attorney General Speed, recently returned from Cape May. Weeks after the executions, the question of their legality continued to plague the president. Again he had sought the opinion of Speed, notwithstanding that he thought of his attorney general as "nothing much—his wife is the better man of the two."

Certainly the very act of questioning this particular government attorney on the matter of the executions was tantamount to asking General Lee what he thought about losing the war. The response could evoke small surprise. Should the trial really have been held before a military tribunal?

"Of course!" Speed's response was by now almost stereotyped. ". . . According to the Constitution in time of war the law of nations constitutes a part of the law of the land and . . . the laws of war constitute the greater part of the law of the land." The opinion digressed to describe assorted "enemies" of the state, including not only "assassins" but also "bush-whackers," a new, odious, and invariably frightening word to Southern householders.

If Attorney General Speed sounded obscure, rambling, and confused, it did not matter. Andrew Johnson, in likelihood, would not have understood anyhow. Even so, the affirmation was scarcely sufficient to banish worries and self-recrimination from the president's mind. In the final analysis, he had signed the legal authorization to hang a woman. Now he must entertain increasing doubts not only as to her guilt but as to the lawfulness of her conviction and her execution.

Stanton, this August, had put himself out of reach of Johnson, journeying to New York and New England. At Fort Lafayette, he visited Stephen Mallory and concluded that the Confederate navy secretary was still of a secessionary mind, not fit for parole.

The president received a special sort of caller as August came to an end: Sarah Frances Mudd, the wife of Samuel Mudd. Along with the others who escaped the noose, Dr. Mudd had been sent not to the penitentiary at Albany but to Fort Jefferson, on a sun-scorched, festering island off

Florida, in the Dry Tortugas. Seventy miles west of Key West in the shark-infested Gulf of Mexico, Jefferson was the largest of the forts. Her husband would perish there, Sarah implored. If the president would not pardon him, could he not be removed elsewhere?

The chief executive was ready with his reply. If Judge Holt would approve papers for the doctor's release, then he, Andrew Johnson, would countersign them. It was a tantalizing if familiar ploy. She hurried to see the jurist.

"Mrs. Mudd, I am sorry," answered Holt. "I can do nothing for you."

Mrs. Mudd, affectionately known to her husband as Frank, had been inspired to visit these two men on receiving her first two letters from Fort Jefferson. "Without you and the children," Dr. Mudd wrote, "what is life for me—a blank void. Time passes very slowly and seems longer than that period" [since he arrived]. However, "this place continues to be unusually healthy and the only fear manifested is that disease may be propagated by the arrival of vessels and steamers from infected ports. At this time there is a vessel lying at quarantine with all hands aboard sick with fever of some description—several have died, and there is not one well enough to nurse the sick—no volunteers from among the prisoners going to them, so the chances of life are small.

"I am now in the hospital. I have little or no labor to perform, but my fare is not much improved. My principal diet is coffee, butter and bread three times a day. We have had a mess or two of Irish potatoes and onions, but as a general thing vegetables don't last many days in this climate before decomposition takes place. Pork and beef are poisonous to me . . . molasses when I am able to buy it, and occasionally (fresh) fish when Providence favored, are the only articles of diet used. I am enjoying very good health, considering the circumstances.

"Sweet, dearest Frank, write to me soon on the receipt of my letter."

SEPTEMBER

Petroleum

B y the autumn of 1865, the fast-growing infant petroleum industry was capitalized at a half billion dollars. The war had not hurt it a bit.

There were 1,100 companies drilling several thousand wells in Pennsylvania, West Virginia (Parkersburg was booming), Ohio, Indiana, Kentucky, and California. It was but eight short years since "Colonel" Edwin L. Drake, a railroad conductor from New England, had struck oil at Titusville, on Oil Creek, some eighty-five miles north of Pittsburgh.

Oil attracted people like John D. Rockefeller. This year, at the age of twenty-six, he had purchased the Excelsior Oil Works, of Cleveland, a city already boasting thirty refineries. Excelsior would soon become the Standard Oil Company, capitalized at $1 million. But little people also were caught up in the fever and frenzy.

"Taking a car on the Atlantic and Great Western Road at Corry [Pennsylvania], after about an hour I fell into a snooze, when bump go the cars, the conductor of the train pokes his head in at the door, 'break in the road, you will pass the night here' . . . Taking a horse the next morning, I climbed the hill that from the east overlooks [Oil City] and the creek. Unless one dipped his pen in mud who could describe that filthiest of cities . . . ?"

The writer, who was not accorded a byline, was on assignment from *The Nation* to the oilfields of western Pennsylvania, in Venango County, some seventy miles north of Pittsburgh. Specifically, he wanted to visit

119

that urban beanstalk of 1865, Pithole City. Nine miles above Oil City on shallow, dirty Pithole Creek, a few yards wide, Pithole had been nothing in May of 1863 but a few farmhouses and their fields.

Now, since oil was struck, its population had sprouted to almost 10,000, including transient teamsters (2,000 at a time), prostitutes, salesmen, lawyers, doctors, and brigands of every size, shape, and degree of moral turpitude. As a possible leaven, on the other hand, there were also platoons of preachers who struggled for spiritual uplift in this later Babylon. Veterans of the war, from North and South, also were drawn by the black ooze—some two and a half million barrels were produced throughout the country in 1865. Pithole alone was pumping a hundred wells.

Finally, the correspondent arrived at the "new reigning beauty of Oildom, euphonious Pithole." He continued: "Everywhere, conspicuous among the trees you see the derricks on the oil well, like steeples of the great temple of Mammon, at which all worship. Derricks, indeed, you see everywhere—in the valleys, on the hillsides, on the tops of hills—with their engines attached, about one in fifty of which is running. Millions upon millions of dollars have been sunk all through this region in the purchase of worthless land at oil-land prices . . .

"The town has the usual appearance of towns in this region, and is a gigantic city of 'shreds and patches.' Most of the buildings are built on land leased for three years. Passing up the street, you see on either side shops and hotels, each laying a different claim to fashion. One is painted, another has a splendid sign, another has its rooms papered. Every other shop is a liquor saloon. It is safe to assert that there is more vile liquor drunk in this town than in any other of its size in the world.

"Indeed, a bar is almost the invariable appendage to every building. Lawyers have bars appurtenant to their offices—each hotel, dwelling house, or shop has its separate bar.

"You pass crowds of persons, in an excited state, hurrying [to and] fro—most of them with haggard faces, old clothes, and trousers stuck in their boots—of that fishy, scarecrow race, specimens of which I had met in the cars. You pass many familiar names—'*stat magni nominis umbra*'— the St. Nicholas, the Fifth Avenue, the Metropolitan, and the like. After a ride of a quarter of a mile you reach the famous United States well, and a strange sight it is. Forth there rushes a stream of oil as large as your arm, with constant gushes of gas. Day and night this stream is vomited forth with unabated force."

Finding the teamsters of especial interest, he singled out one example: "With dark face, shaggy beard, and slouched hat, and trousers tucked into his boots, he sits immovable on his stout team. On every proper occasion he damns his horses with a volubility and versatility of profanity which almost show a divine gift.

"The team jolts on over rocks and trees, down mudholes, down out of mudholes, down ruts . . . out goes a barrel, over goes the team."

A midway certainly, Pithole had become a magnet for circus freaks, including the "fat woman" and the "fat boy." The correspondent attempted to convince his readers that the former was "a buxom young maiden of 800 pounds."

One thing, the boom town sported plenty of rooms for both fat and lean: the Chase, Morey, Bonta, Duncan, Danforth, Metropolitan, Johnston House, Hobbs House, Rochester, and the Astor House. The last named was built in a few miraculous days and christened with a twenty-four-hour ball that Pithole would not soon forget.

There was also "the United States Hotel, like all the rest . . . built of planed boards, unpainted, very loosely put together. Adjacent is a tent with some fifty cots well filled every night and fragrant from proximity to the horse stalls . . . In front of the building is a platform and a long bench. On this through the day and evening, sit gloomy and dirty contortionists chewing the melancholy cud of speculation."

The lobby was an unbelievable hodgepodge of a telegraph office constantly "ticking" away, "a long sink" offering the hotel's sole facility for washing, and, of course, the bar. Whiskey served there, as elsewhere, was "poison," but water tasted like "a solution of salts." The land was so rocky there existed little water anyway. When a bell or, simply, a leather-lunged "whoop!" announced dinner, there was a "wild rush and, often, a physical encounter for seats," then the disappointing menu: roast beef, roast lamb, corned beef, boiled ham, all tasting like it was cut "from the same side of meat."

More formal, surely more respectful was the United States Petroleum Company's assessment of Pithole in its first annual report this year: "The construction of Pithole with its 10,000 inhabitants, its handsome churches and commodious and elegant hotels and a number of large villages surrounding this city, all built within the last six months point to the same conclusion; that petroleum, a great gift of God, for man's benefit . . . will not vanish but continue through time to give a good and cheap light in the houses of the poor, lighten the burden of the taxpayer, increase the national wealth, be useful in the arts and manufactures (as dyes); add a page to the volume of scientific discovery, and flow a steady stream of profit into the pockets of those interested in its production."

There were many facets the authors of the report left unchronicled, such as the grabbag of characters and the crime. Pithole and adjacent fields spawned or nourished a number of legends: Ben Hogan ("the wickedest man in the world"), Stonehouse Jack, Johnny Steel, Marsh Elliott, Pithole Pete, Coal Oil Johnny, Greasy George, and French Kate, a gun-toting, sometimes high-priced whore.

Hogan, basking in his own "wickedness," was handily the most improbable. Before he arrived in the oil fields he had, by reputation, robbed a priest of rare liturgical books, earned tens of thousands of dollars by bounty jumping as a member of the Forty Thieves gang (allegedly enlisting in the Union Army some thirty-six times), spied for both North and South, and even run the blockade as a privateer. Or so it was said. Stonehouse Jack, pretty much Hogan's equal in rowdiness and abiding depravity, finally organized a gang to run Hogan out of Pithole.

But before this worthy goal was attained, Hogan, inevitably, had taken up with French Kate, rumored to have passed as a countess in Paris only after materializing in the bordellos of Brooklyn. Hogan quarreled with her, made up, then denounced her as "the wickedest woman on earth." He added the remarkable but unsubstantiated charge that "she had a great deal more to do with the plot to assassinate Mr. Lincoln than Mrs. Surratt had, and ought to have been hanged in place of her. She was jealous, revengeful and vindictive to an extraordinary degree."

So much for shattered romance. He may have been trying to link French Kate with John Wilkes Booth, who had occasionally visited Oil City the previous year, 1864, bought sixty acres there, and was said to have a share in the major Homestead well in Pithole. The unstable raven-haired actor was remembered as a flashy, drinking character who always had a woman with him. She was invariably a prostitute.

Felonies, thievery, and general crookedness flourished. Even the cumbersome derrick machinery for drilling and pumping was far from safe. If it were not ferociously guarded at night, it might well be gone by morning, all several tons of it. Neither churches nor the U.S. Post Office were sacred so far as hoodlums were concerned. It was practical to set up crosses made of only the cheapest metals or wood. "Selling" the same piece of land, sometimes to dozens of purchasers, was almost commonplace. Signs such as this appeared on posts and on the outside of saloons:

> RESOLVED: if we, the undersigned suckers ever catch the son-of-a-bitch who sold us a share in this venture, it is the sense of this meeting that we jointly and severally agree to boil the bastard in oil, tar and feather him and ride him out of town on the sharpest rail we can find.

People were robbed and rolled to the accordion accompaniment of Hobey Sutton, a former slave with a peg leg, who was hired out by bartenders for other than musical inspiration. They wished that the screams and entreaties of victims, drunk or otherwise, not be heard by other patrons. Hobey teamed up with Hogan and, in fact, any others proffering cash to pay for his music—the louder the better.

Swindling reached an apogee one hot afternoon when a young stranger, newly arrived, sold at least three hundred cords of boiler wood to a man who owned several wells. The young man merely was seated beside the great pile of lumber, eating his lunch, when the other offered to buy it.

"Sure," he glibly replied, setting a figure of $3,000. The customer removed a wad of bills from his pocket. The transaction was consummated.

But the youthful stranger had vanished by the time the purchaser learned the shocking truth. The seller did not own so much as one splinter out of the pile.

After a Sunday stroll "into the beautiful fields nearby," the correspondent for *The Nation* returned to hear "the crack of a pistol." His first conclusion that some men were shooting at targets was quickly proven in error: ". . . On entering the hotel, I found a couple of men handcuffed, one of them shot through the leg. They had broken jail and one of them had 'squared off' at the constable on his arrest, upon which the constable had drawn his pistol and shot him through the leg."

Smart hotel keepers, the writer added, sat up all night with loaded, cocked revolvers or had a trusted clerk double for them.

But Pithole thrived in spite of its frontier abandon, lawlessness, and fraud that had already aroused the attention of the federal government. Added to the wheezing symphony of the pumps and other well machinery was the thud, this autumn, of sledgehammers as the rail line to Oleopolis was completed. Also, more oil lines, from two and a half to six inches in diameter, were being fitted into place, snaking over the hills to barges, major rail heads (and into something brand new called tank cars), or to other centers. Since the dark, heavy substance could be transported much more economically by pipe, the message to the teamsters, who could haul only two barrels per wagon and that at a tedious pace, was clear.

Deadly fights had already erupted between teamsters and the pipeline builders, including their guards. These altercations, added to the ever rising rate of crime, spawned an inevitable evil, the vigilantes. The law-abiding threw up their hands as they despaired, "If the outlaws don't get you the vigilantes will."

Another menace was fire, with at least nineteen serious blazes in Pithole so far that year. The previous month a well known as Grant began pumping so strongly that in a few hours some three hundred barrels had formed a thick, stygian lake over the fields. A curious crowd of several hundred gathered to watch the awesome, uncontrollable spectacle.

They were far too curious for their own well-being. About 7:30 P.M. the petroleum ignited. Flames covering at least an acre of ground billowed a hundred feet into the air as black, oily smoke mushroomed heavenward. Many were injured, and at least one died of his burns.

None knew how to extinguish an oil well fire. It had to burn itself out. Taking cognizance of this ever present peril, a correspondent for the *Times* of London spoke of the "vapour" that had to be carried off from "a wooden spire-shaped chimney," adding: "I have spent many hours in great powder magazines yet, on the whole, I would rather pass a month in them than a day by the great oil wells of Pithole . . . At every turn one meets the warning notices, 'no smoking,' 'beware of smoking,' 'smokers will be lynched,' etc. Yet in spite of everything smoking does go on . . ."

He alluded to the story of "the widow McClintock," who, along with her house and hoard of $80,000, was incinerated one night when an oil lamp exploded. If there was any mourning, it went unnoticed.

"Everywhere," wrote the correspondent for *The Nation*, "there is a sound of revelry. Looking in at the windows, you see everywhere men playing cards, and drinking as always. Beyond the stores . . . in a small house, sleeps after his death agony one of the victims of the fire. Down the hill sits a vigilance committee in secret session . . . further down, the little streams of oil flow on incessantly. Unseen they move this complex of machinery of men and things, with careless hand dealing out to their slaves life or death, wealth or poverty, triumph or despair."

Hobey Sutton's accordion whined while the screams of the robbed and ravished went unheard. Drinking, carousing, whoring, infant Pithole, yet to celebrate its first birthday, luxuriated at possibly the zenith of its existence. None had time to speculate that the wells—all of them—could not only burn but also run dry.

This first autumn following the War of the Rebellion, the cities and towns of America, just as Pithole did, presented many contrasts. In the South want persisted, everywhere.

"Window glass has given way to thin boards," the federal general, Henry Van Ness Boynton, told correspondent Whitelaw Reid. "And these are in use in railway coaches and in the cities. Furniture is marred and broken, and none has been replaced for four years. Dishes are cemented in various styles, and half the pitchers have tin handles. A complete set of crockery is never seen, and in a very few families is there enough to set a table . . . A set of forks with whole tines is a curiosity.

"Hair brushes and tooth brushes have all worn out; combs are broken and are not yet replaced; pins, needles, and thread and a thousand such articles, which seem indispensable to housekeeping are very scarce. Even in weaving on the looms corncobs have been substituted for spindles. Few have pocket knives.

"In fact, everything that has heretofore been an article of sale . . . is wanting now. At the tables of those who were once esteemed luxurious providers, you will find neither tea, coffee, sugar nor spices of any kind. Even candles, in some cases, have been replaced by a cup of grease, in which a piece of cloth is plunged for a wick."

Women's clothing was also "wanting." Wrote Hannah Garlick Rawlings, from Orange County, in the Piedmont of Virginia, to her sister Clarissa in Pennsylvania: "I have not purchased anything scarcely for upwards of four years. And now am in need of everything, both underclothing and dresses . . . There is not a family within the circle of your acquaintance in Spotsylvania [where Hannah had spent the war years] that has not been reduced almost to indigence.

"Henry H. who had become one of the most flourishing men of this very flourishing vicinity, has lost nearly everything. His large mill was burnt by the enemy last summer and he has not now the means to rebuild it."

Noting that all her friends are "no better off," she mentioned that her widowed sister, Anne, had recently moved to a new home about a mile from her previous one "and, while there, had neither cow nor garden, and was without money. It was with the greatest difficulty that she could get bread, and often after breakfasting upon 'corn cake' and buttermilk (the milk supplied by a kind neighbor) she has been utterly at a loss to know where dinner was to come from. My dear, I have eaten bread made from meal that was so sour and musty, I was obliged to hold my breath while I swallowed it.

"Ever since I commenced teaching I have been doing all in my power to educate Anne's children, so as to enable them to take care of themselves, and now I am so glad of it. Bettie will be prepared to take charge of a school herself in the fall, and between us we will provide for Jimmie next year.

"O, Clarissa! We people of the South have drained the cup of bitterness to the very dregs! Hardships and privations of all kinds—the loss of fortune and friends—all these could have been, and *were,* borne without a murmur for the sake of our country. But now, what is there to comfort us! We have no country, our very name is lost to us and we must be identified with the hated 'Yankee.' "

When Hannah contemplated the past five months she tended to feel "as if it could not be reality, and that I have been the victim of some hideous nightmare!"

If she was admittedly a rather poor "loser," she had company. At Cottage Farm, Petersburg, Sara Pryor was not a great deal happier, although more philosophical.

"We had, fortunately, no inclination to read," she continued in her diary. "A few books had been saved, only those for which we had little use.

"A [Union] soldier walked in one day with a handsome volume which Jefferson Davis, after inscribing his name in it, had presented to the general. The soldier calmly requested the former owner to be kind enough to add to the value of the volume by writing beneath the inscription his own autograph, and his request granted, walked off with it under his arm. 'He has been at some trouble,' said my husband, 'and he had as well be happy if I cannot!' "

Some of the articles of furniture were restored after most of the troops marched away, "but nothing handsome or valuable . . . just a few chairs and tables." A crowning insult was the letter from a New England officer who enclosed the photograph of Sara's blooded mare, Lady Jane, and asked for the horse's pedigree; "the pedigree was not sent, but later the amiable [new] owner of Lady Jane sent her photograph. Also his own— on her back."

Then came the tourists, "on their way to visit the localities near us, now become historic. They frequently called upon us, claiming some common acquaintance. We could not but resent this. Their sympathetic attitude offended us, sore and proud as we were."

Her whole house smelled, impelling Sara to eat her meals outside "under the trees, unless driven by the rains to the shelter of the porch. I suffered terribly for want of occupation. I had no household to manage, no garments to mend or make. My little Lucy could not bear the sun, and she sat quietly beside me all day. I could have made a sunbonnet for her, but I had no fabric, no thimble, needles, thread, or scissors.

"Finally, I discovered in the pocket of one of my Washington coats my silver card case with Trinity Church on one side and the Capitol at Washington on the other—objects I had now no right to hold dear. I made Alick drive me in my little farm cart to the sutler's and effected an exchange for a small straw 'Shaker' bonnet which I am sure could have been purchased for less than one dollar. Protected with this, the little girl found a playhouse under the trees.

"A good old friend, Mr. Kemp, invited the boys to accompany him upon relic-hunting expeditions to the narrow plain which had divided the opposing lines on that fateful April morning . . . Ropes were fastened around extinct shells, and they were hauled in, to stand sentinel at the door. The shells were short cylinders, with one pointed end like a candle before it is lighted. Numbers of minie balls were dug out of the sand. One day Mr. Kemp brought in a great curiosity—two bullets welded together, having been shot from opposing rifles."

Her neighbor, Dr. Claiborne, was at this time taking note of a term which had appeared in the American vocabulary: "carpetbagger . . . a new king . . . to represent the civil law, and Adjutant Buttons, to represent the military . . . not one king but a king for nearly every county and city of the commonwealth . . . and with every king an adjutant."

He continued: "The former, light of baggage had one carpet bag, hence his name; but that was filled with provisos, and writs and orders. Lieutenant Buttons was his executive officer, and a scalawag, a low fellow [not?]

to the manor born, and bought with the promise of spoil, was his suborned witness. These men were called sometimes and in some places 'The Bureau,' sometimes the 'Freedman's Bureau.' "

He referred to the new federal entity established by Lincoln shortly before his death and known as the Bureau of Refugees, Freedmen and Abandoned Lands. It was headed by Major General Oliver Otis Howard, of Maine, who had commanded the Army of the Tennessee under General Sherman in the Atlanta, Georgia, and the Carolinas campaigns.

The military, the doctor conceded, might "occasionally contain a gentleman," even though the Lieutenant Buttons variety was "innocent of the smoke of battle." But the "villainy" of the carpetbaggers he found to be unrelieved. All in all, the surgeon of Petersburg could see nothing but trouble ahead.

In Richmond, Susan Archer Weiss, a young friend of Edgar Allen Poe, was picking up the pieces even as were Sara Pryor, Hannah Rawlings, and uncounted others. At the moment, Lieutenant Buttons was of scant concern to her thoughts and immediate challenges. Having belatedly returned to Talavera, in the western part of the city, Susan wrote: "In place of the pleasant, smiling home, there stood a bare and lonely house in the midst of encircling fortifications, still bristling with dismantled gun-carriages. Every outbuilding had disappeared. All the beautiful trees which had made it so attractive—even the young cedar of Lebanon, which had been our pride—were gone; greenhouses, orchard, vineyard, everything had been swept away, leaving only a dead level overgrown with broom-straw, amidst which were scattered rusted bayonets and a few hardy plants struggling through the trampled ground. The place was no longer 'Talavera' but 'Battery 10.'

"In this desolate abode I remained some time."

The aspect of the city itself hadn't changed perceptibly since the reporter from the New York *Tribune* had visited in early July. John Richard Dennett, of *The Nation*, arrived at Rocketts to find a "Broadway and Ninth avenue omnibus" waiting at the landing. It then "rattled us over the ill-paved streets to the hotel."

He continued: "Two rudely painted wooden signs, projecting from the corners of two ugly brick warehouses, told us where stood 'Castle Thunder' and 'Libby.' Of these buildings, the former is used as a city prison; the latter is set apart for the use of soldiers waiting for their regiments, and for the families of Negro laborers working for the United States

Quartermaster. Cannon balls can be seen lying about in the streets, which are little used by any vehicles but army wagons and public.

"Traversing the main street, going up the hill, on which the Capitol is situated, in the centre of what was formerly the business part of the city is the burnt district. For a quarter of a mile one passes nothing but toppling walls, forlorn-looking chimneys, heaps of bricks, with here and there a ruined safe lying in the midst, warped and red from the effects of intense heat. Some Virginia agent of a Hudson Street firm has pasted in half a dozen places the advertisement of 'Hubbell's Golden Bitters' but besides this evidence of enterprise there is very little sign of business activity."

In the surviving shops there were ample stocks, but no customers since none had any money. Dennett believed that Northern merchants had restocked the stores and their "eagerness" to sell he found "quite touching," but "the people could not purchase . . . and the result is that many articles can be bought cheaper in Richmond today than in Baltimore or New York. 'Flour,' says the *Whig*, 'that sold in New York on Saturday for $7 and $8, sold here for $5, and meats that were selling here for 15 to 20¢, there stood on their dignity at 25 to 35¢.' A market with so little money was easily overstocked."

While it would have aroused disbelief in those such as Hannah Rawlings, fashion had reappeared in some quarters of Richmond, along with a resurgence of gaiety. Noticeable finery covered the backs of Northern ladies, creating remarkable contrasts with the local citizenry. Officers' wives, sisters, and friends strolled into "Military Headquarters," near Clay and Twelfth streets, parasols in hand, as band music blared over the city's rubble. This was accompanied by the sound of "dancing feet" that reached others less fortunate "through our closed shutters."

So wrote Myrta Lockett Avary, quoting a letter from a Richmond woman she identified only as Matoaca (perhaps after a community west of Petersburg). Describing the invasion of women from such cities as New York, Boston, and even distant Chicago, Matoaca continued: "Some ladies wore on the streets white petticoats, braided with black, under their dresses, which were looped up over these. Their gowns were short walking length, and their feet could be seen quite plainly. That style would be becoming to us, we said to ourselves, thinking of our small feet—at least I said so to myself. Up to that time we had considered it immodest to show our feet, our long dresses and hoop-skirts concealing them. We had been wearing coal-scuttle bonnets of plaited straw, trimmed with cornshuck rosettes. I made fifteen . . . acquired a fine name as a milliner, and was paid for my work."

Matoaca recalled one that was especially "stunning," sporting "a bit of much-worn white ribbon" which she dyed an "exquisite shade of green, with a tea made of coffee-berries . . . our straw-and-shuck bonnets were pretty. How eager we were to see the fashions! We had had no fashions for a long time.

"When the Northern ladies appeared on the streets, they did not seem to have on any bonnets at all. They wore tiny, three-cornered affairs tied on with narrow strings, and all their hair showing in the back.

"One of the styles brought by the Northern ladies was black alpaca skirts fringed. I got one as soon as I could . . ." Meanwhile, Matoaca commenced braiding a skirt of her own. The prices of materials were "absurd," $75 for a paper of pins, calico $25 a yard, while patterns for a calico dress ran as high as $1,000 ($1,400 for silk). Myrta's correspondent continued: "I am prospering with my needlework. I sew early and late. My friends who are better off give me work, paying me as generously as they can. Mammy Jane has sold some of my embroideries to Northern ladies. Many ladies, widows and orphans, are seeking employment as teachers. The great trouble is that so few people are able to engage them or to pay for help of any kind. Still, we all manage to help each other somehow.

"Nannie, our young bride, is raising lettuce, radish, nasturtiums, in her back yard for sale. She is painting her house herself (with her husband's help). She is going to give the lettuce towards paying the church debt. She has nothing else to give. I think I will raise something to buy window-panes for this house. Window-panes patched with paper are all the fashion in this town.

"The Yankees introduced some new fashions in other things besides clothes . . . one being canned fruit. I had never seen any canned fruit before the Yankees came. Perhaps we had had canned fruit, but I do not remember it."

The resurgence of life and interest in the city was not altogether pleasing to the older generation, especially to those who had suffered from the war more than others. "I confess," an elderly matron was quoted as saying, "I have sometimes of late years been startled by a burst of laughter from a pretty girl," not to mention "somewhat pained by hearing a group of wild girls and clever young men talking in tones better suited to the mill than a drawing room." When *she* was young, "the loud laugh was considered ungraceful and slang words abominable."

This summer, Richmond's most distinguished resident, Robert E. Lee, quit his home on Franklin Street for the relative seclusion of Cumberland County, some thirty-five miles to the west. There, friends had loaned him a cottage, Derwent, near Cartersville, on the James. The air and elevation was healthful to his ever ailing wife, Mary Custis.

No longer under indictment, but nonetheless not pardoned, the former commander of the Army of Northern Virginia, forbidden to wear his uniform, was a man in limbo. Philosophically, he had written to his friend Captain Josiah Tattnall, second commander of the C.S.S. *Virginia (Merrimack)*: "Like yourself, I have, since the cessation of hostilities, advised all with whom I have conversed on the subject, who come within the terms of the President's proclamations, to take the oath of allegiance, and accept in good faith the amnesty offered. But I have gone further, and have recommended to those who were excluded from their benefits, to make application under the *proviso* of the proclamation of the 29th of May, to be embraced in its provisions . . . The war being at an end, the Southern States having laid down their arms, and the question at issue between them and the Northern States having been decided, I believe it to be the duty of every one to unite in the restoration of the country and the reestablishment of peace and harmony."

Lee was restless. Early in August, the trustees of little Washington College, in Lexington, had invited him to become the institution's president. The general replied that he was tired, his nerves ragged from too many well-meaning callers during the final weeks in Richmond, and his very presence could be an embarrassment to the institution in its dealings with the federal government. Besides, he did not feel up to the rigors of teaching a class, or classes, as was expected of presidents of most colleges.

But the trustees wanted him. The college, which dated to revolutionary times as Liberty Hall Academy, still showed its scars from General Hunter's raid. Needed was a figure of prestige to aid in the rebuilding. Lee would not be obliged to teach, he was assured. Furthermore, he would be shielded from curiosity seekers.

Lee accepted. On September 14, Mary Custis wrote to a friend: "I do not think he is very fond of teaching, but he is willing to do anything that will give him an honourable support. He starts tomorrow *en cheval* for Lexington. He prefers that way and, besides, does not like to part even for a time from his beloved steed, the companion of many a hard-fought battle . . ."

Lee's beloved horse was war-weary and gray like his master. If Traveler were ever trim, powerful, dashing, as popular images of the years of strife depicted him, the mount was now slow and somewhat swaybacked.

Laden only with saddlebags, Lee had shipped a few trunks, a desk, a chair, and minor pieces of furniture by canal boat. He chose a northwesterly route to take advantage of river and stream valleys that led just south of Charlottesville and through Waynesboro, atop the Blue Ridge. It was not the shortest way, but it was well marked, heavily shaded against the dying breaths of summer, and spotted with the homes of friends, including two physicians.

Lying south of the Shenandoah, the trail nonetheless often resembled that area of devastation, as delineated by one resident: ". . . The country was almost a desert. There were no fences. Speaking of the condition of the valley after General Sheridan retired, I described wheat-fields growing without any enclosure; someone asked me whether the stock would not destroy the wheat. I said, 'Certainly, if General Sheridan had not taken the precaution of removing all the stock.' We could cultivate grain without fences, as we had no cattle, hogs, sheep, or horses, or anything else. The fences were all gone; some of the orchards were very much injured . . . the barns were all burned; chimneys standing without houses, and houses standing without a roof . . . bridges all destroyed, roads badly cut up, a most desolate state of affairs."

His slouch hat and old campaign jacket covered with dust, Lee was not altogether recognizable. This was agreeable to the general. If he had not sought it before, he now found solace in anonymity, as though it were a salve to his injured pride and shattered dreams for a quite different South.

On the fourth day Traveler wearily limped into Lexington. The town slept on the western slopes of the Blue Ridge, silent save for the late summer hum of crickets, locusts, and tree toads. The next morning, September 19, Lee sat down and wrote his wife about the trip and his greeting by Professor White, "who brought me up to his father-in-law's, Colonel Reid, the oldest member of the trustees of the college, where I am very comfortably quartered. Today I will look out for accommodations elsewhere as the colonel has a large family and I fear I am intruding upon his hospitality."

The college grounds "seem to be beautifully located, and the buildings are undergoing repairs."

The house assigned him was presently occupied. It was an imposing two-story brick dwelling with massive porticoes and pillars, shaded by oaks, elms, and locusts and reminiscent of the former Davis mansion in Richmond.

Commenting on the "beautiful scenery" of his journey, the hot days and cool nights, Lee noted that he was now sleeping under a blanket and found that a fire had been lit in the dining room. "I have thought much of you since I left. Give much love to the girls and Custis . . ."

The Reid family, at first in awe of this distinguished, patrician visitor, was put at ease by Lee's gentle manner and soon spoke with him as though he had long been a member of the household. The latter included some little children who quickly adopted the white-bearded, stately gentleman with the kindly blue eyes.

In a few days, needing some treatment for the sore muscles caused by his journey, Lee visited the famous Rockbridge Baths, eleven miles north of Lexington. Again he wrote home: "I have taken the baths every day since my arrival, and like them very much . . . Yesterday I procured some horses and took them up to the top of Jump Mountain, where we had one of the most beautiful views I ever saw . . . I wish you were all with me. I feel very solitary and miss you dreadfully."

Upon his return to the college, General Lee moved into the Lexington Hotel, although ladies of the town "furnished me a very nice room in the college for my office; new carpet from Baltimore, curtains, etc." Now he concerned himself not only with the incoming freshman class of fifty but with his formal installation, set for October 3.

The ceremonies, he insisted, must be "the simplest possible." This was sharply at variance with the thinking of the trustees, who wanted invitations dispatched throughout the South, bands, long speeches, parades, and so on. The trustees, however, acceded to Lee. He would be sworn in in a recitation room, even now being swept, scrubbed, and polished. Only faculty, students, ministers, and town officials would attend. A local magistrate, Judge William White, would administer the oath. Lee planned to wear a plain gray suit, one that members of the Reid household had described as elegant.

Already at work in the evening on his speech, the South's most famous general would counsel "cheerful submission to the Government, and earnest striving to bring about the old state of peace, industry, thrift and content." He resolved, too, to express "greatest confidence" in President Johnson, a move aimed at "healing the wounds."

Then, putting aside his acceptance speech, under the shadows of the flickering lamp, he started another letter to his wife, on a less optimistic note: "Life is indeed gliding away and I have nothing of good to show for mine that is past . . ."

The leading figures of the Confederacy, widely dispersed, were faring in diverse fashion. Some were now overseas. Kate Thompson, wife of Richmond's commissioner to Canada, Jacob Thompson, still with a price on his head, was writing from Paris to her friend Mary Ann Cobb, in Athens, Georgia: "Passed through the Yankee lines as Mrs. Jones with a brown vail [*sic*] and we sailed from Halifax on the 6th of July . . . After a very safe and pleasant voyage of 11 days we landed at Liverpool.

"I am now in the great city of Paris and enjoying ourselves as much as we can under the circumstances. We are living very plainly but comfortably. We have not much money . . . This city of Paris is the greatest place in the world, as far the superior to England as England is ahead of the United States . . . but I feel I have no home, no country and what an aching void it is in one's heart!"

She noted that "Mr. Thompson" was in "good health" and studying French "hard," but she maintained personally "a perfect disgust for the language." In the French capital she had met "many old friends" including General Breckinridge and Judah Benjamin, and she was "staying in the same hotel with Madame Benjamin." The latter, a lover of the good life and Continental café society, had spent the entire war in Paris.

"There are," Kate Thompson continued, "many other very pleasant Confederates here that you are not acquainted with." In closing, she could report that her husband had received "receipt in full for the last dollar reserving his salary while in the employment of the Government." (This aside was enigma. Had Confederate gold been stashed away in England or France? Or was it worthless paper money? It is doubtful that the fleeing Southerners could have obtained and then carried with them U.S. currency.)

Former Brigadier General Robert Toombs was also in Paris, accompanied by his wife. The veteran of Antietam and Malvern Hill battles had, like Benjamin and Breckinridge, taken the Havana route to freedom. Although he had been a United States senator, the Georgia politician was a relatively minor figure in the rebellion. Never in Davis's cabinet or even in the Confederate Senate, he had manifested undue concern over his personal safety.

Lee, Jacob Thompson, Breckinridge, Toombs—all could find much more to be thankful for than Jefferson Davis. He finally had a visitor: General Dick Taylor, who had obtained his pass to Fort Monroe.

"There were two rooms," Taylor wrote, "in the outer of which, near the entrance, stood a sentinel, and in the inner was Jefferson Davis. We met in silence, with grasp of hands. After an interval he said, 'this is kind, but no more than I expected of you.' Pallid, worn, gray, bent, feeble, suffering from inflammation of the eyes, he was a painful sight to a friend. He uttered no plaint, and made no allusion to the irons (which had been removed); said the light kept all night in his room hurt his eyes a little, and, added to the noise made every two hours by relieving the sentry, prevented much sleep."

Taylor told the former president that he entertained optimism of "obtaining permission for his wife to stay with him . . . Hope of meeting his family cheered him much, and he asked questions about the condition and prospects of the South, which I answered as favorably as possible, passing over things that would have grieved him. In some way he had learned of attacks on his character and conduct, made by some Southern curs, thinking to ingratiate themselves with the ruling powers. I could not deny this, but remarked that the curse of unexpected defeat and suffering was to develop the basest passions of the human heart."

Yet Davis was not really cheered. Still tormented, he wrote Varina, "My strength has greatly failed me, and the loss of sleep has created a morbid excitability, but an unseen hand has sustained me, and a peace the world could not give and has not been able to destroy will, I trust, uphold me to meet with resignation whatever may befall me."

He had not received a "new overcoat" Varina had forwarded, his "daily walks" continued, and all in all "my days drag heavily on."

OCTOBER

A State of Primeval Chaos

As the months after Appomattox passed, time proved a burden to others besides Jefferson Davis, and for differing reasons. In Green Lake, Texas, inland from Matagorda Island, Colonel William P. Lyon, commanding the Thirteenth Wisconsin Infantry Regiment on occupation duty, wrote to his wife, Adelia, in Racine: "The days drag along slowly . . . Coarse food, poorly cooked and very poor water is enough to use up almost anybody; so the sick list is very large. Fully one-third are reported sick."

Nearly everything was wrong. "It has rained terribly most of the time . . . The storm comes from the northeast and is unusual for the season. The water has been over the bottom of our tent several times . . . ague and remittent fevers predominate . . . snakes, scorpions, tarantulas, centipedes, and almost every venomous and loathsome reptile abound here, and the streams are infested with alligators. The boys killed one between seven and eight feet long in the lake close to our camp yesterday, and one eighteen feet long has been killed by the command since it came here.

"We are terribly troubled with mosquitoes. They come in myriads, very large and energetic, and early in the evening drive us under our mosquito-bars."

To avoid the mosquito plague, many of the troops slept in the daytime and danced all night; "they have an old fiddle, and half a dozen fiddlers take turns at the instrument, and a hundred men at a time break it down in regular stag dance style on the prairie by the hour. Last night they wanted to know if the frolic disturbed me, but I told them no, to wade in and enjoy themselves—yet they kept me awake for hours. My bar affords me ample protection and if I do not get sleep at night I take it in the daytime.

"Looking over the camp now, 11 o'clock a.m., you can not see twenty-five men, yet there are 350 at least in it. They are all asleep. The weather is hot . . . from 90 to 95 degrees . . . but during the day we get a breeze from the Gulf, which relieves us greatly."

Food, aside from some "excellent beef," left much to be desired, underscored by a total lack of vegetables: "Our crackers are so old that the worms have taken up their abode in them; but we rap them on the table and nearly all fall out. They are also musty and moldy and are not very appetizing."

Even the uniform allotment had failed the Wisconsin outfit: "No supplies of medicine or clothing, very poor rations and insufficient in quality at that . . . this in addition to being held in service after their contract with the Government has been fully executed is pretty rough treatment for the men who have breasted the tide of war for four long years and whose valor and fortitude have saved the Government from total ruin.

"And the most aggravating thing about our situation is that there does not exist the least necessity for our services. For all any good we do the Government we might as well be in the Fiji Islands, and yet we see no indication that the corps will be mustered out soon."

And so Bill Lyon, from Racine, sat "in this pestilential country, surrounded with more discomforts and in more real danger than have been in for a long time." He was, necessarily, unknowing even as he penned "no signs" of a discharge that in the War Department orders were being written to send the Thirteenth Wisconsin back to their homes and the renewed as well as more grave challenges of civilian existence.

Outside of Edgefield, in the eastern reaches of Nashville, Tennessee, a thirty-five-year-old maiden lady was writing, "The middle of another week of my drowning disagreeable life has arrived." The brittling of the now dull leaves and the steady plop of chinquapins this autumn served but to underscore the unhappiness of Abbie Brooks, a self-employed schoolteacher. Nonetheless, education generally was on a continuing upsurge in the last months of 1865.

In fact, it had leapt 50 percent since 1850, according to the 1860 census, with almost 5 million pupils (a sixth of the nation's population) in 107,527 public schools. Holding forth in predominantly one-room schoolhouses were 130,000 teachers. This meant, among other harvests of creation, that the average soldier in the Civil War, for the first time in the country's bellicose history, was able to write letters home. And he did so in scrawling profusion, usually ungrammatical, but with consistent devotion, homesick, consumed by worries over his family as well himself, in uncomfortable if not miserable surroundings.

Abbie belonged to another, smaller teaching corps, the same 18,000 men and women who staffed the United States' 6,000 colleges, academies, and the private entities such as hers, which did not boast even a structure. A tutor more literally, she could work with her pupils at their homes or in her own.

Most states long since had enacted laws governing education and had levied school taxes, ringing youngsters to class, in 1865, about 130 days out of the year. Opportunities and facilities, however, were unevenly distributed. Pennsylvania, for instance, with a population of nearly 3 million, had 565,000 children in public school, in contrast with Georgia's 56,000 out of more than a million residents.

The slaves in the South were 90 percent illiterate, having hitherto been legislated out of the classroom. Technically this was not the case with "freemen," but it certainly was with the "poor whites," who lived in "filthy poverty, foul ignorance . . . idiotic imbecility . . . Had schools abounded six years ago, I doubt if the masses of the South could have been forced into the war." So spoke Sidney Andrews, thirty-one-year-old former editor of the Alton (Illinois) *Daily Courier*. He was one of the growing platoon of reporters shuffling southward through the backwash of the war.

"The little red schoolhouse," wrote James Shaw, a Mobile, Alabama, newspaperman, "was no feature of the landscape in the lower South. The conception of the State's duty that there prevailed was that the State was a sort of policeman; that it was bound to keep the peace if it could, and punish crime." Beyond that, he believed the state felt no obligations, surely not in the field of learning.

Midway through the war, a Mississippi mother, Mrs. Devlin, packed her daughter in a neighbor's cart and started for the nearest railroad, some miles distant, with the ultimate goal of Canada and education. Still, education was not wholly dead even in the Deep South; one historian called it as unlikely "that the schools vanished into thin air as it is that the students did." In fact, the Mississippi legislature, late in the war, debated a bill to create "the Mississippi Association for Education and Support of Orphans of Soldiers." It failed of passage in favor of an alternative proposal providing for a committee of twenty private citizens to solicit funds for the same purpose. But the surrender of the Southern armies shortly afterward put an end to the proposal.

Abbie Brooks, however, was concerned neither with the literacy of the blacks nor with mass education. Her horizons, perhaps like those of most teachers, were necessarily narrow. Having lived under the federal government for almost the entire rebellion, Miss Brooks knew but a very small flock, sometimes as few as one or two pupils. And her overriding concern was earning enough to eat.

"I am trying," she wrote, "to be submissive to my fate, but it is with an untamed reluctance; if I was doomed to eternal perdition . . . then might I have sorrow, yes the crowning sorrow of sorrows."

At the end of September, Abbie had turned to diary keeping as an outlet, conceivably therapeutic for her all-consuming frustrations. These were often triggered by religious impulse or hauntings of insufficiency. Was she really a good teacher? Was she a hopeless sinner?

Into October she not only poured out the punctuations of daily schoolmarming but sketched the passing vignettes of life in postwar Nashville. But she never confided just what she was teaching. That seemed so obvious to her, hardly worthy of mention.

". . . The remembrances of joys forever departed, the corroding cares of life annoy and worry me, and there seems no balm to cure or charm my troubles and trials from any of their bitterness." Worse, there was often little or no remuneration for her efforts; "they seem to think I have no use for money and teach their children to be accommodating."

And then, the next day, October 4, she mused, "I wonder when I will be visited by some weighty ideas, yes one bright original thought . . ." But that did not inhibit her as she put pen to paper on successive October days, sometimes in the waning sun of late afternoon, often under the light of her worn oil lamp with its tall, blackened glass chimney. "The sun lingers in the heavens like a friend who parts unwillingly. He has shone

The Georgian mansion in Nashville occupied by General Sherman. (National Archives)

*Nashville squalor. Abbie Brooks, the teacher, knew all these "Nashvilles."
(National Archives)*

*The "Limited" arrives in Petroleum Center, Pennsylvania. (American Petroleum
Institute, Shell Oil)*

Much of Richmond survived the fire. This is how sections of the Confederate capital appeared to the Union Army. (Library of Congress)

Ford's Theatre. (National Park Service)

Andrew Johnson, no friend of Stanton or Mary Surratt. (National Park Service)

John Wilkes Booth. (Library of Congress)

Mary Surratt, a simple woman of Southern sympathies who did not understand the mortal peril of allowing potential assassins to meet in her boarding house. (Library of Congress)

A scowling Judge Holt, obedient to Secretary Stanton, measurably speeded Mary Surratt to the gallows, even though commutation to life imprisonment had been recommended by the trial commission. (Library of Congress)

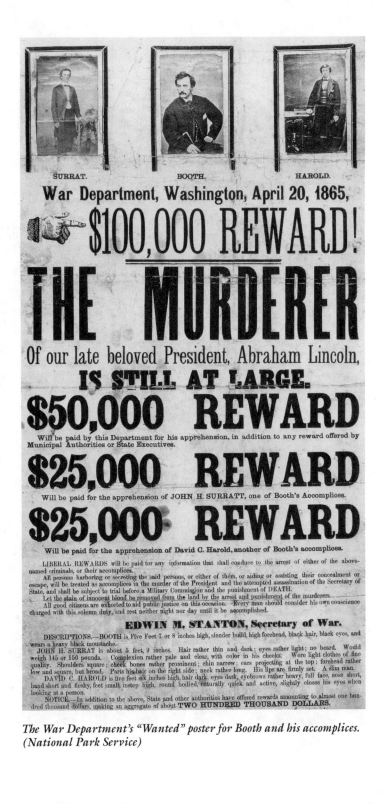

The War Department's "Wanted" poster for Booth and his accomplices. (National Park Service)

The final of Gardner's remarkable sequence of photos of the execution of the "conspirators." The body of Mrs. Surratt is at the far left; Payne, the young giant, is beside her. Public executions were more or less commonplace in the last century. (National Archives)

Carroll Annex to the notorious Old Capitol Prison, where Mary Surratt and others were temporarily lodged, as it appeared after the war. It was razed before the turn of the century to make way for the Library of Congress. Washington was growing, even then. (Library of Congress)

Senator Sumner, no friend of President Johnson, surely his bête noire. (Library of Congress)

Gideon Welles, Lincoln's secretary of the navy, was distinguished by his generous gray wig. (U.S. Navy)

"The City of Charleston lay open to our view... nothing could be more desolate,"
wrote Carl Schurz. (National Archives)

A ruined Atlanta. (National Archives)

Here a crew rebuilds a stretch of track in Virginia. The gentle-man wearing a bowler, at the right, substan-tiates the hunch that foremen even then preferred not to dirty their hands. (National Archives)

The charnel house that was Andersonville prison. Pictures are rare for two reasons: the Confederacy boasted few photographers, and they were less than proud of the camp. (National Archives)

beautifully . . . and now sets gloriously. Jack Frost made a short call this morning, powdering the fences and other objects in his reach . . .

"I am teaching on through an uneventful period of my existence. I eat, drink, sleep and teach school. It is the same treadmill routine daily without variation; but I do wrong to complain. I have very good health, and a use of my limbs. I have enough to eat of a poor quality, with a quiet room to stay in. I had my feelings hurt by asking Dick Scruggs if he could not send after my stove to Mr. Love's. He made more excuses than I thought was possible for him to imagine. As I had paid $12.50 in advance some distance, I thought they would be a little more obliging.

"I am not pleasantly situated. Every sound echoes discontent. I feel it when I retire and when I rise. I am not earning anything with my small school but my condition might be worse."

The next day, October 7, to break the monotony, she boarded the coach for the capital: "I prepared for Nashville this morning and went in upon the accommodation train. A very pleasant arrangement. Mrs. Burton was upon the train and we entertained ourselves by talking. I went to see about my squirrels, found the low bid of six dollars for them. They were so much trouble I concluded to accept the offer. I went to Mrs. White's after I had finished my running about in town. The sun shone very warm upon my back, but I obtained an opportunity to ride soon after crossing the river. I found Mrs. White and Miss Sallie well. Gen. Donaldson's son gave [me] a five hundred dollar bill Confederate money. A keepsake."

And Sunday, "I went to Tulip Street Methodist Church this morning. Before service I enjoyed seeing the people unload from their different vehicles, the ladies dressed in their finest silks which looked as though they were made before the war and others more modern. As it was Conference, the number of preachers and people present was not small. Bishop Kavanagh preached a fine sermon . . . service very long."

The week continued. "I am in school this morning with an additional scholar, Mrs. Woodruff's niece. School duties seem to go along with little or no trouble, if there is monotony there is also smoothness. After school I walked over to Mr. Woodruff's for the purpose of seeing one of my scholars which is sick.

"Business seems brisk at the store. The L. & N. R.R. are putting in a switch in front of the store, and improvement seems to be making rapid strides in the locality . . . It has been another bright day. Many of my scholars are sick and the number in attendance is small."

Then, by Wednesday, October 11, "this is my 4th session in one place, but it has become very dull to me of late. It wearies me exceedingly. I am glad when I see their backs turned towards me going home. Poor children, I try to make myself interesting to them but it is dull music to me. It seems like doing nothing, yes, time lost to me and gone forever. All the pleasure I have is in my room and feeding my pet chickens, which are very tame and gentle. They know the sound of my voice and come rushing to me whenever they hear it. I feed them and they love me apparently very much."

Thursday, the weather was "unpleasantly heated . . . At dinner time I went to see Mrs. Granaghan about borrowing a horse. Mrs. G. put a five dollar bill in my hand which was very acceptable. It was unexpected but it revived me. I love to earn money myself and not have to ask any person for it. I then can be independent and not a fawning sycophant upon any person's bounty.

"After school I went to see Mrs. Woodruff and found three sick children which I had missed from school. John had erysipelas on his face. Charlie had sat down upon a sharp stick, and Toby had cut his foot with a piece of glass. It is now 9 o'clock and the rain is commencing to patter upon the leaves. The ground is very dry."

With a scarcity of doctors, sickness remained ever present. "I sat up all night with Mrs. Woodruff in company with Mrs. Granaghan. The night passed off rapidly for some cause. Mrs. W. was very ill-natured. She would only take her medicine from the hands of the doctor. I had to call him every three hours all night. She is getting very low and extremely cross and irritable. I came home and found Mrs. Scruggs sick. I waited upon her some and went to sleep. I slept a greater portion of the day in order to regain my rest, if possible. I have done nothing all day but sleep. I prepared some bread for baking before I went to bed. A new business for me.

"I arose soon this morning to make light rolls for breakfast. They were only tolerable good. They did not bake well. I spent the day reading from the Life of Patrick Henry . . ."

Life, learning, and monotony in Edgefield, Tennessee, continued.

The desire to improve education went forward elsewhere. In the small eastern Georgia town of Elberton, a number of civic leaders and former military men raised $1,700 to build a schoolhouse. Among them was the well-known lieutenant general, John B. Gordon, who had led the last major counterattack in the defense of Petersburg. Also involved was Brigadier General Alfred H. Colquitt, who had fought with Stonewall Jackson and participated in many of the major battles, including Antietam and Chancellorsville.

The modest edifice would replace a "bush arbor" for "preaching and Sunday school" and other schooling in good weather. So wrote the local chronicler, Kate Hester Robson, herself far too busy to be bored this autumn with her husband, Si, away managing a coal mine. "I had to work. I once tried to plow, but my skirts got in my way. I was young and vigorous, had never been sick, never had headache or backache and never stayed in bed only to keep my babies warm. I was interested again in my gardens and my father sent me more boxes of shrubs, figs, and fruit trees. I guess there was five acres in front of the house, and I laid off drives and walks and terraces. It was on that lot I first planted Pecan nuts and English walnuts.

"I reckon I was always venturesome. When my husband went to his business in Atlanta I would take his hands and mules and plows and have them work on this big front ground, and I got his two-horse wagon broken down hauling big rocks to make a rockery around a tree.

"He said to me once—'don't you mind when I fuss at you for taking the farm hands. I know that ornamental improvement enhances the value of real estate more than anything else.'" The ornamental improvement, it turned out, would enhance the value by exactly $2,000. While Kate landscaped, "other friends who had been impoverished by the war came and bought homes—built cheap houses and began life again."

The women of the South continued to react according to their individual emotions and, like Kate Robson, depending on their physical strength. The erstwhile first lady of the South, Varina Davis, who had resettled on Mill View farm, five miles from Augusta, remained embittered over the treatment that had been accorded her children during her recent residence in Savannah. She poured out her mingled woes and frustrations in a long letter to the commanding officer of Fort Monroe. She hoped Mr. Davis would be moved to better quarters, lest he suffer from "paralysis" and other disorders.

She worried about her husband's not sleeping because of the light kept on in his room, and this in spite of the fact that Jefferson Davis really had but one adequate eye. Vision was not one of his happier endowments. Varina, however, had no way of knowing that the former president of the

Confederacy had been moved to officers' quarters on the second floor, with better, drier air, water, and a hearth. No doubt General Dick Taylor was at least in part responsible.

"On the gallery side of the chimney is a recess with a shelf for books and pegs to hang up my clothes," the prisoner was writing in his diary. Now this well-educated, highly articulate Southerner must wangle some books for those shelves.

Varina continued concerning the harassment of her children while in Savannah: "Little Jeff and Billy went out on the street to play, and there Jeff was constantly told that he was rich; that his father had 'stolen eight millions,' etc. Little two-year-old Billy was taught to sing, 'we'll hang Jeff Davis on a sour apple tree,' by giving him a reward when he did so . . . The rough soldiers doubtless meant to be kind, but such things wounded me to the quick. They took him and made him snatch apples off the stalls, if Robert lost sight of him for a moment.

"Finally, two women from Maine contemplated whipping him, because they found out that he was his father's son; but a man took them off just in time to avoid a very painful scene to them as well as to me.

"Once, when our little boy Jeff had been most violently assailed by an officer's wife in the house, he came up with his face covered with tears after having stood silent during her abuse. I commended Jeff's gentlemanly conduct in making no reply, cautioned him against ever persecuting, or distressing a woman, or a fiend, if it took that shape, but made application the next day for permission to go away to Augusta; was refused, and then prepared the children to go where they would not see such people . . ." The refusal manifestly was rescinded.

"Hourly scenes of violence were going on in the streets, and not reported, between the blacks and whites, and I felt that the children's lives were not safe."

Now, near Augusta, life was better. "The fine country air and the privacy, I have also grown much better; can sleep and eat, and begin to feel alive again with the frosty air, and loving words, and letters which meet me here as in Savannah.

"The whole Southern country teems with homes the doors of which open wide to receive me; and the people are so loving, talk with such streaming eyes and broken voices of him who is so precious to them and to me, that I cannot realize I do not know them intimately. Mr. Davis should dismiss all fears for me. I only suffer for him. I do not meet a young man who fails to put himself at my disposal to go anywhere for me. I cannot pay a doctor's bill, or buy of an apothecary."

While Varina Davis freely acknowledged "kind treatment" when it was accorded by the occupation authorities, for many, including another Southern woman, the war had not ended. Their venom toward the Yankees persisted unabated. "Both ladies and gentlemen [have been] dragged through the streets of Charleston by insolent negro guards in U.S. uniform, and there is not a single provost marshal that has been in Charleston," wrote Eliza Fludd. Eliza, who was related by marriage to the imprisoned former Treasury secretary George Trenholm, obviously had allowed bitterness to guide her angry pen. Federal commanders hanged or shot any of their troops, quite readily, when acts even approximating those Eliza described were substantiated. Bushwhackers, perhaps. And there were so many provosts in the South that their presence had become virtually monotonous, and the subject of quips.

Nonetheless, her house and furnishings in Camden, South Carolina, had been damaged either by Sherman's advancing forces or by the rabble following in their wake.

Writing from time to time this late fall to her sister, Mrs. Joliffe, in Philadelphia, Eliza continued: "It was a daily business for the soldiers (and many officers too) to rob the citizens with open brute force of everything they could lay their hands upon. Thus . . . I am left destitute of everything I owned, but my house with its bare floors and bare walls.

"I am staying on a borrowed bed, and one borrowed table, and four borrowed chairs are all that the house contains. My clothes are so old and shabby that I am ashamed to go into the streets; and I am now sick for want of warm clothing to meet the cool changes of the autumn."

Eliza, however, had not been robbed quite as devastatingly as she had written, since in the next breath she informed her sister: "I have sold the little silver that I had left to provide such necessaries as I cannot do without, and want to make the money go as far as I can, and therefore do not wish to spend it in Charleston where none but 'down cast Yankees' have things to sell, and charge four prices for everything.

"It occurred to me that I could find out through you if I could purchase things at a lower price in Philadelphia. I will enclose a list of what I especially want . . .

"My dear friend, you can form no idea of the suffering there is in the country, more especially in this city, where the heel of oppression grinds the white citizens into the dust . . . You doubtless, as your property lay in Virginia, have been reduced to want, like the rest, and know enough of the sorrows from your friends there. I have known the day when my dear little grandchildren have been crying for food, and we could not get it for them . . ."

Like Abbie Brooks, however, Eliza was certain that "God has never forsaken us in our hour of trial." And, with all her vituperation, she nonetheless believed that the Creator had not "permitted a murmuring thought to arise in my soul." But the "hard life" she had "to struggle with since last January has worn down my frame so greatly that I have suddenly become an old woman in appearance, and feel as if I can never rally again into health and strength."

There were no redeeming virtues or anything approximating such leaven in the character of the Yankees. And as for their relationship to the blacks, they "have completely turned the weak heads of the Negroes, and made them insolent beyond endurance.

"But the respectable class of free Negroes and mulattoes despises the Yankees and their doings as much as the white citizens do . . .

"Even now, my dear sister, we are often in want of necessaries of life, and sometimes I see my poor children cast down, even to tears, because they have expended their last cent for bread and it is not enough for their hungry little ones."

In Eatonton, Georgia, Joel Chandler Harris, who as a boy had watched Sherman's multitudes swarm past his home, tended to second Eliza as well as Dr. Claiborne, of Petersburg, as he tried to adjust to this abruptly altered society. While finding it almost "impossible to describe the condition of the people," he held that "there was no civil law in operation and the military government that had been established was not far-reaching enough to restrain violence of any sort.

"The Negroes had been set free, and were supported by means of a 'freedmen's bureau.' They were free, and yet they wanted some practical evidence of it. To obtain this, they left the plantations on which they had been born, and went tramping about the country in the most restless and uneasy manner.

"A great many of them believed that freedom meant idleness, such as they had seen white folks indulge in . . .

"The leading men of the State were all disfranchised,—deprived of the privilege of voting, a privilege that was freely conferred on the Negroes.

A newspaper editor in Macon was imprisoned, and his paper suppressed for declaring, in regard to taking the amnesty oath, that he had to 'fortify himself for the occasion with a good deal of Dutch courage.' "

The wife of Robert Toombs was ordered by the Freedmen's Bureau to vacate her home "with only two weeks' provisions." This was, of course, before she joined her husband in Paris. The youthful future author added that it was a day of the "carpetbagger and the scalawag—the camp followers of the Northern Army who wanted money and office; and the native-born Southerner who wanted office and money . . . There is no doubt that the indignities heaped on the people led to acts of retaliation that nothing else could excuse; but they were driven to desperation. It seemed . . . that their liberties had been entirely withdrawn."

The effect of these many pressures "was to keep the blacks in a constant state of turmoil. They were too uneasy to settle down to work, and too suspicious to enter into contracts with the whites; so they went wandering about the State from town to town and from county to county, committing all sorts of crimes. As the civil system had been entirely overthrown by the military, there was neither law nor order . . ."

The North, as some quipped, was indeed dragging "the South kicking and screaming into the nineteenth century." Even the convention called in Raleigh to abolish slavery in North Carolina, which it did unanimously on October 8, was accorded much statewide indignation. Andrew Johnson had "compelled" such an action, wrote John W. Moore, a local historian, adding passionately: "This body was the supreme humiliation of our entire history. It was the unwilling penance of a broken and ruined people. It met to do the bidding of haughty and merciless foemen. It but registered the President's decrees.

"North Carolina had been in a state as of primeval chaos . . . The condition of the South was still one of indescribable misery."

If not entirely chaotic, North Carolina had many wounds to lick, much to rebuild and replenish. Correspondents from the North continued to attest to these realities in a defeated land.

Moving through the state by train (infrequently), on horseback, and afoot, a reporter from the New York *Tribune* signing himself E. S. wrote, upon leaving Raleigh: "A remarkable feature of our journey was the absence of travelers. Going out of town in the gray of morning, we met a few country people coming to market with diminutive loads of melons and early produce. Some drove a mule, others a horse or steer. Their vehicles are of the rudest kind, generally consisting of two wheels, a pair of hewn fells which also form the body of the cart, a few rough boards for the bottom, and perhaps two sides and a tail board hold the produce, the dried corn blades for the horse's fodder and the driver sitting on top.

"In some cases, nearly the whole family comes to town, walking behind their humble carriage and sometimes going barefoot."

Eight miles south of Raleigh he stopped for lunch—"or breakfast?"—at the farm of a Mrs. Whittaker. It was a slim meal since she had no coffee, or much of anything: "No meat in the house. The smokehouse had been stripped of bacon—the barn and crib of fodder and corn. The soldiers had left them nothing. She was 'right glad' the war was over and hoped never to hear of war again." She had lost one of her two sons.

All through their conversation "a coy damsel" listened through a partly opened door, and "dodged away" as the reporter walked near. E. S. thought this characteristic of young Southern women; "they always ran away like scared partridges upon our approach."

It was a new invasion from Yankeeland, so far as Southerners viewed the influx. There were travelers of every genre of endeavor, or lack of it, and physical description: teachers (mostly female), ministers (or so-called), pitchmen accenting the hawkers of fast medicinal cures, prospectors, carpetbaggers, correspondents, hustlers (male and female), and the merely curious. For young men who had no taste for fighting—and had avoided service through one ploy or another—this was a safe time to visit the battlefields.

All returned with their own stories, their impressions, convinced they had experienced quite an adventure.

Railroading remained an especial source of fascination, in great measure because of its manifest uncertainty. A writer for the New York *Herald* happened to think this autumn that "railroad transportation is rapidly becoming in the South what it used to be before the war."

But Richard Dennett, pushing along much the same route of the Virginia Central to Lynchburg, came to other conclusions. He made the trip with the knowledge that only a few days previously a train had gone off a trestle, killing two passengers and injuring almost everyone in the coaches. Worse, marauders had robbed them while they lay stunned. He described his trip: "Every hour or two the train is stopped; the passengers get out and drink water at the tank that is supplying the engine; Negroes beside the track are busy chopping the wood short for the furnace and throwing it on the tender; nobody seems to be in any hurry. When two screams from the whistle give the signal, we leisurely get aboard again.

"It was understood that passengers for Lynchburg were to change cars at the Junction, while the other train proceeded to Danville. At the depot, I could find no one to tell me when the train would leave, nor whether it would start from that station. The train itself, meantime, was nowhere to be seen, nor could I learn where it was to be found, 'till at last a man who had heard me several times making fruitless inquiries, told me it was 'up thar a short piece,' pointing to a curve in the railroad.

"Getting a Negro to carry my trunk, I walked along the track for a quarter of a mile 'till I came to an engine and three freight cars, into one of which I put my luggage. Some Negroes loading freight thought the train went to High Bridge and Far'ville.

"A white man whom I approached on the subject 'reckoned it did,' and went on chewing tobacco. A conductor I could not find, but finally a brakeman whom I asked, after carefully scrutinizing me as if to see if I might be trusted to keep a secret, told me that it didn't go to Lynchburg, but was the Lynchburg train."

Yet another traveler, reaching Richmond at 4:00 A.M., mused on "a peculiarity of southern railroads that they always either arrive, or start at four o'clock in the morning."

Other writers, pressing tediously through the South, professed to find reasons for the erstwhile Confederacy's want and privation. Sidney Andrews evoked harsh memories as he visited in late October the infamous stockade in Florence, South Carolina, about a hundred miles from either Wilmington, North Carolina, or Charleston, South Carolina.

"Florence," Andrews wrote, "is a name rather than a place; or, say, a point at which three railroads centre, rather than a town. There is a hotel, and a church, and a machine shop, and two so-called stores, and three barrooms, and twenty-five or thirty residences, and a great pine forest. There is a long, broad street, at one end of which is the hotel—a somewhat pretentious two-story wood building, with a wide and lofty piazza in front, and an ungainly tower in the centre. At the farthest end of the street are the stores and the machine shop. Midway are the apothecary's and the hospital, and a vacant law office. Back of the street, in the pines, are the dwellings which constitute the town."

Andrews found the stockade to be about a mile and a half northeast of the center of Florence, spread over some sixteen acres of swampy, "malarial" ground, the "breeding place of agues and fevers and typhoids and rheumatic complaints—the rank and pestiferous home of diseases and death . . . Everything remains as the Rebels left it . . . The walls of the stockade are sixteen feet high, built of unhewn logs some nine or ten inches in diameter, set deeply in the ground . . .

"Here is the city of the living dead."

Of an estimated 13,000 federal prisoners incarcerated here, about one third perished.

This was all history so far as General Grant was concerned. The Confederacy was crushed, wholly unable to bear arms again. The federal army, he informed the War Department on October 20, could be safely reduced to 80,000 from its wartime peak of more than one million men. At present, the Regular Army's strength was 210,000, though another 50,000 could be called back "in case of emergency." The mustering out had been conducted "so quietly" since April "that it was scarcely known save by the welcomes to their homes received by them."

The general added, "The apprehensions felt by some of disturbances and disorder at so vast a force being suddenly thrown upon the country to resume the occupations of civil life after having been so long absent from them, proved entirely unfounded." As to the South itself, there had been "no collision of any importance between the soldiers of the rebel army returned to their homes and our troops. Everywhere submission was perfect, and all that was asked by them was permission to resume the ordinary pursuits of civil life."

As a postscript, Grant recalled, "At the beginning of the war our small Regular Army was barely adequate to protect our overland routes, and our Indian frontier and garrison our seacoast works. At its close, we practically had no Indian frontier, as the mines of the Rocky Mountains had scattered settlements at numerous points along their slopes, and the force employed in protecting these settlements and the overland routes was double that of the whole Regular Army at the beginning of the war."

On October 27, Alexander H. Stephens arrived home in Crawfordsville, Georgia. From Liberty Hall he wrote in his diary, "Thanks be to the Giver of all good, the Father of all mercies, and the bestower of all blessings, I am once more at home! I am sitting in the same room and at the same table from which I arose to suffer arrest on the 11th of May."

Two weeks earlier, President Johnson had paroled although not, at the time, pardoned a descending echelon of the Confederacy's leaders. They included, in addition to Stephens, Postmaster Reagan, Secretary of the Interior Trenholm, and the Richmond jurist John A. Campbell, who, like Alexander Stephens, had been a lukewarm secessionist. Stephen Mallory, whom Stanton had found in August not sufficiently penitent, and Clement Clay were not yet forgiven.

Stephens parted company in New York with Reagan, "a clever, upright honest man" but one with "few opportunities for education or culture in his youth." Although Stephens called on many friends en route south, his long-sought visit was at the White House. The president granted him an hour and a half.

"I gave him my own views very fully and freely upon the subject of Negro suffrage," Stephens wrote. "I told him the adjustment of that question belonged exclusively to the States separately, but in my judgment the States ought not to exclude the blacks entirely from the polls. I outlined the plan of a classification I had thought of, but said I believed it too late now to consider such a change in our system. As things are, I thought the principle should be established of allowing the franchise to such members of the black race as could come up to some proper standard of mental and moral culture with the possession of a specified amount of property. Such an arrangement would be right . . . [and] my inference from the conversation was that his policy was to have the Negroes, as soon as possible, removed from the country as the Indians were."

The nation, reeling from the war like a man badly mauled by night prowlers, remained in a state of flux. Many, like Alexander Stephens, were beating homeward to the South after sojourns forced or voluntary in the North. But others saw opportunities outside of the stricken states of Dixie. They were packing for northerly climes. One was Charles Colcock Jones, Jr., thirty-four, a Savannah lawyer, whose wife, Eva, was ill in Augusta, not far from Crawfordsville.

"My darling wife," he commenced a hurried note, "this will be handed to you by Mr. Sconyers who leaves here in the morning with two wagons loaded with corn and groundnuts . . . I sent mother some potatoes and a sack of groundnuts. I wanted to have sent a pig, but the weather has changed so warm that I am afraid the sum of two days would affect it. You will find, darling, your dried peaches with the wagons. I send also for mother three baskets of eggs."

Then, on October 27, turning to the greater preoccupations on his mind, Charles wrote again to Eva, advising her that his friend Mr. Ward wanted him to accompany him to New York "to recommence the practice of law there." He continued: "What do *you*, my precious one, say to this? I feel that your wishes must first be consulted in the matter. So completely have we been broken up here—so impossible do I find it to procure a house, and so uncompromising does everything appear that I think it becomes us to pause and weigh well the present before any plans are formed for the future. It would appear that under Providence we are brought to a pause, almost I should say to a full stop."

Much weighed "very heavily" on Charles; Eva's health, the Georgia heat, poor professional opportunities in the South, the welfare of "our dear little daughter," and also reflections on their tenth wedding anniversary the next day. Noting that he was enclosing a photograph of his father, he paused as he realized that night was upon him: ". . . The twilight is fading away, and I write almost in the dark."

NOVEMBER

The Quick and the Dead

As the winds of November brought their chill presentiment of winter, the war's legacy of hate, vengeance, premature death, and even suicidal despair persisted.

On the tenth, in Washington, D.C., another man was penning a few words to his beloved: "My Dear Wife: this Bible I read to where you see the marks, where I left off reading . . . I must leave you without the means to live, to the miseries of a cold, cruel world. God bless you."

And a shorter note accompanying a copy of the New Testament "to my dearest child Cora." She was ten.

It was shortly before 6:00 A.M. on a bright, cloudless Friday. Captain Henry Wirz, C.S.A., from his cell in Old Capitol prison, had completed the terse messages in anticipation of morning orders already made known to him. He was to be hanged.

A military commission headed by Major General Lew Wallace, a member of the court that tried the conspirators, and prodded along by the same judge advocate, Joseph Holt, had been meeting since summer to try the former commandant of Andersonville Prison.

The charges of which the wizened, bearded forty-three-year-old native of Zurich had been found guilty were many and damning. He did "conspire" along with others of the Confederacy, including Jefferson Davis, "maliciously, traitorously and in violation of the rules of war to

153

impair and injure the health and to destroy the lives . . ." of some 13,000 federal prisoners.

"In furtherance of his evil design," he allegedly neglected proper lodging, food, and medical attention; nor did he provide sanitary conditions, according to the commission. The hapless Confederate officer was charged not only with torture—from fastening prisoners in stocks without water and pinioning them with balls and chains to unleashing vicious dogs to snarl and tear at them—but also with personally committing the murders of thirteen prisoners.

That Wirz was a physician as well as a banker by education made his alleged conduct all the more incomprehensible. He still suffered intense pain from a right arm mangled in the fighting at Seven Pines during the Peninsular campaign. Sometimes he carried it in a sling. Those few who had rallied to his defense claimed that the pain had affected his emotions and his reason. Still another factor and a contradiction could be raised by military men: where else was a lowly captain ever given command over tens of thousands?

Certainly Wirz's superior, Brigadier General John H. Winder, who rose from provost marshal of Richmond to head all Southern prisons east of the Mississippi, should have been in the dock beside the obscure, diminutive Swiss or even instead of him but for one notable circumstance. Winder had dropped dead of a fever before Appomattox. The stroke of fate had been frustrating to Edwin M. Stanton, who had long ago placed the Southern prison boss on his retribution list. Thus Wirz could be considered a stand-in for his deceased superior.

Andersonville became a symbol of bestial inhumanity when it was established late in the war, in 1864. It was stretched across the pine barrens of southwestern Georgia to relieve pressure on the Richmond prisons and others such as the Florence stockade. The citizens of the capital of the Confederacy had become resentful of the drains on their meager sustenance because of the thousands of Union captives in Libby, Belle Isle, and Castle Thunder.

Certainly the blockade was in great measure responsible for the cutting off of food supplies. Moreover, the South's entire transportation system, especially the railroads and canals, was breaking down—more from deterioration than enemy action, although Union cavalry had regularly disrupted Southern trackage.

The prisoners' rations were set, optimistically, by the Confederacy's quartermaster and commissary: "Beef, one pound, or bacon, one-third of a pound, corn meal, one and one-fourth pounds, with an occasional issue of rice, beans, molasses and vinegar," also salt. The unrealistic goal was never realized, not even as a month's rations. It quickly became apparent that the scrubby region would not supply sufficient or wholesome provisions, including corn or beans, to sustain Andersonville's more than 31,000 prisoners.

Just before Wirz's trial, Major General Wilson, who had organized the capture of Jefferson Davis, dispatched Captain James M. Moore, a quartermaster, to the vacant charnel house that was Andersonville. He reported that it was situated on the Southwestern Railroad, "60 miles from Macon, and but one house in the place except for those in the compound itself." He continued: "The country is covered mostly with pines and hemlocks, and the soil is sandy, sterile, and unfit for cultivation, and unlike the section of country a few miles north and south of the place where the soil is well adapted for agricultural purposes . . . It is said to be the most unhealthy part of Georgia . . . At midday, the thermometer in the shade reaches frequently 110 degrees; and in the sun the heat is unbearable.

"The inhabitants of this sparsely settled locality are, with few exceptions, of the most ignorant class, and from their haggard and sallow faces the effects of chills and fever are distinctly visible.

"The noted prison pen is 1,540 feet long and 750 feet wide, and contains 27 acres. The deadline is 17 feet from the stockade, and the sentry boxes are 30 yards apart. The inside stockade is 18 feet high, and the outer one 12 feet high, and the distance between the two is 120 feet . . . The ground is filled with the holes where they had burrowed in their efforts to shield themselves from the weather."

Moore found the trenches for the dead to be only two to three feet deep, and some even more shallow as the topsoil had washed away. Without coffins or, often, clothing, the corpses had been placed but twelve inches apart.

In the summer of 1864, rampaging units of Sherman's army further disrupted any semblance of the camp's organization and inspired the removal of healthy prisoners to Charleston. The Confederacy, ever shorter of food and, in fact, of supplies from shoes to soap, desired a complete exchange of all prisoners. But General Grant took a tough, unyielding stand.

"It is hard on our men held in southern prisons not to exchange them," he wrote, "but it is humanity to those left in the ranks to fight our battles. Every man we hold, when released on parole or otherwise, becomes an active soldier against us at once either directly or indirectly. If we commence a system of exchange which liberates all prisoners taken, we will have to fight on until the whole South is exterminated."

Nonetheless, without reciprocal guarantees, the South, desperate to be relieved of the burden of so many prisoners, in November 1864 sent some 13,000 sick and wounded to the ports of Charleston and Savannah, where federal transports waited. But only 3,000 soldiers in gray—or whatever clothing—were exchanged in return.

In April 1865, with the surrender of General Johnston's army, Andersonville was abandoned. There, Wirz, laboring under the illusion that he had been included in the parole provisions of that last, large Confederate army, was arrested.

The trial commenced on August 23, not in the penitentiary of so recent court-martial notoriety, but in the Court of Claims room in the west wing of the U.S. Capitol. Wirz arrived from his cell (number 9, on the third and top floor) in Old Capitol prison, just across the street. The defendant was dressed in a faded Confederate uniform from which all insignia had been removed and wore, before being seated, an "old-fashioned" silk hat.

If Captain Moore's sketches of Andersonville were grim, so was the entire trial. Its spectators included, nonetheless, well-perfumed women. They fanned themselves, often leaned forward to catch the full innuendo of an unpleasant recall, and rarely changed expressions. It was the French Revolution's Place de la Concorde all over again.

For the prosecution Judge Holt had appointed a special judge advocate: sad-faced, bearded Colonel Norton P. Chipman, himself a wounded veteran of the fighting before Fort Donelson. The colonel had marshalled a formidable battery of about 150 witnesses, contrasted with 32 for the defense. Chipman's case proved a monotone of repetition. One stark piece of testimony—or sworn deposition—was heaped atop another until horror itself became commonplace.

"I am sick," wrote Sergeant John L. Ransom, of the Ninth Michigan Cavalry, who somehow found paper and pencil to keep an Andersonville diary, "just able to drag around. My teeth are loose, mouth sore, with gums grown down in some places lower than the teeth; and bloody legs swollen with dropsy." His entry was dated June 15, 1864. He continued on the subject of "raiders," prisoners who preyed on the sick and feeble.

"Raiders now do just as they please, kill, plunder and steal in broad daylight, with no one to molest them. Have been trying to organize a police force, but cannot do it. Raiders are the stronger party. Ground covered with maggots. Lice by the 1400 thousand million infest Andersonville. A favorite game among the boys is to play at odd or even, by putting their hand inside some part of their clothing, pull out what they can conveniently get hold of and say, 'odd or even?' and then count up and see who beats . . . Some of the men claim to have pet lice which they have trained . . . am gradually growing worse . . ."

"I have seen men die suddenly there," recalled Samuel J. M. Andrews, of the Seventeenth Illinois Infantry. "I remember distinctly seeing two men fall over and die upon the spot, or rather fall over dead . . . I saw one patient in the hospital with ball and chain attached to his ankle; he was so weak that he was hardly able to walk."

John A. Cain, of the California Cavalry Battalion, San Franciso, told of coming to Andersonville with a group from Richmond. "It was raining very hard when we arrived there, about two o'clock in the morning. We were drawn up in line four deep, about 1,000 of us, and were marched through water about knee-deep; a great many of the men were very sick and feeble . . . Being very dry, I started to the swamp to get some water; in the dark I fell into a hole headlong."

The hospital, he testified, "was only a few boards thrown together very temporarily to shed the rain off those very sick lying in there." When a visitor entered the hospital, patients would plead to be brought water or to be assisted to the "sink" for a drink. The latter was a sort of cistern into which the camp's one inadequate creek flowed.

Cain described how the prisoners tried to make small fires, "which a hat would cover up," out of pitch pine roots for warmth and for cooking meals and occasional "very coarse beef" or "mule flesh," seasoned with the daily ration of "about a teaspoonful of salt." Often Cain ate his meal and meat raw, despairing of keeping the fire going against the often incessant rain.

Thomas N. Way, from an Ohio regiment, said he had been punished for fifteen minutes by being tied up by his thumbs. When he escaped and was recaptured he was confronted by Wirz, who said, "Well, you're back again. I'm going to take care of you this time. I'm going to put you in the stocks, you God-damned son-of-a-bitch!"

Another former prisoner testified that while Wirz was carrying a loaf of cornbread to reward an informant (concerning a planned tunnel) a soldier, sick with dysentery, struggled to his feet and pleaded for food. Wirz allegedly struck him over the head with a riding crop, knocking him down. Shortly, the man died.

William H. Jennings, a black man with a bad wound in his left thigh, treated improperly if at all, was sentenced to thirty lashes for not working, then taken off all rations, including water, for twenty-four hours. Jennings testified he saw another man in the stocks dying after bloodhounds had twice bitten him.

Albert Kelley, of the Fortieth Ohio, swore that men were being robbed of their blankets and canteens by sentries.

Alexander Kennell saw prisoners in balls and chains. One, also clamped into stocks, died from exposure in the cold pinewoods night. H. Pond, of the Second New York Artillery, claimed that Wirz snatched away a prisoner's photograph of his wife and two children, then trampled it in the mud.

Some of the most damning testimony came not from a former inmate but from a Confederate surgeon, Dr. Joseph Jones, of the Medical College of Georgia at Augusta. When he visited the camp in August—the month of the most deaths, nearly 3,000—he was wholly unprepared for "this gigantic mass of human misery." He went on to report filth almost indescribable: "The haggard, distressed countenance of these . . . complaining, dejected, living skeletons, crying for medical aid and food and cursing their Government for its refusal to exchange prisoners, and the ghastly corpses with their glazed eyeballs staring up into vacant space . . . amongst the sick and dying, formed a picture of helpless, hopeless misery, which it would be impossible to portray by words or by the brush . . ."

Dr. Jones asserted that he found "hygiene defective" in the extreme. "The attendants, who appeared in almost every instance to have been selected from the prisoners, seemed to have in many cases robbed the sick of their clothing, money and rations, and carried on a clandestine trade with the paroled prisoners and Confederate guards without the hospital enclosure, in the clothing, effects of the sick, dying and dead Federals.

"The supply of rags for dressing wounds was said to be very scant, and I saw the most filthy rags which had been applied several times, and imperfectly washed, used in dressing wounds . . . The manner of disposing of the dead was also calculated to depress the already desponding spirits of these men . . . When a patient dies he is simply laid in the narrow street in front of his tent [this was called Broadway by the more cynical] until he is removed by Federal Negroes, detailed to carry off the dead . . . In the dead house the corpses lie upon the bare ground."

To this testimony, Horatio B. Terrell, of the Seventy-second Infantry Regiment, added, "One man would go to the heels of a corpse and the other to the head, and they would swing him into the wagon. They would pile them in just like dead hogs from the slaughterhouses."

As to cooking, Dr. Jones maintained it was "of the most defective character." Five large iron pots like those used to boil sugarcane appeared to be the only utensils in a hospital counting never less than 2,000 patients. The surgeon found that the soaring mortality rate was caused not by climate but by diet, which produced "scurvy and its results and bowel infections." He listed gangrene (not surprisingly) and even heart attacks as other killers of the prisoners.

Dr. Jones was but one of the assorted visitors from the Confederacy to the prison. For example, Howell Cobb and other well-known Southern statesmen had been seen there. None had taken any steps to improve the deadly conditions.

In substantiation of the prosecution's charge of murder, William Willis Scott, of the Sixth West Virginia Cavalry, said that he was going for a bucket of water when "a sick man . . . sitting on the side of the bank" asked Captain Wirz if he could get out.

" 'Yes, God damn it, I will let you out,' " Wirz was said to have replied, "and with the revolver he struck the fellow over the head and shoulder several times." Although the prisoner was able to return to his tent, Scott found him dead three days later, "pretty badly bruised around the head and face."

James K. Davidson, of the Fourth Iowa Cavalry, asserted, "I have heard Captain Wirz say that he was killing more damned Yankees there than Lee was at Richmond . . . I have seen men who were starved to death, thousands of them . . . I saw the chain gang . . . I saw hounds . . . I saw one man who was bitten by the dogs . . . I saw two men shot there by the guards."

Ogden Scudder, the cousin of Willis Boughton (from Sheffield, Illinois), was taken prisoner while fighting in Sherman's Atlanta campaign. At Andersonville, he was treated "barbarously." There, "the boys [were] starving, sick and dying . . . Bodies of those who died were thrown in shallow trenches and covered over with a small amount of earth.

"We were herded together in a damp, almost boggy place and fed one pint of corn meal, ground cob and all, for each person, as a day's ration. We were allowed one stick of stovewood each for fire to cook our meals. By several throwing in together, we managed to make a bed of coals. Around the camp to mark its boundary a dead line was chalked. Any unfortunate who stepped over that line was mercilessly shot. Andersonville was an example of other camps to which we were transferred.

"We were starving and losing our strength. At night should I turn on my back, my chum had to turn me over before I could rise to my feet. The nights were cold, and we suffered in every way.

"In a few weeks, we were started on a weary march for Libby Prison. Weak and hungry, we even dared to leave the ranks to snatch dry bones from the sand by the wayside. With these we made soup. We were given resting spells, and more starving at the Florence prison camp and then at Charleston. Finally we reached Richmond and were confined in Castle Thunder, an old tobacco storehouse. The guards here were ordered to shoot any prisoner who dared to look out of a window."

After weeks of testimony, which at least one of the newspapers labeled "lurid," Wirz appeared visibly shaken. Much of the time he lay back on a sofa which had been brought into the room. This was partly because his arm hurt. He complained, too, that he had been accorded inadequate spiritual aid. As a consequence, Father Boyle, of nearby St. Peter's Church, was summoned to minister to him when needed.

In early October, Wirz commenced a fragmentary diary. Back from the chambers in the U.S. Capitol in late afternoon, he sat in the emptiness of his prison cell and scribbled his forlorn jottings: ". . . A beggar crippled, with my health and spirit broken, why o why should I desire to live?

"I owe it to myself, my family, my relatives, even the world at large to prove that there never existed a man so utterly devoid of all humanity, such a fiend incarnate as it has been attempted to prove me to be . . . I see very well that I am a doomed man.

"I am tired and worn out, whichever way I turn my eyes everything looks gloomy and dark." Then, in a rush of anger, he scrawled in heavy pencil, "What a mockery the trial is!"

Henry Wirz's court-appointed attorneys, Louis Schade and O. S. Baker, tried but did not achieve much more success in defending their client than had their predecessors in exonerating Mary Surratt and her codefendants.

Even the witnesses they summoned on his behalf tended to produce additional damaging testimony.

The Reverend Peter Whelan, for one, who was a prison chaplain, asserted that the defendant "was always calm and kind to me . . . I have seen him commit no violence . . . I have never heard of his killing a man, or striking a man with a pistol. Captain Wirz afforded me every facility to visit the prisoners and afford them any relief that was in my power."

Nevertheless, he recounted the hanging of six prisoners, condemned by the Confederates as well as by the captives for "raiding," plundering, and other violence. Wirz, after their "court martial," according to the Reverend Mr. Whelan, delivered the six under armed escort to their fellow prisoners, stating, in the manner of Pontius Pilate, "I now commit them to you. You can do with them as you see fit!"

The clergyman recounted that the six "begged" him to intercede, but he claimed to have been unable to help. Although one of the condemned broke away and scurried "into the swamp," he was caught and hanged along with the rest.

Other witnesses called by defense counsel, largely from Confederate quartermaster or medical ranks, were in agreement that the countryside was too infertile to supply adequate nourishment, that the rail connections were poor and in disrepair, and that rations were provided as they became available. But all, to the disappointment of the accused's lawyers, agreed that Wirz did little or nothing to ameliorate the prisoners' sorry state or even initiate a board of inquiry to improve living and eating conditions.

When one of the incarcerated, Robert Kellogg, was led to state that he had observed "no instances of personal cruelty committed by Wirz, as I understand it," he erased any benefits by blurting, "His character was cruel and brutal . . . We saw that we were badly treated and miserably provided for."

Defense counsel winced.

About the most positive testimony for the defense was that of Martin S. Harris, Fifth Regiment, New York Volunteer Artillery, who expressed the opinion that "General Winder was responsible" for the conditions and that the prisoners, because of their unruly conduct, only worsened matters.

Thus it turned out that the very candor of the defense witnesses served but to augment the prosecution's case. And so the terrible chronicle of a few cataclysmic months at Andersonville unfolded, day after day, week after week. Were it not for the mute presence of nearly 13,000 graves, the testimony would have sounded improbable, at least exaggerated. Through his counsel, Wirz stated, "I have never denied that the prisoners were mistreated, but it was not my fault."

He did deny any deliberate killings or the use of vicious dogs—he was merely a soldier obeying orders—and again and again he said that he had been paroled and was not subject to arrest. He said he was a "scapegoat" for the higher-ups.

The military court remained unimpressed.

Colonel Chipman, prodded by Judge Holt and encouraged by the previous record of General Wallace, was on the scent of blood. He sought to involve personages of the Confederacy with much more impressive pedigrees: Jefferson Davis, former secretary of war James A. Seddon, Alexander Stephens, and certainly Judah Benjamin and Breckinridge, except for the fact that the last two were on the other side of the Atlantic, beyond his grasp. Colonel Chipman, however, ended by snagging a very small fish, Robert Garlick Hill Kean.

Head of the Bureau of War in the War Department in Richmond, Kean had supervised several dozen young women clerks. They filed and copied reports. Neither he nor those who reported to him were concerned with policy decisions. A testy, die-hard secessionist, Kean in his diary blasted all members of the occupation forces, from generals to sentries, as "tyrants" or "satraps." Like Davis, he had been unable to make peace with the Union, but unlike Davis, he remained a free man.

In the absence of the defendant, Colonel Chipman questioned Kean and drew forth only denunciation of the Union and its policies. "The whole," he would later write, paraphrasing his criticism before the commission, "had no reference whatever to Wirz, but was obviously designed to inculpate Mr. Seddon [the first secretary of war] and Mr. Davis."

All in all, Kean was a most embarrassing witness. Chipman, after considering the possibility of indicting, dismissed him and sent him back to Richmond on the next train.

The newly released onetime vice president, Stephens, though not summoned, would be penning his own thoughts on prisons in general and Andersonville in particular. In Davis he had never noticed any "disposition to be vindictive towards prisoners of war," and he himself (Stephens) had urged the release of "all prisoners on parole of honour, whether the authorities at Washington exchanged or not." Conceding that although "great and unavoidable suffering" was "perhaps occasioned by subordinates," Stephens concluded that "war at best is a savage business; it never has been and never would, perhaps, be waged without atrocities on all sides."

At long last the trial was over. It had been too soon after the fact for proper judicial objectivity. Perspective was absent. Time had not yet leavened the passions of the great majority. It was strikingly obvious that if a thousand more witnesses were to be summoned, the same horror would unfold with only the names, the specifics, the nuances, and the inflections changed.

October had all but ended. Outside the Old Capitol the leaves fell, to make pretty patterns of red, yellow, and brown, contrasting with the drab brick of the ugly prison structure.

And at this time Wirz's wife, Elizabeth (Saville), paid him a visit. Some said she had been living in Georgia, others Kentucky, where Wirz had briefly practiced medicine before the war. He had wedded her eleven years before, his first marriage having ended soon in divorce. She too had been married earlier, with two children by her first husband. This had been a tragic year for the Wirzes. Two of their three daughters had died since early April.

Elizabeth came to her husband's cell twice. Present each time was Lafayette Baker, in recent days promoted by Stanton to the rank of brigadier general in spite of the fact that he was under indictment on charges of false arrest and selling pardons to Southerners. Detective Baker, undaunted, condemned Wirz as "a disciple of Nero," and made certain the couple's conceivably last reunions would not be private.

According to the War Department's mogul of detectives, the conversation between the two was matter of fact, to the extent even of their calling each other by last names. In any case, Baker did not measure it by the emotions that might have been expected. At this second and last meeting, the detective thought Elizabeth was passing something to him as they kissed.

Baker maintained in his report that he rushed over to Wirz, grabbed him by the neck, and forcibly removed a small waxed pill from his mouth. Upon examination, it was said the pill contained strychnine. Since Baker, however, had a firmly founded reputation for the dramatic as well as for fantasy, the whole incident may not have happened outside of his own imagination.

Although the commission had obviously judged Captain Wirz well before the trial began, the verdict and sentence were not made known to the accused until November 6, only four days before the date set for his execution, but four times the ephemeral interval accorded those convicted of conspiracy in July. There were no apparent provisions for appeal, review, or, needless to say, executive clemency.

But the little captain from Switzerland was not surprised. He was said first to have called to a prisoner in the adjoining cell identified only as General Briscoe: "General, I'm going to be hung!" Then, during the ensuing three days: "I'm damned if the Yankee Eagle has not turned into a damned turkey buzzard! . . . I do not fear death . . . I'll haunt my persecutors!"

When Father Boyle asked him Thursday evening to forgive the judges who had passed sentence, Wirz snapped that he could not forgive those who had "falsely sworn an innocent man's life away."

He ate a large supper of fried oysters and slept so soundly he had to be awakened at six o'clock the next morning. When warders brought him a black robe, with an attached hood, the captain quipped, "Soon I will have a white gown."

The Swiss consul general, John Hitz, called on Wirz at about this hour. The evening before, Hitz had written a long, flowery appeal to President Johnson, concluding, "For the credit of the two Republics who gave birth and fostered this errant child, Henry Wirz, if in your Excellency's judgment, tempered with the mercy of our Redeemer upon the cross, you can possibly spare this additional sacrifice of life, I beseech you to do so by commuting the sentence of Henry Wirz to solitary confinement for life."

In addition to the efforts of Louis Schade, the defense counsel, there was but one other recorded appeal for clemency: from a citizen simply identified as Estwick Evans.

Hitz was accorded a cool reception by Wirz, who pointed out that he had never renounced his Swiss citizenship. He wondered why "his country had not interceded on his behalf well before this 11th hour?"

As the consul walked out of the door, shaking his head, Major G. H. Russell, the provost of the District of Columbia, sent a deputy to request that Wirz sign a "register." He did not say if this was for routine prison records or to satisfy a morbid desire to augment an autograph collection. The former prison warden commented wryly, "This is the last signature I will ever write. Farewell CSA!"

He continued to wear what had been described at the trial as a "grim smile." Whether he did not understand, was indifferent, or was completely stoic none who had been with him during the past months could discern. But most conceded he was a brave man who appeared to know how to die.

Still carrying his shattered right arm in a sling, Wirz was led out into the November sunshine at about 10:15 A.M. The same kind of rowdy crowd that had witnessed the execution of Mary Surratt and the other three was today at the Old Capitol. They were not only thronging the wooden-fenced front yard surrounding the gallows but roosting high in the branches of trees and crowding the windows and rooftops of neighboring houses to glimpse a man's last gasps. Women were not in short supply.

The photographer Alexander Gardner was back, his paraphernalia set up and ready. George Alfred Townsend, of the New York *World,* was among the press contingent, most of them wearing top hats and morning coats, almost like the traditional executioners of Great Britain. They had all of them become experienced hands at these grisly rites. Others, charged with civilian or military crimes, had died this year on the same stark scaffold.

The lonely and friendless captain was allowed to sit on a wooden chair, about on a level with the noose, while Major Russell read the sentence and specifications. Wirz had to know them by heart. Impatiently, the "rabble," as Townsend would write, shouted, " 'Down with him! Let him drop!' " The high-pitched female cries, not unlike those of their forebears in Paris, were discernible in the chorus.

At 10:32 A.M. the rabble's lust was sated. At once, as Townsend wrote, "a regular Fourth of July cheer went up."

The next morning, his newspaper observed that there had thus been "another addition to Stanton's collection."

That same Saturday, November 11, in lower Manhattan, someone else who played a role, if conceivably negative, in Secretary Stanton's accumulation of victims remained deeply distressed. Preston King, as one writer would observe, "in mind, temperament, physical constitution and experience . . . was not well fitted for the vast, intricate and perplexing duties" of the office of collector of customs.

"Burdened with immense direct responsibilities, overborne by politicians and office seekers, straining every nerve to give to each relatively petty case the care and attention demanded by the greater . . . Mr. King was rapidly and fearfully exhausted."

This particular reporter, however, did not remember or perhaps was unaware of a Friday the past July when Annie Surratt cried and screamed on the White House stairs, and Preston King would not allow her to pass up to President Johnson's suite. But King could not forget.

His friends urged him to get away, take a rest, forget his troubles, if he could. With this suggestion he complied in part, spending some days at his home in Ogdensburg, New York. In fact, he had been there most of the past week. But his family remained worried, so much so that they encouraged a relative by marriage, a Mr. Bridges, to rent a room in the Astor House, at Broadway and Vesey Street. There King resided, in a suite supposedly once occupied by Daniel Webster.

But the 275-pound former legislator appeared to worsen. Casually, he observed to Bridges Friday evening that he would like to go up to the hotel roof and "fly away." In the same breath he had to admit he probably would not "fly very far."

His old associates, including Navy Secretary Gideon Welles, were aware of his past mental aberrations and of the fact that he had been admitted to the celebrated Hartford Retreat asylum some twenty-five years ago. It was now suggested that he consult with the well-known Dr. Brown, of the New York Insane Asylum.

King seemed to agree with this counsel. He made an appointment for Monday morning, the thirteenth.

Saturday evening, about eight o'clock, the collector of customs entered a general store at West and Barclay streets. He wanted twenty-five pounds of shot for "waterfowl shooting." With that impressive quantity, he would have been able to bag or at least shoot at a remarkable number of ducks, geese, or other game birds.

Although this fact did not appear to surprise the clerk, the customer's method of transporting the purchase did. He tried to stuff the lead pellets, divided between two bags, into the pockets of his capacious overcoat.

They didn't fit. Finally the clerk connected the two parcels by a rope so that King could balance them over his shoulder. He walked off into the night with his curious burden.

Sunday passed.

Early Monday morning, November 13, King arose before dawn, dressed, and left the Astor House via the ladies entrance, on Vesey Street.

Then he made his way down to the Hudson ferry terminal at Christopher Street. The first boat for Hoboken left at 7:30 A.M. Patiently, Preston King waited, holding two heavy bags on his lap.

On time, the ferryboat *Paterson,* with a customary toot, was off across the river. Barely clear of the slip, it paused to allow a Europe-bound liner to thump past. When the ferry was about two hundred yards from the docks, a young man and two children in the stern noticed "a very heavy man" tie two bundles around his waist and take off his hat. The breeze from the ferry's headway picked it up and blew it along the deck. The young man retrieved the hat and started for its obvious owner. ". . . your hat, mister!"

The obese passenger for Hoboken then did a shocking thing. He stepped onto the railing, hauling himself up with obvious effort, and was gone.

In disbelief, the man and the two children ran to the side to see two legs protruding above the churning waters. Then they vanished under the dirty flotsam of the Hudson.

If violent death in the wake of a war that had claimed in excess of 600,000 lives had become commonplace, natural death had itself to be accepted as a corollary of life. In an era when forty years was the average life span of a man or woman, child mortality—as high as two hundred deaths per thousand—could be rationalized only as the will of God. But this was scant solace. Death always lurked, just beyond the windowsills.

Private soldier and ranking officer alike awaited with apprehension that letter from home. Sooner or later it was apt to bear word of the loss of a son, a daughter, a newborn. Sometimes there had been epidemics, including typhoid, scarlet fever, bilious fever, measles, and pneumonia. There were mysterious ailments such as infant cholera and the croup. Often the children simply expired, and the doctors, if any were in attendance, had no idea of the cause.

General Sherman lost two sons, his beloved Willie just before the Atlanta campaign and the other, an infant whom he had never seen, immediately after. Abraham Lincoln and Jefferson Davis both buried sons while in their executive mansions. It was about all the two presidents had in common.

These passings rarely were chronicled in the local papers, other than through paid notices. But to those who cared, it was darkness suddenly falling, a void that would persist. Little more than a week after Preston King had disappeared beneath the Hudson, a citizen of Atlanta, John C. Whitner, was advising a relative, Professor William Rutherford, in Athens: "I have but a few moments . . . and write with a heavy, aching heart . . . I have sad, sad news to communicate and wish you or sister Mary Ann or some of the family to break it to our Mother. Our darling little niece Mary Willis Erwin is no more. She died today about 1 o'clock and, as I trust, now reposes in the bosom of our Savior God. Her sickness was very short and her disease throughout very much resembled her father's." The father was thought to have had apoplexy.

"She was well Friday evening. About dusk she and Eliza were at my store. That night she had a chill, was quite sick yesterday, but no one dreamed her end was so nigh—not even half an hour before her spirit took its departure. We all are crushed to the ground . . . a sweet flower is thus rudely nipped by the frost of death."

This November a number of persons in particular had reason to consider themselves lucky to be alive. Among them were Dr. Mudd, Captain Waddell, and twenty-two men and women brought together quite by chance. The twenty-two happened to be in or near the Hotel Wyoming, on Greenwich Street, in New York City, on Sunday, a week before Preston King's fatal decision.

At 11:00 A.M. the stillness had been shattered and church bells damped by an explosion heard even across the river in Jersey City and Hoboken. Windows in an entire block were fragmented as the glass showered onto the street in tinkling discord. Curb stones were cracked and thrown around like shrapnel. A barber's pole was split in several pieces as if it had been struck by lightning. Horses bolted, hauling their wagons along with them.

As the twenty-two who either were passing by or were seated in the lobby of the Wyoming struggled to their feet or felt themselves apprehensively for cuts and bruises, William Stoddard, the proprietor of the dingy, second-rate hostelry, began to reconstruct the chain of events that had preceded the stupendous blast.

During the final days of August, a youthful German, Theodore Leers, arriving from Hamburg on the steamer *Donau,* had checked into the Wyoming. (He was one of the more than 248,000 immigrants coming to the United States this year; this was nearly half the number of servicemen who had perished in the four years of the Civil War.)

Among the voyager's several pieces of luggage was a heavy, medium-sized square box. He had moved out the last of October, leaving that strange package behind. Stoddard, for no special reason, had brought it into the office, where it was used variously as a stool or a footrest for polishing boots.

Then, this Sunday morning, the box suddenly began to smoke. The bartender and another man trundled it into the street, where it detonated just as the two were walking back inside. Not until the next day, when Theodore Leers had been located, was the mystery unraveled. The box, which Leers readily admitted he had forgotten, contained "chemical oils." It had been given to the immigrant in Hamburg by a representative of the Swedish engineer Alfred Nobel, with the suggestion that he might become an agent in America for the oily substance.

The young German, however, took a casual view of his parcel. With a blanket on top, it made a nice headrest when he was asleep in steerage. And, as the hotel clerks had found, it was the right shape to sit on. Leers surely did not know that he was introducing nitroglycerin to the United States, nor would he have understood the substance's significance. The inventor Nobel would shortly patent nitroglycerin as dynamite. Nobel, who was refining and perfecting what a French scientist had discovered fifteen years earlier, had obtained his first explosion in 1862. Two years later, Nobel's small plant outside of Stockholm blew sky high, taking his youngest brother, Emil, with it. Nonetheless, by the spring of 1865 Nobel's Hamburg factory was in full swing, with the output increasing.

Thus, several months too late to conceivably alter the outcome of the Civil War, an explosive at least fifteen times the strength of gunpowder had crossed the Atlantic Ocean.

On November 5, James Waddell navigated a salt-encrusted C.S.S. *Shenandoah* into the Mersey River, hauled down the Confederate flag, and surrendered his command to the Royal Navy. He went ashore at Liverpool, a free man, having eluded U.S. Navy patrols throughout a remarkable 23,000-mile, four-month cruise. Still afraid that he would be hanged as a pirate if he returned home, the tough sea dog would spend a decade in England while joint U.S.-British claims commissions struggled to place a monetary value on the depradations caused by the *Shenandoah, Alabama,* and other British-built raiders.

And in Maryland Jere Dyer, the brother-in-law of Dr. Mudd, received unhappy news: the convicted surgeon had attempted to escape aboard one of the steamers that ran infrequently from Fort Jefferson to the mainland. "I was put in the guardhouse with chains on hands and feet and closely confined for two days," Dr. Mudd wrote. "An order then came from the major for me to be put to hard labor, wheeling sand . . . I am now thrown out of my former position, chief of dispensary, and not likely to be reinstated. I know not what degree of degradation they may have in store for me . . .

"Four prisoners have died during the short time I have been here; the last one died the morning I made my attempt to escape . . . We have a disease here which is termed bone fever, or mild yellow fever, which has attacked at least three-fourths of the inmates of the Fort. It lasts generally but two or three days; during the time, the patient imagines every bone will break from the enormous pain he suffers in his limbs . . ."

November was ending. The trees around the White House were bare. The leaves lay dead and brown on the ground. Little of a historic year remained except ghosts and memories, few of them pleasant. There was not only Dr. Mudd but also Mary Surratt, Henry Wirz, and all of the political prisoners Lafayette Baker had clapped into the infested fastness of Old Capitol.

There was much to haunt Andrew Johnson and others of his administration, including Edwin Stanton, Attorney General Speed, and Judge Advocate Holt. The president, perhaps because his health and his presentiments still plagued him, decided it was time to redress some wrongs, if belatedly. First, citing the fact that *habeas corpus* had been suspended almost two years ago (actually throughout most of the war), he wrote: "I Andrew Johnson, President of the United States, do hereby proclaim and declare that the suspension aforesaid and all other proclamations and orders suspending the privilege of the writ of *habeas corpus* are revoked and annulled."

It would take effect in two days, Friday, December 1. All eleven seceding states, however, would be excepted, along with the District of Columbia and the territories of New Mexico and Arizona. But since the nation's capital was excluded, the restoration of this all-important legal right would not have benefited Mary Surratt even had it been effected in the late spring.

A concerned Johnson did not stop there. He ordered the Old Capitol emptied and turned over to the quartermaster for more mundane use, for example, warehousing such military necessities as clothing, tools, tents, and oats for horses.

At the same time, the chief executive instructed Secretary Stanton to disband Lafayette Baker's overzealous detective corps. Baker was falling from favor anyway. Not only had he been indicted, but a report by a subcommittee of the House of Representatives would comment on Baker's recent testimony, "It is doubtful whether he has in any one thing told the truth, even by accident."

Furthermore, Johnson directed that there must be no more censorship of the telegraph, which was also under the snooping scrutiny of the War Department. This was a violation of privacy of which very few citizens had been aware even during the war.

With a few strokes of his pen, President Johnson had accomplished much. But the excesses had persisted, and they overwhelmed the president's remedies, to the mounting horror of the Supreme Court. Arbitrary arrests, executions decreed by military commissions or courts-martial (mostly unpublicized), and lives blighted by suspicion and hearsay if not perjured testimony—all this would remain a blot, and the issue of more than 13,000 political arrests would not go away.

DECEMBER

A New City Is Springing Up

On Tuesday, December 5, Andrew Johnson addressed Congress—the convening of the thirty-ninth—for the first time. He thanked the Almighty for the return of peace and looked forward to responsible state government again, with all its prerogatives. Slavery, "the element which has so long perplexed and divided the country," must be abolished by amending the Constitution. The freedmen should be enfranchised, but it would be an unconstitutional "assumption of power" for the president to attempt to do so.

It was a literary, balanced, and philosophical message that met with instant acclaim from all save the radicals. Johnson, who had been exposed to no formal education, had not written a word, nor would he likely have been capable of so doing. George Bancroft, the eminent historian, had composed the document with moderate consultation from the chief executive.

He did not touch on the industrial or technological miracles that the Union performed during the war years, leaving this, perhaps, for his generals, admirals, and cabinet officers to describe in their separate reports to the new Congress. Johnson alluded briefly, however, to the desirability of the "free circulation of men and merchandise . . . Commerce should be free and unobstructed." This he saw as a way of linking the states more closely.

Bancroft, the literary graybeard, might have served up figures for the

173

president to describe the nation's economic growth in the short violent years since 1860. The three quarters of a million sewing machines (representing the output of seventy-four factories) had tailored their own industrial revolution. Some said as many as a thousand new machines, selling for an average of $60 apiece, were being produced every day.

In addition to 500,000 pairs of shoes for the Union army, these wondrous creations clicked out millions of uniforms and components of clothing, hats, gloves, underwear, suspenders, horse blankets, and on and on. The ability to produce such items speedily helped to triple the North's consumption of wool over the years from 1860 to 1865, to 200 million pounds.

Agriculture, stimulated by mechanical advances, flourished proportionately. Since thousands of field hands were away in the army and horses had galloped off to war or were victims of disease (veterinarians being scarce), machines had become a necessity. These included steam-propelled harvesters, rotary plows, threshers, binders, and lesser but greatly improved implements such as the "self rake." With reference to the latter, the enthusiastic comments received by the McCormick Company from a farmer named George Sherrill were typical: "[I] tell you what we done with the machine. In the first place we cut our grass which worked beautiful and then we cut our oats with the self rakes which worked as perfect as anything ever had of the kind. Now sir, in my estimation there can be no machine to work more beautiful in grain and grass. It is good enough for me."

Each of the estimated 250,000 reaping machines in use was capable of cutting ten acres of grain a day. Such mechanization enabled wheat production alone in the Northern states to surge from some 145 million bushels in 1860 to about 200 million a year by war's end. Agriculture was materially boosted by the establishment of the Department of Agriculture in 1862 and the passage of the first Morrill Act, endowing primarily agricultural, or land-grant, colleges in the states. In no way had the Confederacy been able to compete with this.

A process for condensing milk had been invented and put into production four years before the war by Gail Borden. But it was consumed only in small quantities by Union soldiers, who preferred fresh milk, and that usually from cows confiscated from Confederate owners. For the most part Billy Yank drank rivers of coffee. Some troopers claimed they could gulp down one or two quarts at a sitting. Canned food, mostly vegetables, was in existence but it did not reach army commissaries, which continued to buy dried and salted edibles, from pork and beef to codfish.

There were 200,000 manufacturing plants in the North by 1865. They ranged all the way from one- or two-man basement shops to the thirty-eight large arms plants, led by the huge Springfield (Massachusetts) Armory, which were producing about a million rifles, muskets, carbines, and revolvers annually by 1865. As impressive as the production was the fact that most of the weapons had interchangeable parts. The uniformity system, as it was originally called, had been appreciated in both Europe and the United States for at least half a century. Hitherto, no one had applied it on a large scale, not even for the simplest of products.

Buttressed as it was with English imports, the South nonetheless could not hope to match the volume of ordnance gushing out of the North.

The restless, inventive minds of Americans were responsible for 6,000 patents in 1865. Curiosity in general, however, was not confined to the western shores of the Atlantic. Sir Morton Peto, a member of Parliament, had just returned to Great Britain from a year's study of business in the United States. He had a book-length report to write, and he was proud that it "bristles with figures." Among them: "The value of the agricultural implements and machinery in use on farms . . . amounted in 1860 to $246,118,141 . . . an increase of more than 63 per cent over the estimate for 1850 . . . [and] it is a curious fact, that with all their labor-saving implements, many of which have never found their way into use on this side of the Atlantic, the Americans are continually calling for improved innovations . . . 'The farmer must be relieved from the drudgery of hard and continuous muscular exertion, such as mowing by hand and cutting the grain with the sickle.'

"The plough which at the present time excites most attention in America is an implement called the 'rotary spader' . . . With four horses [it] spades the earth 8 inches deep and 3 feet wide, at the rate of five or six acres a day. It is thus a very labour-saving machine, but its heavy cost ($200) is against it."

Relatively smug about the superiority of the British textile industry, Peto sniffed, "The greatest number of hands claimed to be employed in the cotton factories (of whatsoever description) in America in 1860 was 122,028; in England our operatives in cotton factories numbered in the same year . . . 405,256."

Somewhere along the way during his voracious probing, Peto came up with the general figure of $2 billion as the "value of the products of manufacturing industry in America," at least in 1860, and tried to define the term and the scope alike of "manufacture." He wrote as well, of "all the corn that is ground at the mill, all the trees that are sawn and planed, all the fish that are caught out of the seas and rivers, all the boots and shoes that are made out of leather . . ." even about pianos, dresses, liquor, soap, and coal. Sir Morton was impressed with printing and the number of newspapers in America, 400 daily "and no less than 3,266 daily, weekly, biweekly and monthly. Nearly 10 million copies of these papers are in circulation: or one daily and weekly paper to every third person in the whole population. The number appears prodigious."

He also found that the more than 153 million pounds of printing and stationery paper in the United States was within about 34 million of Great Britain's considerable output: "pamphlets, duodecimos, quarto volumes, publications of Congress, books got up at cheap rates, and volumes on the production of which no labour, trouble, care or cost whatever has been spared." Peto was especially impressed with a "Tribute Book," honoring the "self-sacrifice and patriotism" of those who fought to preserve the Union. "I do not think I have ever seen a book superior to this as regards paper, letterpress and binding."

He was wide-eyed over the East Coast's "infinite variety of bays, harbors and rivers, some of which could accommodate even the *Great Eastern*." He credited the canals with carrying about one third of the approximately "9 million tons of produce annually conveyed from west to east." The large canals of the United States, however, unlike the lacy network in England, froze in the winter, and the railroads were inadequate to compensate for the loss of haulage. He listed the principal eastern railroads as the New York Central, the Erie, the Atlantic and Great Western, the Pennsylvania Central, and the Baltimore and Ohio.

It appeared to Peto that "a vast mass of produce is yearly destroyed" because of inadequate transportation. Corn, cattle, petroleum, and "the traffic of the wonderful coalfields" was not being moved properly because of the lack of trackage; "the existing railroad requirements of the West are, in fact, insufficient."

As for the South, now "disburdened . . . of an incubus" with the end of slavery, he saw bright prospects, including the likely doubling of cotton production within five years. ". . . All that is wanted is capital and enterprise. Those States have at command all the resources that soil and climate can afford . . ."

But Carl Schurz, reporting to President Johnson this December after his Southern tour, did not find the word "disburdened" quite so applicable. He thought the "whole agricultural labor system" had been "turned upside down." Though the slaves "had heard of Mas'r Lincoln's Emancipation Proclamation in a more or less vague way," they and their masters did not face the complexities of freedom until the war's end and "to most of the southern whites this problem was utterly bewildering. Many of them, honest and well-meaning people, admitted to me with a sort of helpless stupefaction that their imagination was wholly incapable of grasping the fact that their former slaves were now free."

The conclusions of other observers would fall somewhere between Schurz's pessimism and Peto's optimism. There were positive signs along with the negative. For example, Union soldiers on garrison duty were aware of new stirrings in the South. For one, Captain Peter Eltinge, of the 156th New York Volunteers, with the provost marshal's office in Lexington, Georgia, near Athens, found that business already was "brightening up" in Atlanta.

He thought it might be a good place for himself and his brother George, also on duty, to set up business, since "several persons from Lexington have gone to Atlanta and they all report a healthy condition of affairs there." On other scores, he wrote variously to his father and sister Kate: "The people seem to take very little interest in public affairs. For the past month there has been a great religious excitement here. Protracted meetings have been held all over the country and many have been converted. This excitement is now about over and I think the people will pay more attention to Political affairs.

"It is very important that every good and honest man in the South should put his shoulder to the wheel now and do all in his power to bring the States back into the Union. Most of the Southerns accept the issues of the war and especially in regard to Slavery. They consider that institution gone beyond a doubt and never expect to see it reestablished in this Country. Some of the people feel very sore yet over the loss of their Slave property. It was a bitter pill for many of them."

He had been to barbecues and to dances, and "the people all treated me very kindly notwithstanding I am a Yankee . . . The people of the South you know have always been noted for their hospitality and I don't think they have lost it." He admitted regretting he had sent his father a check for $150 and hoped the latter would "send me $50 as soon as possible . . . Please send about $10 in every letter you write as I shall need it."

Two correspondents arriving in Georgia at the same time agreed with Peter Eltinge's optimism. Sidney Andrews, observing that Georgia was "the richest and most enlightened of the Gulf States," continued: "From all this ruin and devastation, a new city is springing up with marvellous rapidity. The narrow and irregular and numerous streets [of Atlanta] are alive from morning till night with drays and carts and hand-barrows and wagons, with hauling teams and shouting men, with loads of lumber and loads of brick and loads of sand, with piles of furniture and hundreds of packed boxes, with mortar-makers and hod-carriers, with carpenters and masons, with rubbish removers and house builders, with a never-ending throng of pushing and crowding and scrambling and eager and excited and enterprising men, all bent on building and trading and swift fortune-making."

Observing that Chicago "in her busiest days" could scarcely show such activity, Andrews marveled that every horse and mule available had been put to use to haul wagons through the rutted streets. The four railroads which served Atlanta and constituted a prime reason for the city's military value during the war were said to "groan" with traffic, and, although partially rebuilt, they could not keep up with the demands of the "nervous and palpitating city."

He continued: "Men rush about the streets with little regard for comfort or pleasure, and yet find the days all too short and too few for the work in hand. The sound of the saw and plane and hammer rings out from daylight till dark, and yet master-builders are worried with offered contracts which they cannot take.

"Rents are so high that they would seem fabulous on Lake Street [in Chicago], and yet there is the most urgent cry for store room and office room. Four thousand mechanics are at work, and yet five thousand more could get immediate employment if brick and lumber were to be had at any price. There are already over two hundred stores, so called, and yet every day brings some trader who is restless and fretful 'till he secures a place in which to display another stock of goods.

"Where all this eagerness and excitement will end no one seems to care to inquire. The one sole idea first in every man's mind is to make money.

"Meantime, Atlanta is doing more than Macon and Augusta combined.

The railroad from here to Chattanooga clears over one hundred thousand dollars per month, and could add fifty thousand more to that enormous sum if it had plenty of engines and rolling stock. The trade of the city is already thirty per cent greater than it was before the war, and it is limited only by the accommodations afforded, and has even now spread its wings far out on streets heretofore sacred to the privacy of home."

John Richard Dennett, the tireless writer for *The Nation,* journeyed to Atlanta at the same time. He arrived by the Georgia Railroad, which was now operating the entire 160-mile distance from Augusta. Impressed by the "comfortable and commodious" cars, he also marveled that the train rattled along at "more than fourteen miles an hour." Dennett saw "burned buildings . . . rails fantastically twisted and bent, and ruined locomotives . . . a most cheerless and mean-looking place."

He added: ". . . The mud was almost ankle-deep. It had rained for three weeks. People walked slowly, treading with careful steps in the foot-prints—slowly getting narrower in the soft mud—of those who had ventured before them. The middle of the city is a great open space of irregular shape, a wilderness of mud, with a confused jumble of railway sheds, and traversed by numberless rails, rusted and splashed, where strings of dirty cars are standing, and engines constantly puff and whistle. In one place I saw beside the track a heap of bones and skulls of animals, collected from battlefields and the line of march for some factory, mould-ering and blackening in the wet weather. Bricks and blocks of stone and other rubbish were everywhere.

"The gray coats are almost as numerous as the blue uniforms, often very dirty, of the white and Negro soldiers, some of whom are always on guard in the streets. White women are but seldom seen, perhaps because the sidewalks are nearly impassable; the men are obliged to wear the bottoms of their trowsers [sic] tucked in their boots. Negroes of all colors abound.

"But though Atlanta, in spite of its newness, has a cheap and squalid look, which is depressing, it evinces much energy and life."

Atlanta, "I tell you, will be the best place in the south for a carriage repository," John Bridges, working for a wholesale druggist on Alabama Street, wrote to a friend, E. W. Webster, in Plainville, Connecticut, who manufactured various vehicles. The city, Bridges averred, expressing the enthusiasm of many, "is being rapidly built up and will be much larger than ever before." Although worried about high freight rates, Bridges guessed that he could probably sell two or three wagons a week.

As a start, he suggested that Webster ship him three carriages without tops, three with, and two or three wagons. "There is nothing of the kind here, and I know of no one going in the business . . . All the business here is cash. Nobody talks of credit. Let me hear from you soon. If you do not accept my plan, I want to make it to others . . ."

Marietta, just northwest of Atlanta, had been damaged in the early days of Sherman's campaign when the Union general was repulsed by General Johnston at Kennesaw Mountain. Now Marietta too was rebuilding and the object of many seeking new areas of habitation. William Sydnor Thompson, formerly of the Stonewall Brigade, was studying law in Marietta and tutoring merely to pay his expenses since he had taught in Tennessee at the outbreak of war. Even now he was but twenty-two years old.

"This is the place to obtain success," he wrote his father, Warner, who lived in West Virginia and was in poor health. "Business working lawyers are needed. When [the] RRs are completed, which [work] is now in progress, there will be an interminable amount of business carried on here, and men of the right stamp will be needed. Looking twelve months ahead, I see the most brilliant prospects for enterprising and business men.

"Marietta had before the war a population of three or four thousand inhabitants. It has that no. now with one-half the town in ruins. Settlers from all parts of Ga., Tennessee and Kentucky are flocking in here, and they are of a class to benefit any community in which they may reside. At present no more money than is absolutely necessary is in circulation; but plans are being formed for building up the place, which cannot fail to put in circulation a large amount of capital. I consider it a lucky day when I determined to 'strike' for Georgia."

On prospects of agriculture, Thompson observed the soil, tending too much to sand and clay, "susceptible of improvement" but "well adapted" to crops such as sweet potatoes and melons. Markets were plentifully stocked with edibles largely from other areas. Beef at twelve cents a pound and butter at forty cents were typical of the price range. However, "the great drought that has prevailed here during the past six months has [created] or will create a great deal of suffering among the poorer classes." Thompson admitted that he was living "on the fat of the land." But he needed tobacco, since the local crop was "of an inferior quality," and hoped that his father or someone would express him ten plugs of "that thick" Virginia variety.

A traveler through Marietta who chose to remain anonymous paused to observe citizens with "a degree of destitution that would draw pity from a stone." Yet women came "from a distance of ten to fifteen miles afoot, leaving homes entirely destitute in order to get a few mouthfuls to save the lives of their helpless children."

Many former slaves, the observer noted, were loath to abandon their masters, fearing to starve otherwise. "They [the slaveholders] all told me that no man in the country had more than two bushels of corn left.

"There are 35,000 men, women and children in the counties of Georgia immediately surrounding Atlanta who are dependent upon the United States Government for support and preservation from death by hunger."

In other areas of Georgia, Alabama, Texas, and Arkansas the canvas this December was just as dark, gray at best. Callaway Campbell found living in Murray County, northwest Georgia, not measurably improved since war's end. To his young sisters, Mary and Nancy, in Petersburg, Virginia, Campbell wrote: "We have no mail here except along the line of the railroad . . . The towns are being built up again very rapidly. The negroes about here seem quite peaceable and quiet and hardly appear to know whether they are free or not, for when they flood into the towns they are frequently arrested and punished by the troops, sometimes they hire them out to the highest bidder or others they put to work on the streets . . . It is a great pity that the poor indolent creatures are not in Africa where the breadfruit grows almost without cultivation."

To his grandmother he would complain that "from having 12 head of horses and mules I was left without one, and 60 head of hogs reduced to six head . . . I have been trying to sell my land on the little Tennessee River . . . Money matters are very tight here."

In Gordon County, adjoining Murray to the south, Elisha Lowery, writing of the "scarcity of money" and the high price of corn, noted, "I believe that there is poor women and children here that will suffer if not starve to death for bread . . ." He added that "our country is full of Negroes going from house to house begging to get to work just for something to eat. The men that has no family can make out . . . but them with little children and women and children is going about starving and freezing." Like Callaway Campbell, Lowery complained of the "derangement of the mail," but presumed it was caused "by the washing away of the bridges."

In Alabama it was reported that "by far the greater suffering exists among the whites." Their plight was worsened by a summer drought which "nearly ruined" the corn crops and also hurt potatoes. In Texas, cotton grew luxuriantly only to drop out of the bolls and rot on the earth for want of hands to harvest it: "The planters made contracts with their former slaves to remain with them and save the crops, but they . . . deserted at the first opportunity." Thus cotton became a disaster this season in parts of Texas.

In the hills of the far South, especially in Georgia and Alabama, misery was intensified this Christmas season. An official of the Freedmen's Bureau noted especially "widows with large families of small children" without homes. He saw "about thirty persons for whom shelter must be provided or death will speedily follow their present exposure."

Governor Isaac Murphy, of Arkansas, spoke of "thousands suffering . . . for want of food and raiment and who unless speedily relieved will, in many instances, during the winter die from the effects of hunger and cold." He continued: "The desolations of war in our State are beyond description. Suffering and poverty are, perhaps, more general in this than other rebel States, from the fact that during the entire war an internal and bloody strife existed between the Union element and their rebel neighbors . . . Guerrilla bands and scouting parties have pillaged almost every neighborhood north of the Arkansas River, also in the country south of the river, lying near the Indian boundary. It would be safe to say that two-thirds of the counties in the State are in destitute circumstances, and many will suffer for food and clothing this winter and spring, unless relieved by the noble kindness of the people of the Northern States."

But in Tennessee, long under the sternly protective wing of the federal government, it was a different story. One resident, Abbie Brooks, of Edgefield, could continue to indulge in the luxury of day-to-day personal concerns, sad, wistful, or happy: "The poetry of my youth has all vanished. Moonlight and midnight are the same if I am well and there is no perceptible discord of the machinery of my employment.

"The golden sunset, the beautiful and rich coloring of the forests, the luxuriant landscapes and the murmuring waterfall all pass before me as matters of fact. Everybody seems the same way, the world has grown cold and heartless." Then, as December moved along, "I succeeded in borrowing a horse from Mrs. Granagan, and after school rode down to Mr. Adams. One of the Negroes dressed my large black chicken for market, and I took a foot mat made from corn husks. I prepared these things to buy the children some candy. I have promised them a treat in the form of a Christmas tree although it will be in advance of Christmas. I design it as a parting gift to them for the last day of school."

Then, she made another trip to nearby Nashville, after arising before daybreak. Accompanied by a friend, Johnny Adams, she wrote, "I wanted to see Mrs. McFerrin. We found them all well. The children came running to meet me as soon as they saw me. 'Miss Abby has come!' echoed over the place in all directions. They all seem to have a warm corner in their bosoms and a kind spot in their hearts for me. Mrs. Mc. invited me to come and spend several days with them, saying that I would be welcome."

Abbie Brooks returned to Edgefield on horseback, with Johnny Adams. Although she bared her other emotions, the schoolteacher did not divulge her relationship with the young man. Was he a casual friend or something much more intimate?

The next day, Sunday, while "the wind blows . . . like rain," out of habit she went to church, where the sermon "was not particularly interesting . . . The congregation was small as usual. There are but few in the neighborhood who seem to care whether they go to church or stay at home."

Before December reached its midpoint, she wrote, "I am so weary with teaching that I cannot bear to see the scholars come into school, although they seem very much attached to me . . ." And with this entry Abbie ceased her diary writing forever and faded into the limbo of unrecorded history.

In South Carolina there was growing confidence in spite of the pessimism Carl Schurz had voiced in his appraisal of the seceded states: "No part of the South I then visited had . . . suffered . . . as much . . . as South Carolina, looked upon by the Northern soldier as the principal instigator of the whole mischief and therefore deserving of special punishment."

From Charleston, Lewis M. Ayer, a former brigadier general, was writing to D. A. Jacques, a New Yorker who was preparing a guidebook for Northerners emigrating south. Without reservation, Ayer described the Barnwell district, in southwest South Carolina, as "a beautiful, undulating country, interspersed with oak and hickory . . . admirably watered by innumerable creeks and rivulets . . . the middle country of South Carolina, the healthiest portion of the whole world.

"Our facilities for getting our crops to market are very good indeed . . . Our wagon roads are very good all the year round." He added that additional transportation included the South Carolina Railroad, while the Port Royal Railroad was "in a fair way of being soon completed." Barge traffic could use the Savannah and Edisto rivers.

Ayer was not so sanguine about the freedmen, who "express a willingness to work . . . but they don't believe a word of it, and can only understand freedom as synonimous with idleness."

Writing to General Ayer, H. C. Smart, of Barkers Mills, South Carolina, noted that he was "anxious to purchase 8 or 10 mules or horses. I am prepared to make cash settlement. Was entirely stripped of horses, cows and money by the Federal Army. I have contracted for about 35 laborers for the next year and if I can get the mules and horses to work with I think there will be no time in making the money to pay for them by next August or September."

And Charleston merchants were advertising in several newspapers addressed to "the Merchants of the South," to "advise you of the fact that Charleston is again a market for the purchase of goods."

To the north, Richmond was showing new life, if not at the same lusty pace as Atlanta. "The burnt district," wrote Whitelaw Reid, "comprising nearly all the business portion of the city, south and east of the Capitol, was beginning to rise from its ruins. Between a fourth and a third of it would soon be better than before the conflagration, with which the Rebels signalized their abandonment of the city. But business was greatly overdone by Northern speculators who had rushed down with heavy supplies of goods immediately after the surrender. The first pressing necessities satisfied, the Virginians were too poor to trade largely."

Northern loans, some of which he thought were as high as a half million dollars, he believed responsible for getting the railroads operating again. The Virginia Central, for example, ran west to Staunton, with connections all the way to Chattanooga, Atlanta, and Mobile. The tracks to Wilmington, North Carolina, which carried so much food from the blockade runners to wartime Richmond, were repaired and again busy. The trains continued to Charleston, "a few gaps being filled by stage lines." And the James "swarmed" with rival steamers all plowing for Baltimore.

Nonetheless, Asbury Christian spoke for many Richmonders when he wrote, "The year 1865 was the darkest in all the annals of the city." There would be a "sigh of relief . . . when it had gone into the past."

Slavery, too, officially went into the past. On December 18, the Thirteenth Amendment, abolishing it, was ratified. The amendment had been approved by the legislatures of twenty-seven states, including all in the South except Mississippi. This in itself was interesting since none that had seceded had yet been readmitted to the Union.

But certainly not all went along with Washington's policy toward the conquered South. Robert Waring, editor of the Charlotte (North Carolina) *Times,* wrote a vitriolic editorial that was reminiscent of the wartime Southern press. He wrote of the "grinding despotism" imposed on the occupied states, the continuing "serfdom" of the people. Arrested and tried for sedition, Waring was fined but $300 by a military court and not imprisoned. It was not his first brush with the law. He had been jailed in New York in 1861 after raising his hat to a Confederate flag. Richmond papers had earlier experienced similar problems with the occupying forces.

Then there was the more serious case of Admiral Raphael Semmes, who had been anticipating a Christmas at home with his family in Mobile, where he was establishing a law practice. He was stunned when, on the fifteenth, a group of federal officers banged on his door. They bore an arrest warrant, signed by Secretary of the Navy Gideon Welles. The former commander of the C.S.S. *Alabama* had briefly led a small, ragtag group of soldiers and sailors at Danville, Virginia (Davis's last temporary capital), before being paroled with Johnston's army.

Washington still considered Semmes a pirate. President Johnson, the admiral wrote, had acted like "a traitor to his State" (Tennessee), a "charlatan" who "cowered in his struggle with Congress."

Taken to Washington, Semmes was confined first in the Navy Yard, next to the Marine Barracks, and finally in the Old Capitol. Once more it had been returned to its erstwhile role after being closed to prisoners for only three weeks.

Gideon Welles, whose spectrum of likes and dislikes contained only sharp blacks and whites, did not apologize for the seemingly illegal arrest, noting in his diary there remained "some nice points" to be decided. Welles was angered because Semmes, like so many other Confederate officers, had "deserted" the government "in disregard of his obligations and his oath." He had "made it his business to rob and destroy ships and property of his unarmed countrymen," and he had also continued the fight in Richmond "without ever being exchanged." Welles was expressing a familiar Northern pique because the admiral had made his way to sanctuary in England after the *Alabama* was sunk, in June 1864. Semmes remained in prison for several weeks before an irate General Grant, joined by equally incensed navy officers and members of Congress, demanded the release of an honorable warrior who had already been paroled and who had meticulously observed the rules of warfare.

In late December, the legislative branch belatedly remembered Jefferson Davis, that "ugly elephant on Johnson's hands," in the words of Horace Greeley. The Senate adopted a resolution asking the chief executive "upon what charges or for what reasons" the former leader of the Confederacy continued to be a captive and "why he has not been put upon his trial."

(The secessionist executive had just been visited in Fort Monroe by his pastor, the Reverend Mr. Minnigerode, of St. Paul's in Richmond, who prayed with him, read the scriptures, celebrated communion, and "gave him peace of mind," according to press reports.)

The upsurge of interest in Davis appeared to take by surprise not only the chief executive but also Stanton, Attorney General Speed, and Judge Advocate Holt. It was as though all four had momentarily forgotten the proud, austere man. Once roused, Johnson's secretary of war and his legal lieutenant responded with long memoranda and generally conflicting opinions.

Speed and Stanton, in agreement that Davis and some others, including Clay and Mallory, were guilty of high treason, nonetheless now concluded that "the civil courts have alone jurisdiction of that crime." They professed to some frustration that such legal bodies were not yet sitting in Virginia.

Holt, on the other hand, still felt compelled to defend his "military tribunals," which had effectively hastened Mary Surratt, Henry Wirz, and the three others to the gallows. In an indictment rambling to thousands of words and citing examples of perfidy in Roman history as well as the Napoleonic Wars, the judge advocate renewed earlier charges that Davis was surely involved in an attempt to "kidnap or kill" Lincoln, then hold him (as a cook!) in Libby Prison should he survive. Davis, Holt reiterated blandly, was at least privy to raids on New England and plots to burn New York City for which one Confederate officer had already been executed.

Without recommending in so many words that Davis be hanged, Holt concluded by urging that a "military court . . . such as tried and condemned his alleged confederates in guilt" should be summoned to try the erstwhile leader of the rebellion on charges of "violation of the laws and usages of war . . . his monstrous crimes against humanity."

Still confined in Fort Monroe along with Jefferson Davis, Clement Clay at last received a visitor, his wife. Virginia Clay had for months haunted Washington's officials, ranging in rank from Johnson and Stanton through a descending order of prestige to Attorney General Speed and assorted congressmen. Finally, she obtained the long-sought pass.

At the prison, however, Major General Nelson Miles, the commandant, at first refused to honor the pass. Keyed up as she was with anticipation, Virginia Clay threw herself at the general's feet. She screamed and clutched at his trousers.

It was too much for the white-haired prison surgeon, Dr. Henry Vogell. "Miles, for God's sakes, let the woman go to her husband!" he implored.

So the two were reunited.

December wore thin.

"Christmas has come and gone without disturbance of any kind," wrote forty-two-year-old Catherine Ann Devereux Edmondston, of Halifax County, in eastern North Carolina, on the Virginia border. Her family owned two handsome plantations, Looking Glass and Hascosea.

"We dined with father," she wrote, "and found that he was in the same unsettled condition as regards labour for the coming year as ourselves. Two of his people and one of ours have since Christmas signed a contract for '66, but all the rest exhibit the force of inertia in a most striking degree . . . They will do nothing but sleep and get wood for themselves, and even tho' living under his roof, eating his bread and burning his wood, with but two exceptions they refuse to do the daily necessary plantation labour. They admit they do not know what will become of them."

The only two freed slaves who escaped Catherine's censure were Owen and Dolly, who "turn with scorn and abhorrence from even the mention of wages . . . More faithful, cheerful, or affectionate ones it would be hard to find."

The last day of December Catherine recorded as "a miserable, unsettled, annoying day to us all, but especially to Mr. E. who has been busy with the Negroes—settling accounts, and discharging those he does not wish to keep. Amongst the number is Henry—poor fellow, made worthless by emancipation!"

Throughout the nation, the press took especial note of the passing of 1865. All editors agreed it had been a momentous year. The New York *Herald* devoted many columns to a month-by-month chronology, observing, "Was there ever such a speedy transition from war to peace, from hostility to submission?"

In its Sunday, December 31, edition, the New York *Times* editorialized: "Very hopefully the New Year dawns upon us. 1865 brought to us the priceless honors and blessings of Victory, Union, Peace and Freedom. Starting from this assured vantage-ground, the year 1866 cannot fail to add to the list, prosperity and progress . . . With the Union once more made perfect, with law triumphant and vindicated, with freedom assured, with health and peace reigning throughout our borders, what grand and happy record may we not hope for our country during the New Year?"

But in the South it was a time for soul-searching and sober reflection. "Both as individuals and as a people," wrote the Columbia (South Carolina) *Phoenix,* "we have been in the deep waters of affliction . . . the debris of our burnt city, the widespread desolation of our entire county and the graves of thousands of our noble dead all speak to us in strains of eloquence and in songs of sadness."

On New Year's Eve, in Warrenton, Virginia Mosby sat up all night with her sick daughter, Vic. She would write, "How many visions passed rapidly through my head, where we would all be this time next year, how many that are now full of joy and gayety will be numbered with the silent nations of the dead. Oh! that with the coming year we may be more thoughtful and determined to enter into it with determination to be more useful here . . . or for eternity."

1866

JANUARY

The Union Pacific

As blizzards howled over the plains of Nebraska Territory and icy rains drenched the earth, the most ambitious project since the ending of the war hammered westward: the Union Pacific. To meet it, unwinding eastward from the coast was the Central Pacific.

Thousands were involved in this peacetime counterpart of a military operation. Rail gangs proved to be a melting pot: both federal and Confederate veterans, blacks, Irish and German immigrants. They rested and brawled in "hells on wheels" or "tent towns," which sprang up like dragons' teeth about fourteen miles apart along the right-of-way, "sown amidst the plains and deserts and mountains."

Chinese coolies, ultimately about 11,000 of them, worked on the Central Pacific, signing up as they left the immigrant ships in California. The dangers they faced, especially in handling blasting powder (sodium nitrate or potassium nitrate, both highly unstable), inspired the maxim, "not a Chinaman's chance."

The coolies subsisted largely on tea, rice, dried oysters, abalone, and bamboo shoots. They were entirely satisfied with wages of one dollar a day and slept where they lay down.

In early January, the railroad was nearing Fremont, which was the first settlement of any note. It had arrowed more than forty miles west from Omaha since July, when the first spike was driven into the sun-baked prairie clay. But nothing had rolled smoothly.

Land was cheap, and federal charters and subsidy loans were encouraged. But money, since the financial panic of 1857, was scarce. Joint financing from many investors and companies, mostly in the East, had been a prerequisite to the building of the railroad. Those who risked their capital ranged from bankers to a Massachusetts manufacturer of shovels. Even though Abraham Lincoln provided all the support possible at a time when salvaging the Union was the first priority, speculators were skeptical.

There had been several false starts. One such was a route due west out of Omaha which had to be abandoned because of the hills and grades. And Omaha itself was not the most desirable point of origin. Established but a decade before, in 1855, it had seen its first white settlers only ten years before that. This was during the Mormons' trek to Utah Territory. Since no railroad served this ugly, dirty frontier town of some 1,800, supplies had to be trundled by wagon from Des Moines, 133 miles overland, or shipped via the Missouri River from Kansas City—itself no vineyard—more than 170 miles to the south. Both Kansas City and Omaha were hot in the summer, bitter in the winter.

At Kansas City, there was a rail connection with the East by way of the Hannibal and St. Joseph Railroad and the Missouri Pacific Railroad. The Union Pacific builders rather favored the waterway, operating six large steamboats of their own to carry all manner of supplies, from rails and ties to salt pork and shoes.

Everything had to be hauled in. The country was virtually barren, even of stone and lumber. Local cottonwood, as one example, could not be treated so that it would make sturdy ties with a reasonable span of usefulness. Hardwood from Michigan, Indiana, and even as far east as Pennsylvania had to be transported at an added expense of $2.50 a tie. River freightage of rails (from Pennsylvania) was $1.35 a ton.

The very magnitude of this undertaking had captured the nation's imagination. In the summer, Speaker of the House Schuyler Colfax, of Indiana, had journeyed 2,000 miles across the continent (starting from Atchison, Kansas) in Ben Holladay's celebrated Overland Stage Line. The flamboyant pioneer Holladay employed his own armed guards to beef up U.S. Cavalry escorts, which were not always available. In the speaker's party was Samuel Bowles of the Springfield (Massachusetts) *Republican*.

All along the way people asked the writer, "When do you think the Pacific Railroad will be done?" or "Why don't or won't the government, now the war is over, put the soldiers to building this road?" Everyone wanted it completed "as soon as possible." It had become *their* railroad.

Bowles wrote: "Tender-eyed women, hardfisted men—pioneers or missionaries, the martyrs and the successful—all alike feel and speak this sentiment. It is the hunger, the prayer, the hope of all these people . . . hope for 'home,' and what home can bring them in cheap and ready passage to and from, or reunion with parent and brother and sister and friend . . . 'home' they call the East. It is a touching and pathetic, though almost unconscious tribute . . .

"What are the possibilities and probabilities of the great continental railway? What of timber, of water, of coal for fuel; the steep grades and high ascents of the two great continental ranges of mountains to be crossed, the Rocky and the Sierras; and the snows they will accumulate upon the track in the winter months? These are the suggested and apparent difficulties to the building and operating of the Pacific Railroad."

Optimistically, Bowles was certain the trains, as the tracks were laid, could carry the wood and other supplies along and, ultimately, there would even be "steam from petroleum." It was, however, "a shame" that the railroad had not already stretched across the plains to the Rockies, where it would face the challenges of running several hundred miles above sea level.

Although construction gangs were preparing to go into winter quarters at Fremont and elsewhere, their progress had been notable. Tracks, in spite of the cold and driving snow, were being spiked down at the rate of one mile a day. The quality of the rails and the roadbed was so good that trains could steam along safely at thirty-five miles an hour. There was freight and makeshift passenger traffic serving such growing clusters of habitation as Bellevue, Papillion, Elkhorn, and Valley.

Travel habits were changed, week by week, with the westward progress of the Union Pacific. "All freight and passenger service by horse, mule, and ox trains were abandoned from Omaha as a point of departure," wrote Frank Reardon, a member of the railroad's mechanical department, "and transferred to the end of the track . . .

"I found Omaha filled with a heterogeneous collection of humanity in which all races, nationalities, creeds and colors were in evidence; many with no visible means of existence as well as others better fixed financially, but owing to the limited facilities of the town for the caring of so many transients, they were compelled to sleep in abandoned freight wagons or in any nook or place that would afford temporary shelter.

"It was compulsory upon those leaving Omaha for the 'front' to provide buffalo robes or blankets for sleeping purposes, as no provisions had been made or could be furnished except to a very limited extent at the few stage stations then being abandoned with the progress of the railroad.

"During construction, no passenger equipment was in service. Boards (were) nailed around inside of box cars or, if preferable, the passenger was welcome to a seat upon a flat car loaded with railroad iron. Such was all the convenience available. The price was the same for either. Terms, however, were easy as the passenger had the privilege of walking if accommodations as mentioned were not desirable.

"There was no coal in the country. Fuel for locomotives consisted generally of green cottonwood, which the enginemen declared sprouted after being put in the fire box, a condition which seriously impaired the steaming qualities of the engine. I had left Omaha at 7 P.M., and arrived at Fremont, 46 miles out, the next morning. There was no delay other than stopping to wood-up or at a stand-still with blower on in a desperate attempt to coax steam enough to proceed for a few miles, when a repetition of the same conditions would be experienced."

Travelers, aside from those connected with the Union Pacific and government commissioners (who had already accepted the existing trackage), were many and assorted: organizers of the Young Men's Christian Association, bankers, preachers, hotel and saloon builders, lawyers, doctors, patent medicine men, adventurers, the idly curious, and, of course, prostitutes. The whistle stops along the right-of-way were already Pithole boomtowns in capsule, steamy, brawling oases amid the harshness of the plains winter.

Grading had been completed fifty miles beyond Fremont along the flat bed of the Platte River. Preparations had been started for a 1,500-foot-long truss bridge over the Loup Fork River. Some of the know-how gained in the war when bridges had to be rebuilt under fire quickly—and well—was useful in this phase of the railroad's engineering.

In fact, Major General Grenville M. Dodge, veteran of the Atlanta campaign and now chief engineer for the Union Pacific, wrote of the semimilitary nature of the operation, not only for its precision but because of the fact that the trains were well supplied with rifles and other arms and that a gang of tracklayers "could be transmuted into a battalion of infantry at any moment." It was estimated that more than half of the laborers had fought in the war.

He added: "The men who go ahead (surveyors and locators) are the advance guard, following them is the second line (the graders) cutting through the gorges, grading the road and building the bridges. Then comes the main body of the army, placing the ties, laying the track, spiking down the rails, perfecting the alignment, ballasting and dressing up and completing the road for immediate use. Along the line of the completed road are construction trains pushing 'to the front' with supplies. The advance limit of the rails is occupied by a train of long box cars with bunks built within them, in which the men sleep at night and take their meals."

Immediately following "come trainloads of ties, rails, spikes, etc. which are thrown off to the side. A light car drawn by a single horse gallops up, is loaded with this material and then is off again to the front. Two men grasp the forward end of the rail and start ahead with it, the rest of the gang taking hold two by two, until it is clear of the car.

"At the word of command it is dropped into place, right side up, during which a similar operation has been going on with the rail for the other side . . . Close behind the track layers comes the gaugers, then the spikers and bolters. Three strokes to the spike, ten spikes to the rail, 400 rails to the mile . . ."

The operation in eastern Nebraska was being carried forth in a friendly climate, where Indian tribes were existing more or less in proximity to the whites. In fact, a treaty with the Omahas in 1854 had opened up not only a site for the city but the immediate prairie for railroad builders. In September 1865, at Fort Smith, Arkansas, representatives of the Cherokees, Shawnees, Choctaws, Chickasaws, and seven other tribes had signed treaties of loyalty to the United States, avowing peace and friendship and also abolishing slavery. At the same time, the tribes of the Southwest renounced all existing agreements with the defunct Confederate government.

But farther to the west and north, Indians disputed the migration of settlers, who needed the land, sources of food, or, at the least, rights-of-way.

"All the tribes of the Indians east of the mountains and many west are in open hostility," wrote Major General John Pope, commanding the Department of the Missouri, in St. Louis. "They attack the mail coaches, emigrant trains, and small posts continually. The United States is required to protect the great overland routes."

Largely forgotten amid the greater issues of the war, settlers in the Dakota and Montana territories had been constantly terrorized and murdered. The warriors of the Sioux chief Little Crow had wiped out entire families in western Minnesota. Losses among the immigrants in the years since 1861 had ranged as high as one thousand. By the time of Appomattox, more than 50,000 persons had abandoned their farms and outpost cabins and fled back to St. Paul, Minneapolis, and the well-established towns and cities along the Mississippi.

In November 1864, a vengeful Colonel J. M. Chivington led a wild, whooping band of local volunteers into a village of Cheyennes and Arapahoes along the Big Sandy River in Colorado. There they slaughtered some five hundred Indians, largely women and children. No quarter was given. The brutal carnage added more fuel to the fiery confrontation.

On July 27, 1865, at Fort Laramie, Brigadier General Patrick E. Connor, commanding the District of the Plains, had reported another attack at Platte Station, Dakota Territory. It resulted in the death of one officer and twenty-five men, together with the wounding of another twenty-five; "bodies scalped and horribly mutilated . . . Indians say that they do not want peace and expect an increase of 1,000 more to their force. They are now three miles west, destroying telegraph line."

And a week later, also from Fort Laramie, another dispatch, "200 Cheyenne Indians attacked station near Big Laramie . . . killing 4 men and 1 woman, and taking as prisoners 1 woman aged 15 years and 1 girl baby aged 2 years—a fate worse than death."

These incidents were but punctuation in a continuing attrition. To counter such attacks, General Connor set out the end of July on what was known as the Powder River Indian Expedition. With him were 2,500 men—about half of the number requested, short of ammunition and supplies—"and many barefoot horses."

Throughout the month of August the cavalrymen rode across the wild lands along the Powder and Tongue rivers, which wound through southeastern Montana Territory and northeastern Wyoming (part of Dakota Territory). Scouting forays and one small action involving the expedition's Pawnee scouts culminated, on August 29, when the soldiers came across a large Arapahoe village, situated on a mesa. This group was under Black Bear and Old David.

Here, along the Tongue River, just inside of Wyoming, at 9:00 A.M. the soldiers tore into the migratory settlement just as the warriors were about to break camp. It was all part of "the glorious work of annihilating savages." So wrote twenty-four-year-old Captain Henry E. Palmer, of Centerville, Ohio. The cavalrymen galloped into the village amid a pandemonium of "more than a thousand dogs . . . barking," some 3,000 ponies whinnying and at least seven hundred braves emitting their "fearful yelling."

The bugle sounded the charge and, according to Palmer, "my horse carried me forward almost against my will and in those few moments, less than it takes to tell the story, I was in the village in the midst of a hand-to-hand fight with warriors and their squaws, for many of the female portion of this band did as brave fighting as their savage lords. Unfortunately for the women and children, our men had no time to direct their aim; bullets from both sides and murderous arrows filled the air; squaws and children, as well as warriors, fell among the dead and wounded. The scene was indescribable."

After emptying his revolver into the prone bodies of three warriors, Palmer turned his attention to a fellow trooper whose tongue had been pierced by an arrow. Without hesitation, the captain cut out the arrow. General Connor himself was nearly trapped while pursuing the retreating foe "fully ten miles from the camp." When he returned he found his men reducing the encampment to ashes, burning everything—buffalo robes, furs, blankets, lodge poles, tepee covers, even dried buffalo meat, in one huge pyre. Atop it were placed the bodies of the one officer and twenty-four cavalrymen lost in the engagement.

Although he acknowledged that the Indians "made a brave stand trying to save their women and children," Palmer reasoned that "we must either whip the Indians and whip them badly or be whipped ourselves . . . We had accomplished a grand victory. Two hundred and fifty lodges had been burned with the entire winter supply of food and clothing for the band. The son of the principal chief (Black Bear) was killed, 63 warriors were slain and about 1,100 head of ponies captured."

Samuel Bowles, during his transcontinental journey, praised General Connor's "new energy" in his campaign to inflict upon the Indians "sharp punishment." He asserted that if they could not live in peace, "extermination it must be, else we may as well abandon this whole region; give up its settlement, its subjugation to civilization, its development to wealth and

Christianity. It is the eternal contest between barbarism and civilization
. . . The red man of reality is not the red man of poetry, romance, or
philanthropy. He is false and barbaric, cunning and cowardly, attacking
only when all advantage is with him, horrible in cruelty, the terror of
women and children, impenetrable to nearly every motive but fear,
impossible to regenerate and civilize."

There were some, nonetheless, of different mind, one of whom was
General Pope. He boiled upon reading a memo from General Connor,
stating, "You will not receive overtures of peace or submission from
Indians, but will attack and kill every male Indian over twelve years of
age." The instructions, thumped the commander of the Department of
the Missouri, were "atrocious" and must be "countermanded" at once.

Then, in a long, philosophical letter to General Sherman, still commanding the Military Division of the Mississippi, Pope lamented the fact
that "the Indian, in truth, has no longer a country." The general continued: "His lands are everywhere pervaded by white men; his means of
subsistence destroyed and the homes of his tribe violently taken from him;
himself and his family reduced to starvation, or to the necessity of warring
to the death upon the white man, whose inevitable and destructive
progress threatens the total extermination of his race. Such is today the
condition of affairs on the great plains and in the ranges of the Rocky
Mountains.

"The Indians, driven to desperation and threatened with starvation,
have everywhere commenced hostilities against the whites, and are carrying them on with a fury and courage unknown to their history hitherto.
There is not a tribe of Indians on the great plains or in the mountain
regions east of Nevada and Idaho of any consideration which is not now
warring on the whites . . .

"The first demand of the Indian is that the white man shall not come
into his country, shall not kill or drive off the game upon which his
subsistence depends, and shall not dispossess him of his lands. How can
we promise this, with any purpose of fulfilling the obligation, unless we
prohibit emigration and settlement west or south of the Missouri River?
So, far from being prepared to make such engagements with the Indian,
the Government is every day stimulating emigration and its resulting
wrong to the Indian . . . Where under such circumstances is the Indian to
go and what is to become of him?"

Expressing the opinion that it was "useless" to talk of an "unmolested home" for the tribes, much less subsisting them, he foresaw the ultimate "dispossession" from their lands, and "whatever may be the abstract wrong or right . . . the only practical question to be considered is, how this inevitable process can be accomplished with the least inhumanity and the greatest moral and physical benefit to the Indian.

"We are surely not now pursuing such a course, nor are the means used becoming to a humane and Christian people. My duties as a military commander require me to protect the emigration, the mails, and the settlements against the hostile acts of the Indians. I have no power . . . to do this except by force. This necessity demands a large military force on the plains, which will have to be increased as the Indians are more and more driven by desperation, and less and less able to protect the game, which is their only means of life.

"The end is sure and dreadful to contemplate."

Indians remained an ever hovering menace to the railroad builders. They were especial anathema to the "rodmen," or surveyors who plotted the course of the rails dozens of miles ahead of the main party. Weather, food, and shelter also contributed to the loneliness and dangers of their mission.

"With the first streak of dawn, the camp was alive, campfires blazing in the dim light of the morning, horses stamping at their feedboxes attached to the wagons and loudly munching their corn, and the entire camp preparing for the commencement of the day's journey . . ." So wrote young Arthur N. Ferguson, a rodman with the Union Pacific. Among his many vignettes was this description of a typical day: "Immediately after breakfast, which consisted of meat, bread, potatoes and strong coffee, the stove was turned upside down and all the fire and ashes emptied out. Before it was hardly cool, it was lashed up in its accustomed place behind the wagon. Soon everything was tumbled in—teams hitched on, and we were all rolling over the prairie westward.

"During the entire morning our route lay over a high rolling prairie with here and there an occasional cabin and a few acres of sod-breaking, where some hardy pioneer was striving to make a home for himself and little ones."

Ferguson was encountering a unique type of dwelling of the plains, used not only by settlers but also as permanent shelters by the friendly Pawnees. The tough fibrous grass roots of the area made sod blocks the nearest thing to concrete. The young son of Colonel Josiah B. Park,

William Lee, who lived in one for a year, would describe his sod house in some detail. A simple one-room structure, the average sod house had two windows and two doors, with a roof either of the same natural material or of canvas, and, as a bonus, it was "exceptionally warm in winter and cool the following summer."

The interior, young Park wrote, "was what you made it. Generally partitioned into several rooms, with burlap for a wall covering. Not decorated as artistically as some Fifth Avenue homes, but quite likely affording as much satisfaction in the way of comfort. The burlap was . . . the product of grain sacks . . . The stables and other necessary out-buildings were of the same earthy material." In the summer, grass and wild flowers lent an unusual prairie beauty to the place.

Continuing his journals, Arthur Ferguson reported that when the party reached deeper into Indian country, in the vicinity of Fremont, "some three or four men . . . turned their faces homeward." This in spite of an escort of sixty soldiers of the Twelfth Missouri Cavalry. "Very much dissatisfied . . . at times on the point of rebellion against their officers, they said that they had enlisted for the war, to fight rebels and not to go out into the western wilderness to fight Indians."

Then, "about six miles from Elm Creek," the young surveyor wrote of the first Indian alarm: "As we were approaching the creek, which comes out of the high bluffs to the north, and is densely timbered, we saw mounted men running to the timber, and in the darkness of the evening could not distinguish who or what they were. Our troops, however, at once deployed right and left and advanced at a brisk trot with carbines unslung and sabres ready for any emergency.

"They soon disappeared among the dark shadows of the timber and in about an hour's time the bugle recalled the troops. They were unable to find any traces of them, and whoever or whatever they were had made good their escape among the rough bluffs and canons to the northward. This little affair stirred up our camp considerably and gave us plenty to talk about around our campfire for that night . . .

"It is a busy and lively night after the day's march to see the troopers busily engaged in rubbing down their animals, and they seem to have quite an affection for them, calling them by pet names and bestowing a great deal of care upon them. Their campfires burn . . . after nightfall and the solemn tread of the sentinel, with bright gleaming carbine, assures one if, in the still hours of night we are attacked, the enemy will receive a warm reception.

"West of this point the country becomes wilder and more desolate."

The cavalry also scouted the country for food, often returning "with game of various descriptions" strapped to their saddles. Then, another scare: "While we were all, save the pickets, soundly sleeping, we were startled by a shot, which in the dead hour of night, caused every man to spring from his bed, weapons in hand. I caught up my carbine and rushed out just as I had sprung from my bed, and found myself in the midst of fifty or sixty excited men. The guard while on duty opposite the island had in the dim distance seen a man slowly wading around the point and close in the shadow of the overhanging willows. He discharged his piece at him, when he suddenly disappeared. Whether he was hit and had fallen into the water, or whether he disappeared among the bushes, we were unable to tell. However, our camp soon quieted down and we had no further alarm during the night."

And still another, in a day or so. A "black speck" was seen in the distance, first thought to be a buffalo, but in a few moments "the glass plainly showed the object consisted of two men with their horses, who were moving rapidly in our direction.

"The troops in advance called a halt, and the entire train came to a standstill, to await the arrival of the two individuals."

They turned out to be division engineers, with bad news. Instead of going home, as all expected, the party must tent for the night and then continue onward. "By morning the weather had grown very cold, the sky covered with heavy, leaden clouds which indicated snow. The air blew very cold and chill. Notwithstanding the severe weather, we had to triangulate the Platte. The men were compelled to wade the river, which in places was up to their armpits . . .

"Tonight our campfires burn brightly and we have a strong guard on, as we are in the midst of hostile Indians. They have made several attacks in the past few days and have killed quite a number of whites. Several companies of cavalry have passed up the road to some ranches 20 or 30 miles on, where the Indians are now making strong and vigorous attacks and the assistance of the troops have been asked by scouts.

"In the morning, by daybreak, we started down the river, intending to go some 15 miles and then go into camp as soon as possible . . . during the day we passed the new-made graves of some ten or twelve men who had recently been killed by savages. They were some fifteen feet from the road, among the tall and rank prairie grass.

"About 4 o'clock in the afternoon, it commenced snowing, and in a short time we were in the midst of a furious storm. We hastened on the party as fast as possible to a dense body of cottonwood timber on the river bottom which, after reaching, w : proceeded as fast as possible to pitch our tents, the snow storm increasing in violence fast . . . The tents were up, but inside them the tramping of many feet had turned the snow into water and mud . . ."

The party slept under the illumination of "blazing fires" built by those unfortunate troopers who had no tents. "The horses were fed with large quantities of cottonwood limbs, the bark of which they seem to relish. Night, however, passed away and the morning broke on a cold and desolate camp. The storm had ceased, but everything was cold and cheerless. Nearly a foot of snow covered the entire camp."

The group split up, Ferguson starting for the dread lands adjacent to the Republican River, on Nebraska's southern border, winding in and out of Kansas, "the worst Indian country in the entire West . . . Large bodies of troops have been killed in this region after hard battles with the Indians, and months afterward their bones have been found bleaching on the prairies."

It was also "the great buffalo country of the West, and sometimes a black, surging mass can be seen extending in every direction as far as the eye can reach, the herd running up into thousands." Generally ignoring the buffalo, the cavalry took after the equally plentiful antelope, "wasting their ammunition by shooting them in sport," then leaving the carcasses for the wolves, coyotes, and buzzards.

". . . This is a terrible country, the stillness, wildness and desolation of which is awful. Not a tree to be seen, nothing but a succession of hill and valley with occasionally the bed of a large lake [or] a salt spring . . . not a sign of man to be seen, and it seemed as if the solitude had been eternal."

Then, in a valley, "we saw what we supposed to be a war party of Indians. Our troops trotted briskly forward, when the band started on full run, and we discovered that instead of savages, it was a large troop of wild horses . . . They were as fleet as deer and [the soldiers] could not get within musket shot."

Frustrated that they had found no targets to their liking, such as Indians, the cavalrymen started shooting at wild horses, antelopes, "nearly everything that came within range of their guns." At one point, Ferguson casually inquired how much ammunition was left.

"Only one or two rounds," a trooper replied, with fine nonchalance. Others could count not one bullet. "It was," Ferguson would observe in understatement, "very careless on their part."

Food was low: "All I have had today to eat has been a few lumps of white sugar, and a few wormy crackers (hard tack) . . . we have no water for ourselves or animals, but we have drunk a small keg of vinegar."

Then, with the little remaining ammunition, one of the soldiers bagged a large buffalo, "but it was almighty tough for it was an old bull with nearly all its teeth gone."

And the weather, always the weather, "very cold and stormy, and we have occasional snow. The troops have no covering and they suffer very much . . . the weather has become intensely cold . . . all day we toiled over the divide, the cold bleak wind striking to the bone . . . the severe weather of a winter campaign."

Across the 7,000-foot Sierra Nevada, where the Central Pacific was struggling eastward, conditions were yet worse, with snow ten feet deep in places. Some storms lasted two weeks with scarcely a letup. Nonetheless, according to John R. Gilliss, an engineer: ". . . The storms were grand. They always began with a fall in the barometer and a strong wind from the southwest. The thermometer was rarely below 20 degrees at the beginning of a storm, and usually rose to 32 degrees before its close so that the last snow would be damp and heavy, sometimes ending in a rain. The storms ended and clouds were scattered by cold winds blowing over the eastern range of the Sierra Nevada; these raised the barometer and dropped the temperature at once . . .

"Snow slides or avalanches were frequent . . ."

He wrote of men being crushed to death in their shelters, or even houses, although others were rescued after being buried for as long as fourteen hours under the snow.

Construction on the Central Pacific had commenced in Sacramento in January 1862. California had not been distracted by the war as had the Eastern and Midwestern states. In four years, the line had progressed a little over fifty miles, about the same as the Union Pacific, to Colfax, California (named after the speaker of the house). The slower rate was the direct result of the terrain, especially the necessity to smash and blast through mountains. No fewer than fifteen tunnels had been planned, for a total length of well over a mile.

Beyond Colfax lay the challenge of the Sierras. Like military objectives, they remained to be conquered by the engineers. The very names of the areas ahead were awesome and formidable: Cape Horn and Dutch Flat, Alta and Grizzly Hill, Cisco, Donner Pass, Truckee . . . and some lesser-known terms of demarcation familiar only to the engineers.

Officers of the Central were men who became synonymous with California: Leland Stanford, formerly a wholesale grocer who was both the president of the railroad and governor of the state; Mark Hopkins and Collis P. Huntington, hardware merchants; and Charles Crocker, who had made his fortune in dry goods.

"The work of grading has been continued without cessation," Leland Stanford wrote to President Johnson. "The grading between Newcastle and Colfax was very difficult and expensive, increasing as the line was pushed up the mountain slope. The cuttings have been deeper, the embankments higher, and more rock work encountered as the line has progressed eastward.

"Several expensive trestle bridges have been constructed across deep ravines, some as high as 100 feet in the center."

Both snow and rain hampered construction. Snow brought tunnel work to a halt. Rain combined with melting snow to turn wagon roads into quagmires, "nearly impassable," according to J. H. Strobridge, construction superintendent. He elaborated: "Large numbers of pack animals had to be brought into use, and on them were carried nearly all supplies, even hay and grain, over steep mountain trails, to the construction camps. Account the very wet and terribly muddy conditions, it was impossible to have the goods needed for use. Obliged to use pack horses for the mountain trails—had to pack even bales of hay distances of 25 miles and for four or five miles all supplies were taken over this way."

But the weather and mud did not appreciably ruffle the Chinese, as Stanford advised the chief executive: "As a class they are quiet, peaceable, patient, industrious and economical. Ready and apt to learn all the different kinds of work required in railroad building, they soon become as efficient as white laborers. More prudent and economical, they are contented with less wages. We find them organized into societies for mutual aid and assistance. These societies can count their numbers by the thousands, [and] are conducted by shrewd, intelligent businessmen who promptly advise their subordinates where employment can be found on most favorable terms.

"No system similar to slavery, serfdom or peonage prevails among these laborers. Their wages, which are always paid in coin each month, are divided among them by their agents who attend to their business according to the labor done by each person. These agents are generally American or Chinese merchants who furnish them their supplies of food, the value of which they deduct from their monthly pay."

They were coming west from all sections of the East and Midwest, not only toward California but to Texas, already "echoing to the Longhorns' hooves." Former Confederate cavalrymen became especially expert cowhands. They started out from thousands of villages, towns (such as Sheffield, Illinois), and cities, jauntily, joking.

"John Cannon," wrote Willis Boughton, "declaring that as a loyal Tammany man he might meet and marry an Indian queen, joined one of those caravans [of covered wagons] knapsack strapped to his back, trudging beside the schooners, and we saw him no more."

In fact, "the lure of the New West drew many families from our village. They had been pioneers at Sheffield, and the town was becoming too crowded; so they pioneered again into a newer country, several becoming farm owners in Iowa and Missouri.

"The lure entrapped even the Rev. Mr. Lyman, the beloved preacher of the Congregational church. It was not in poverty and rags or even in a threadbare gown that he preached the doctrines of the Sermon on the Mount—yea and the new commandment.

"The whiteness of his dwelling accorded with the purity of his life. He owned and tilled 40 acres of rich prairie land in order to relieve his parishioners of the burden of sustaining their church.

"In public places he always appeared neatly and perfectly attired for one of his calling. He befriended the Negro slave, for he came from the land of Charles Sumner. He saw evil in the saloon, and strove to rouse a sentiment in favor of local option." (This initiative was opposed with considerable enthusiasm.) "He condemned the traveling circus, but if there was a menagerie attachment, he led his entire family to reserved seats in order to show his approval."

When this solemn parson with the puritanical impulses announced he was going west, many in Sheffield, especially the barkeepers, breathed a sigh of relief. He sold his well-kept, fertile fields and house to the village doctor and started packing.

"I must live where my children can have the advantage of college life," he asserted. Word soon came back that the Reverend Mr. Lyman had settled down in Grinnell, Iowa (where temperance and self-denial were somewhat more de rigueur than in Sheffield), on a "larger tract of land" and hoped to pay tuition bills at Grinnell College through his crops.

At about this time, new tidings of Indian assaults filtered back to Sheffield. Boughton told of the return of a resident who carried his own scalp in his pocket. A band of Indians attacked his crew working on the Union Pacific. He was knocked down and his scalp sliced from the top of his head. A troop of soldiers followed the savages and killed the one who carried his scalp.

"He recovered it and had it tanned. His hair was long, black and silky. He had a bag of small nuggets of gold which he sold to Sheffieldites at fabulous prices."

The possibility of being scalped, however, of starving, freezing, or becoming hostage to a host of other dangers and discomfitures, at best uncertainties, did not slow the tide of western migration. Whether to work on the railroad, like the man who toted his scalp, to seek fortunes in California, or merely to settle on cheap or free land somewhere in the far West, men singly or accompanied by their families quit the cities, the villages, and the farms of the East.

Hosts of Americans had heeded Horace Greeley's editorial in the New York *Tribune*, "Go west, young man, and grow up with the country."

It little mattered to the readers that the distinguished if liberarily light-fingered Greely had quietly lifted the catchy slogan from an earlier article in—of all newspapers— the Terre Haute *Express*.

FEBRUARY

Like a Smile on the Lips of the Dead

"On a cold windy day in February, Martha Haines and I landed at Yorktown, Virginia, and were met by the superintendent of schools which had been established by the Friends' Freedmen's Association of Philadelphia. We soon learned that teachers and 'missionaries' were needed at Fort Magruder: this place was about ten miles from Yorktown."

The writer was Margaret N. Thorpe, like Abbie Brooks a teacher, but not in the same tradition since the latter was more of a private tutor. Margaret, petite, blonde, with large blue eyes, was one of a growing army attempting to augment the work of the Freedmen's Bureau in bringing mass education to the former slaves.

The war-spawned Freedmen's Bureau, under army control, was starting toward its ambitious goal of educating 150,000 in 2,500 schools. Already, more than 11,500 blacks in Virginia and 19,000 in Louisiana were learning their three Rs. In Goldsboro, North Carolina, three hundred students crowded into one small schoolhouse. An earnest black preacher harangued this flock when the assigned teachers paused for breath, according to a reporter for the New York *Tribune* who happened by.

The program appeared altogether so promising that the New York *Times* editorialized, "There is some danger that the next generation of Negroes in the South may be more intelligent and better educated than the whites. So much public attention and effort are devoted to the former, and the latter seem so entirely left to their own resources (which are scanty at best)."

Southern women, perhaps the majority of them, did not accept either the "nig schools" or the Northern teachers in good grace. In North Carolina, for example, these predominantly young women from New England or the Midwest had to board and eat together, usually in homes commandeered by the army and sometimes protected by the soldiers. In extreme cases, teachers for the Freedmen's Bureau were not permitted to disembark from coastal steamers in ports such as Wilmington, Charleston, or Savannah until federal authorities forcibly interceded.

Thus Margaret was fortunate at least to have arrived unimpeded at her destination. For several days she stayed at the Mission House, "a large frame building occupied by the superintendent, matron and five teachers . . . [and] had charge of the Yorktown schools and the distribution of clothing, medicine, garden seeds, implements and the many other gifts sent by northern friends.

"After our few days visit we journeyed to Fort Magruder in the old wagon, irreverently styled 'the Ark', over one of the worst kind of roads in the world, a wornout corduroy. We found Fort Magruder was a small earthwork erected by General [John B.] Magruder to impede General McClellan's advance up the Peninsula [in 1862] . . . Inside the fort were three small houses, one of brick was occupied by the Freedmen's Bureau officer and his family; the other two were frame and were vacant and dirty."

Margaret and Martha chose the better of the two houses and commenced cleaning. The place was composed of but two rooms, one of which served as a parlor, dining area, and bedroom, the other as kitchen. "Over the latter presided a tall, black, utterly incompetent woman who put cleanliness, punctuality and expedition amongst 'de vanities,' a peculiarity of character which we continually met, and which was a great hindrance in our work."

The two teachers set up housekeeping in quarters hardly "luxurious," without carpets, easy chairs, a wardrobe, a furnace, or a stove other than that in the kitchen. In fact, their "large open school room" had but one wood stove, necessitating heavy clothing and walking to and fro while teaching to keep warm. The schoolhouse itself, located just outside the fort, was a long, low log building, with some benches, a few desks, one table, but no maps or blackboards. Through holes in the walls and roofs of both the school and Margaret's residence the snow and rain would drift in, "waking us at night by falling on our faces."

Barely prepared, Margaret and Martha were confronted on opening day by a "motley assemblage . . . every shade of color, from jet black to blue-eyed blondes. Cold, dirty, and half-naked but eager to learn, none seemed to care to know what we intended to give in the way of clothing and food, but anxious to feel sure that they would have the privilege of coming to school every day.

"Their respect for 'white ladies' awed them into quietness and obedience—but with each other they were like snarling puppies, not so much from ill humor as the result of a training that had taught them neither self-respect or respect for anyone but those with white skins."

School opened at 9:00 A.M. for the youngsters, usually about seventy-five in number—and then from 3:30 to 5:00 P.M. the teachers turned their efforts toward "some of the older children and a few grown women, writing and sewing. We had no difficulty in keeping them attentive to study and work, as they looked upon it all as a 'great privilege.'

"Many of the children were very comical indeed. We sometimes questioned whether it had not been within a very recent period that they had lost their caudle [caudal, or tail] appendage and acquired the power of speech!

"Frequently a little black hand would be raised and when the owner was given permission to speak we would be told, 'cussin' in dis ere corner.' Upon investigation would be told that the offender had most likely said nothing worse than 'he never had no right to say, I never knowed my lesson, [and] if dat chile da' say dat again I'll wash him black mouf,' or 'dis gal say I'm a black nigga, ain't no mo' nigga dan she is!' "

Three hundred blacks lived in a settlement outside of the fort, which was known as the camp. The teachers spent "much time" visiting there, distributing clothing, medicine, garden seeds, and implements for carpentry, and generally offering advice on the inhabitants' many problems.

". . . We never had clothing enough to supply those who really needed it, and we would sometimes cut up army blankets into garments. I well remember one night when Martha and I sat up until 2 o'clock making a suit for a little boy. He received it so joyfully the next morning and by night it was in shreds! Not that 'Buddie' had been so careless, but the blanket was shoddy.

"Insufficient clothing and protection from inclement weather, also poor and often not enough food were some of the causes of frequent sickness, so that we distributed quite an amount of simple medicines, but at one time during this winter we felt that the demand for castor oil was becoming exorbitant. Upon close observation found that the cup to hold the oil was always brought by a child with a pathetic story of a sick baby at home. We soon found that even if the 'sick baby' was not purely imagination, it never received the oil for that always was used by the school children on the bread they brought to luncheon."

Such was the shortage of butter.

Night school for the adults, some of them elderly, was so popular that it often continued an hour after the nine o'clock scheduled closing "before we would have the courage to say 'now you must go!' Nearly all the night scholars were grown men and women, some so old that their bowed heads were covered with white hair. One man with daughter and granddaughter lived three miles from the schoolhouse and very seldom missed their six-miles walk."

Although the advent of the Ku Klux Klan was a few months off, many of the older blacks were nervous, largely because of excesses by some of the troops. Often the student with the daughter and granddaughter arrived with sword and gun, "both so large and clumsy and rusty we concluded they were relics of the Revolution." After the weapons were placed in a corner of the room, "the poor old worn white head bent over his pages as he patiently spelled the words over and over, and his triumph when he mastered one was most touching, often he would say, 'isn't this a most blessed privilege . . . Many a time I have been whipped for being found with a book, for I always wanted to learn to read.' "

Two young oystermen from the York River invariably arrived munching on corn bread. This sustained them on their long walk, in lieu of dinner. Sometimes, Margaret and her friend Martha varied the evening courses by discussing "moral and social subjects" instead of arithmetic or grammar. They would "try to impress upon them the necessity of being cleanly, thorough, punctual, honest and any other subject we felt might be helpful. One night as I talked, an 'uncle' on the front bench began rubbing his hands and exclaiming 'what a deliberate oration!' "

The schoolhouse appeared to exist "in the middle of a barren plain," since the country was flat, the soil was poor, defying vegetation, and the fences had been torn down during the war, "and we loved to stand 'outside de do' on moonlight nights and watch the dusky forms coming from all directions, and listened to their clear and often beautiful voices singing the weird plantation hymns and songs.

"One crowd would frequently march under the direction of a young man who had been a soldier. He was a fine specimen of the real African, intensely black and straight as a pine tree . . . [singing]:

> " 'The Lord come in on apple tree, the bell done ring,
> I'm gwine home.
> Two white horses, side by side, come along
> sinner, come along.' "

The challenges and ennui encountered by teachers were matched by other facets of life in Tidewater Virginia.

"I wish," wrote Margaret, "I could give you an idea of Virginia roads. Imagine the worst possible, and then think they are five times worse and you may have a slight idea of what we went over and through and around in a drive to Hampton to see a horse that Martie had purchased." (More than half a year after the end of hostilities, a good, healthy horse or mule was hard to find.) "We left Yorktown at 4 o'clock in the afternoon in an open 'buggy.' The drive is about 20 miles and with our good horse we expected to arrive at headquarters in three hours; instead of that, we were over five hours.

"On our way, we asked an old woman how far it was to Hampton. 'Hampton, honey, you'd better git up and git!' and 'git' we did. Sometimes up, up, up and sometimes down, down, down. When we got out of our carriage, one of Martie's overshoes came off, and although it was carefully sought, it was never found. So you can picture the mud; we never succeeded in finding the bottom . . ."

And still, with all the sacrifices and discomfitures experienced by the Northern schoolmarms, resentment against them festered within the Southern women.

"It never occurred to the men, women and maidens [of the South] who visited all the poor, sick, old and feeble Negroes in their reach," wrote Myrta Lockett Avary, "breaking their night's rest or their hours of recreation or toil without a sense of sacrifice—who gave medicines, food, clothing, any and everything asked for to the blacks and who ministered to them in neighborly ways innumerable—that they were doing the work of a district or parish visitor." Such, snapped Myrta, Southerners had been doing ever since the slaves arrived "by way of New England."

The terms "missionary," "educator," and "philanthropist" were anathema to the author. "Holier than thou" she thought would be a better tag.

"Newcomers were upon us like the plagues of Egypt," she railed. "Deserters from the Federal Army, men dismissed for cause, followers in its wake, political gypsies, bums and toughs . . . Yankee schoolmarms overran the country!"

There had also arisen the anomaly of freed slaves caring for their erstwhile masters. When the slaves could no longer do this, through changed circumstances, both slaves and those for whom they had worked were filled with a sense of loss and emptiness. For example, Old Abram, Sara Pryor's trusty, informed her sadly that he better "scuffle along," since he could take care only of himself now.

Sara had "reached the end of all our resources." The cow, Rose, her constant wartime companion and milk source, had died; her two pigs had "fulfilled their destiny long ago"; the turnips and potatoes were consumed. Army rations, even dried cod and fodder corn, had ceased.

Worst of all, minus the helping arms of Abram, "without food or fuel we could not live in the country." (Just where the farm was has never been determined.) So she prepared to move her children into Petersburg until such time as her husband, Roger, could earn enough in his new law practice in New York to ask his family to join him.

"The afternoon before our departure from Cottage Farm," she wrote, "the weather was so deliciously balmy that I walked over the garden and grounds, thinking of the great drama that had been enacted on this spot.

"The spring comes early in the lower counties of Virginia. Already the grass was springing, and on the trees around the well which had so often refreshed General Lee, tender young leaves were trembling. Spring had come to touch all scars with her gentle finger tips. Over all the battle-torn ground, over the grave of the young soldier who had lain so long under my window, over the track ploughed by shot and shell, she had spread a delicate bloom like a smile on the lips of the dead.

"Much of my last night at Cottage Farm was spent at the window from which I had watched on that anxious night of my first homecoming. The home had been polluted, sacked, desecrated—and yet I was leaving it with regret. Many a hard battle with illness, with want, with despair, had been fought within those walls. It seemed like a long, dark night in which neither sun nor moon nor stars had appeared; during which we had simply endured, watching ourselves the while, jealous lest the natural rebound of youthful hope and spirit should surprise us, and dishonor those who had suffered and bled and died for our sakes."

In the minds of some Virginians, even the antisecessionists, nothing was going along as it should. Far less reconciled even than Sara Pryor, John Minor Botts, former federal legislator and Unionist once jailed in Richmond for his open attacks on the Confederacy, was testifying passionately before the Joint Committee on Reconstruction. This had recently been convened by Congress. Wholly dissatisfied with the president's handling of affairs, he told the committee: "At the time of the surrender of General Lee's army, and the restoration of peace I think there was not only a general but an almost universal acquiescence and congratulation among the people that the war had terminated, and a large majority of them were at least contented . . . but from the time that Mr. Johnson commenced his indiscriminate system of pardoning all who made application . . . they became bold, insolent and defiant; and this was increased to a very large extent by the permission which was immediately after the evacuation of Richmond given by [federal officers] . . . to the original conductors of the public press before the rebellion to reestablish their papers . . . without restriction or limitation." And from then on, Botts charged, "the spirit of disloyalty and dissaffection" flourished, fueled by "the licentiousness of the press.

"Was the war in all its horrid consequences designed to establish a democratic oligarchy here in the South and eventually take over the general government with all its patronage and power [given] to this pack of bloodhounds? Or was it designed to preserve the Union, maintain liberty, and wipe out forever all national parties?"

Seeking answers to these and related questions, President Johnson dispatched his friend Ben C. Truman on a fast winter swing around the South. Sometime staff officer, sometime correspondent and presidential secretary, Truman found himself focusing on the Southern attitude toward the conquerors: "There is a prevalent disposition not to associate too freely with northern men, or to receive them into the circles of society. But it is far from insurmountable. Over southern society, as over every other, woman reigns supreme, and they are most embittered against those whom they deem the authors of all their calamities [more] than are their brothers, sons and husbands."

Noting that the younger women of the South "are much superior to the southern men both in intellect and energy and their ascendancy over society is correspondingly great," he continued, "But the stories and rumors to the effect that northern men are bitterly persecuted and compelled to abandon the country I pronounce false. If northern men go south they must expect for a while to be treated with neglect, and sometimes with contempt; but if they refrain from bitter political discussions and conduct themselves with ordinary discretion, they soon overcome these prejudices and are treated with respect."

Truman found, as a sort of paradox perhaps, that the white officers who had commanded the black regiments, certainly "the most offensive" of all Northern units, had tended in particular to remain in the old areas of their campaigns: "Large numbers of ex-Federal and ex-Confederate officers are engaged together in mercantile pursuits and in cotton planting. Nearly all of the cotton plantations in Florida are being run by such parties. The banks of the Mississippi are lined with plantations which have been leased by northern men and Federal officers. Arkansas and White River plantations are generally being run by officers who have served under [Major General Joseph Jones] Reynolds, while a large number of the Red River plantations have been placed under cultivation by officers of [Major General Andrew Jackson] Smith's command." Both Reynolds and Smith had served in the U.S. Army.

"Fourteen officers of a colored (Kentucky) Regiment are engaged in planting and raising cotton near Victoria, Texas. The First National Bank of Texas, at Galveston, has for president ex-Major General [T.F.] Nichols, of the late Confederate Army, and ten of its directors are also ex-rebel officers, while the cashier is ex-Major General [William T.] Clark, of the Union Army, and who formerly commanded a division of colored troops.

"In all of these connections the utmost harmony prevails. Notwithstanding the above facts—and I could multiply them—I maintain that in many sections of the South there is a widespread hostility to northern men which, however, in nine times out of ten, is speedily dispelled by individual contact, and the exercise of generous regard for private opinions . . . all who can be spared from industry of the North to go south can readily find places of business where they can live in quiet and prosperity."

Even in ruined Columbia, some "places of business" could be found again. On the seventeenth of February the Columbia *Phoenix* "turned the rules" in order that the columns of the paper would all be bordered in black. It was the first anniversary of the burning of South Carolina's capital.

"On this morning in the year 1865," the *Phoenix* editorialized, "the sun rose upon their city in all its completeness and natural beauty . . . The rising sun of the following day rose upon a mass of smoking ruins and a forest of chimneys throughout the entire length of the city . . . thousands of homeless wanderers were seen scattered over our streets, our parks, our fields . . . Columbia probably lost between 12 and 15 hundred buildings the night of February 17 . . .

"The 20,000 inhabitants of Columbia had not realized what war was, nor the ruin and desolation it brings . . .

"We must go to work. Thus far, with limited means and with very depressed feelings and with a very gloomy prospect in future; the merchants and real estate owners in our city have done well. About 200 buildings have replaced those destroyed and before five years the city of Columbia will reassert her rights and be one of the most beautiful and attractive cities in the United States . . ."

Across the border in Georgia, where the Savannah *Herald* was reporting resumption of daily train service to Augusta, as well as to Thomasville, in the state's southeast corner, there persisted strong feelings about the future in general and slavery in particular.

"The war is ended," wrote Willis Willingham, of Lexington, to his friend Captain Peter Eltinge, home on leave in New York, "but its consequences will be seen and felt for an age to come. Man is a belligerent animal, hence histories' bloody pages tell of little else than blood and carnage; and yet what stupendous folly it is to go to war!"

Taking exception to a previous comment by Eltinge that Georgia "has not quite come up to the President's requirements in relation to reconstruction," Willingham insisted that the state had "toed the mark square up" but along with the rest of the South was disappointed in not having congressional representation [which] "should exist between the North and South . . . as it would have been if the [Southern] members had been received into Congress at once."

He lashed out at the Radical Republicans for seeking "Negro suffrage at once" and labeled as "preposterous" the capacity of a race "very little superior to the Monky tribe" to vote. Willingham was convinced the South "had rather live as she is under military rule than have Negro suffrage."

He asserted that his "desire above all things," however, was for the country to "be quiet, and fraternal feelings . . . restored throughout the land . . . the South has committed suicide, she is ruined irretrievably. There are some persons who express hope that the South will yet blossom as the rose—but they are mistaken. The rose bush of the South was cut up root and branch by emancipation of the Negroes."

Gloomily, he predicted that the former slaves "will not work much as freedmen," and the North would suffer for lack of cotton, since the freedmen "never will work much unless forced to do so."

He was seconded by Ella Gertrude Thomas, living in the badly damaged plantation Belmont, near Augusta. "We owned more than 90 Negroes," she wrote, "with a prospect of inheriting many more from Pa's estate. By the surrender of the southern army, slavery became a thing of the past and we were reduced from a state of affluence to utter beggary, for the 30 thousand dollars Pa gave me when I was married was invested in Negroes alone."

Since Ella robustly interpreted the Bible as not merely condoning slavery but as decreeing it "must be," she admitted that "for a time I doubted God!"

More outspoken was Clement Clay, writing to his wife, Virginia, from Fort Monroe: "I think the utter subversion of our political and social systems and sudden enfranchisement of four million slaves a great crime, and one of the most terrible calamities that ever befell any people; that generations yet unborn will feel it in sorrow and suffering; and that nothing but intense hatred and vindictive rage could have so blinded the North to its own interests and [to] those of humanity as to induce the consummation of this act of wickedness and folly.

"I look for nothing but evil to both blacks and whites in the South from this sudden and violent change in their relations; intestine feuds and tumults; torpid indolence and stealthy rapacity on the part of the blacks; jealousy, distrust and oppression of them on the part of the whites; mutual outrage and injury, disquiet, apprehensions, alarms, murders, robberies, house-burnings, and other crimes; the blighting of hearts and homes and the destruction of industry, arts, literature, wealth, comfort and happiness."

At the very least, Clay was prone to exaggeration, but his thinking was not wholly in discord with that of many Northerners. "I am not," wrote a New York *Times* correspondent who signed himself Quondam, "of the number who believe that the free Negro will do as much work as the slave, and that their production *per capita* will be as great as before. Anyone well acquainted with the race knows their improvidence, recklessness and need of direction . . . [though] they are for the most part civil, obedient, and docile."

The emancipation of the slaves was, demonstrably, secondary to the preservation of the Union. Lincoln himself had written Horace Greeley on August 22, 1862, "My paramount object in this struggle is to save the Union, and it is not either to save or to destroy slavery. If I could save the Union without freeing any slave, I would do it; and if I could save it by freeing some and leaving others alone, I would also do that."

As a Midwesterner, the president had grown up on rather neutral ground, where a black face was scarcely a common sight.

Now, the question of what to do with the legally freed remained in the forefront. Ben Truman, in his journeys, concluded, the "vast majority" in that section of the nation held that "the Negro occupies a middle ground between the human races and the animal . . . It is the former slave owners who are the best friends the Negro has in the South . . . while it is the 'poor whites' that are his enemies. It is from these he suffers most. In a state of slavery they hated him; and now that he is free, there is no striking abatement of this sentiment . . . Everywhere, the inoffensive Negro is exposed to their petty and contemptible persecutions . . .

"The cruelties and all its outward forms have entirely passed away; but, as might have been expected, glimmerings of its vassalage, its subserviency, and its helplessness linger."

There had also been the matter of relocation. In fact, this had been a recurring possibility during and immediately after the war. Abraham Lincoln had endorsed an ill-starred colonization off Haiti in 1863. A smaller group sailed from Baltimore in October 1865 for Liberia. Johnson was but one of a number of Northern leaders after the Great Emancipator who favored or hoped for some sort of resettlement for the former slaves. Secretary Seward, with reservations, went along with such reasoning.

This February, General Sherman was reviewing for President Johnson a situation which was responsible for ever increasing unhappiness among the landowners of Georgia's Sea Islands. He stressed the need to provide for the vast numbers of blacks who had followed the army from the interior of Georgia, "as also of those who had already congregated on the island near Hilton Head [South Carolina] and were still coming into our lines. We agreed perfectly that the young and able-bodied men should be enlisted as soldiers or employed by the quartermaster in the necessary work of unloading ships, and for other Army purposes. But this left on our hands the old and feeble, the women and children . . ."

Stanton had come to Savannah shortly after the occupation and talked with the old blacks, "mostly preachers." According to Sherman, the secretary of war came away "satisfied the Negroes could, with some little aid from us by means of the abandoned plantations on the Sea Islands and along the navigable rivers, take care of themselves." Knowing that the army had no right to "convey title," the general issued order number 15, valid only for the duration of the military occupation, "aimed to make provision for Negroes who were absolutely dependent on us."

Frances Butler Leigh was one of many who had fled from the Sea Islands. Now, at last, she had quit her wartime home in New York for Butler's, the family plantation on St. Simons Island. Her journey southward was a sad and sentimental one. She had paused in Richmond, where, after some searching, she "found the grave I was looking for . . . There he lay, with hundreds of others who had sacrificed their lives in vain."

She continued to Greensboro, North Carolina, presumably accompanied by her father and a German maid acquired in New York. The hotel in Greensboro was "a miserable tumbledown old frame house, and the room we were shown into more fit for a stable than human habitation; a dirty bare floor, the panes more than half broken out of the windows, with two ragged, dirty calico curtains over them that waved and blew about in the wind. The furniture consisted of a bed, the clothes of which looked as if they had not been changed since the war, but had been slept in, in the meanwhile, constantly, two rickety old chairs, and a table with three legs.

"The bed being entirely out of the question, and I very tired, I took my bundle of shawls, put them under my head against the wall, tilted my chair back, and prepared to go to sleep if I could. I was just dozing off when I heard my maid . . . a little German girl, give a start and exclamation . . . a huge rat had just run across the floor . . . We spent the rest of the night shivering and shaking with the cold, and knocking on the floor with our umbrellas to frighten away the rats, which from time to time came out to look at us.

"At four in the morning my father came for us, and we started for the train, driving two miles in an old army ambulance."

From then on, Frances' journey was a potpourri of trains, wagons, an "old broken-down stage coach," former army conveyances, and more trains until she finally arrived in Columbia, South Carolina. Frances was unprepared for the "long line of blackened ruins . . . it was too horrible!"

On to Augusta, Georgia, she progressed, where she slept all of three hours, and soon east toward Savannah. During this journey, "we were jolted and banged over a road composed entirely of ruts and roots, until I thought I should not have a whole bone left in my body." But there was consolation: "It was a lovely evening . . . the moon rose full and clear. The air, delicious and balmy, was filled with the resinous scent of the pine and perfume of yellow jessamine, and we were a very jolly party, four gentlemen, with ourselves, making up our number, so I thought it good fun on the whole. In fact, rough as the journey was, I rather enjoyed it all . . ."

In Savannah she thought the people "crushed," but she found "no bitterness towards the North; they are too sad to be bitter; their grief is overwhelming. Nothing can make any difference to them now: the women live in the past, and the men only in the daily present, trying in a listless sort of way to repair their ruined fortunes.

"They are like so many foreigners, whose only interest in the country is their own individual business. Politics are never mentioned, and they know and care less about what is going on in Washington than in London. They received us with open arms, my room was filled with flowers, and crowds of people called upon me every day, and overwhelmed me with thanks for what I did for their soldiers during the war, which really did amount to but very little." Frances, modestly enough, did not confide the reason for their gratitude. It was understood, however, that she had visited Confederate prisoners in the Manhattan area and at the notorious Elmira camp, New York State.

Her father went ahead to Butler's on St. Simons. He bore somewhat surprising news on his return. All the Negroes left at the island had remained there, and there were others in addition, including some who had been sold several years before.

"They received him very affectionately," Frances wrote, "and made an agreement with him to work for one half the crop, which agreement it remained to be seen if they would keep. Most of the finest plantations were lying idle for want of hands to work them, so many of the negroes had died . . . Many had been taken to the Southwest, and others perferred hanging about the towns, making a few dollars now and then . . . so most people found it impossible to get any laborers.

"My father also reported that the house was bare, not a bed nor chair left, and that he had been sleeping on the floor, with a piece of wood for a pillow and a few negro blankets for his covering. This I could hardly do, and as he could attend to nothing but the planting, we agreed that he should devote himself to that, while I looked after some furniture. So the day after, armed with 500 bushels of seed rice, corn, bacon, a straw mattress, and a tub, he started off again for the plantation, leaving me to buy tables and chairs, pots and pans."

When Frances' furniture arrived it more resembled "the possessions of an Irish emigrant than anything else; the house linen fortunately was in pretty good order, but the rest I fancy had furnished the overseer's house in the country ever since the war; the silver never reappeared. So I began my purchases with twelve common wooden chairs, four washstands, four bedsteads, four large tubs, two bureaux, two large tables and four smaller ones, some china, and one common lounge, my one luxury—and this finished the list."

At last, the end of the journey, on the ferry to St. Simons, but "we stuck fast on a sandbar in the river where we remained six hours, very hot, and devoured by sand flies, till the tide came in."

They arrived at the town of Darien at 1:00 A.M. in bright moonlight. Her father was waiting, and they "were rowed across to the island by four of our old negroes." Then the plantation:

"The floors were bare, of course, many of the panes were out of the windows, and the plaster in many places was off the walls, while one table and two old chairs constituted the furniture. It was pretty desolate, and my father looked at me in some anxiety to see how it would affect me, and seemed greatly relieved when I burst out laughing. My bed was soon unpacked and made, my tub filled, my basin and pitcher mounted on a barrel, and I settled for the rest of the night.

"The next morning I and my little German maid, who fortunately takes everything very cheerily, went to work, and together we made things quite comfortable; unpacked our tables and chairs, put up some curtains (made out of some white muslin I had brought down for petticoats) edged with pink calico, covered the tables with two bright-colored covers I found in the trunk of house linen, had the windows mended, hung up my picture of General Lee . . .

"I have one large pot, one frying pan, one tin saucepan, and this is all; and yet you would be astonished to see how much our cook accomplishes with these three utensils, and the things don't taste *very* much alike."

One meal at least was supplied by a former slave, who shot and presented the family with a turkey, inspiring Frances' conclusion, "The negroes seem perfectly happy at getting back to the old place."

Elsewhere in the nation, life and endeavor had glowed brilliantly, only suddenly to sputter out. For example, at February's close, in the oil fields of Pennsylvania, there was continuing disaster.

Workmen using the so newly introduced nitroglycerin were blowing themselves up as frequently as the railroad builders in the west. Fires were incinerating wells, derricks, and occasionally entire communities. This month, eight wells at Bennehof Run, Petroleum Center, Pennsylvania, were burned to charred holes. They had been ignited by sparks from a pumping engine. The town itself was narrowly spared by the conflagration, which would never have started if the engine operators had been sober.

There were further leavenings to the oil boom. In the fall, the Homestead well in Pithole stopped flowing. The sudden drying up of the Seine in Paris could not have evoked more incredulity.

Production in a few wells dwindled, but most, like toppling tenpins, simply expired, without so much as a final squirt of the black stuff. The economy of Pithole was ruined.

Hotels closed, one by one, followed by the bars. There was no one to drink what liquor remained. Preachers turned the keys in the front doors of their churches, packed up, and trudged off. Certainly there were many more souls elsewhere wailing for salvation.

On the heels of the men of the cloth were the bankers, lawyers, doctors, and, last but scarcely least, the prostitutes.

Suddenly there were no more strident arguments, no more shootings, no more wheezes of the pumping machinery. A strange silence fell over a town that was barely a year old.

". . . Operators, speculators, businessmen and others quickly departed," was *The Nation*'s amen. "The eager throng of oil pilgrims had disappeared and Pithole was deserted."

Torn bits of newspapers, with dates not old at all, bills, receipts, letters telling of a frenetic optimism blew to and fro through silent, snow-flecked streets. Shutters banged out eerily their own requiem to shattered hopes and headlong, mindless greed.

Pithole had become the nation's newest, and surely youngest, ghost town.

MARCH

The Ides

In the Shenandoah, Jim Huffman, having brought new life and zest to his local log church and Sunday school, had turned to domestic concerns: "I thought if I had a helpmate I could weather the tide better and glide more sweetly. I needed everything but a wife, but I did not know that.

"I began to look around and when I found one I thought would suit, she was 25 miles away and I had no suitable horse nor conveyance; yet I managed to make a trip about once a month."

Courtship, it turned out, had to be conducted under continuing challenges. One old horse, warworn anyhow, needed to be shod. Then, when Huffman started out, a "big rainstorm" halted him dead. Another time he was riding "a little black woolly colt and it was raining to beat the band.

"When I got to the river, it was flush, very muddy and full of big round rocks. The little rascal had never seen the river and was afraid and went blundering along with his head up in the air, looking up and down the river."

As his rider had feared, the colt stumbled, drenching him. "I hit him with my umbrella and broke the staff and still the rain came down. My homespun clothes were wet, it was still raining and I had 19 miles to go. This made it gloomy for me . . ."

Undaunted, "after deliberating and considering the ups and downs and inconveniences," Jim Huffman decided this courtship was already too difficult and "protracted." He went to the popular Farrar and Clippinger's store in Harrisonburg and bought sufficient cloth for a tailor to make him a decent wedding suit. They were married, and, "after a sumptuous supper at the home of the bride (about 40 guests), the first half of the night was spent in an old-fashioned jollification and a good time.

"Next day we drove down to mother's, where another nice supper was served to a jolly crowd." So, with little money but robust determination, Huffman started married life, still struggling to ford the Shenandoah River and working long hours to realize his investment—$4,000—in a combined grist and sawmill.

Soon the mill was leveled by fire. No matter, he borrowed money and built another. And no more little "woolly colts," since Huffman now boasted a "four-horse team fully harnessed and equipped with fly straps, wagon with bed, and an extra horse for the other team . . ."

Jim Huffman was driving, if not necessarily for success, toward the comfortable family life of a miller and farmer in Page County, Virginia.

In Petersburg the life of another Virginian, Sara Pryor, remained in flux. Her children were showing progress in school, especially in the Romance languages, she was earning money giving piano lessons, and her husband, Roger, was experiencing modest success in his New York law practice. With a $50 check came the optimistic assurance that his family should be able to join him in a few months. This so heartened Sara that she took the short train ride to City Point to inquire about steamer schedules.

"City Point," she would write, "lately a place of strategic importance, where the great ships of the Federal Army [*sic*] were anchored, where Mr. Lincoln had been entertained by General Grant, where General Butler had long made his headquarters—was now silent and deserted. Not a shade tree, not a 'shanty' remained to mark the occupation of the Federal troops.

"An unsheltered platform afforded the only place for a traveler to rest while waiting for the boat, unless he could content himself with the dust-covered seats in the forlorn little [railroad] car and the limited view from the narrow, dirty car window. Out on the platform, seated on his own boxes, the traveler could see the sweep of the noble James River, broadened here into a sea as it took into its bosom the muddy waters of the

Appomattox. Landward there was little to be seen except an unbroken waste of dusty road and untilled field."

If no shanty existed nearby, there was a "small log cabin," in front of which "a suspicious hen was leading her brood as far from the engine as possible, and a pig in an odoriferous pen was leaping on the sides of his sty and clamoring for breakfast." At this point "a languid Negro woman" appeared from the cabin and confided she had come outside only "to see the boat pass."

Elsewhere in the South, other people were similarly picking up their lives as though reopening a book to a brand new chapter after it had been abruptly closed.

"Our town," wrote Mary Ann Cobb to her mother, from Athens in mid-March, "has been quite gay since you left. We have not had the opera but we have had concerts and exhibitions innumerable . . . the young ladies of the town gave a concert at the close of which the audience called for Dixie, and it was sung with a great deal of spirit. I suppose such exhibition of rebel [nostalgia] is the cause of our having a Yankee garrison with us now."

From Atlanta, a schoolteacher, Jennie Lines, the wife of Sylvanus Lines, was making a journal entry at the same time: "The war has been over almost a year, the last battle was fought on the river between Columbus, Georgia and Gerard, Alabama, and in the streets of Columbus.

"My experience of that last battle is too sad to write and I shall jump the two last years and commence keeping a domestic journal . . . Night before last we had a little shower, the first we had in three weeks, the wind has been blowing from the northeast ever since and the cold is increasing. Fruit trees are in bloom and our garden is mostly planted and nearly all the seeds up . . . Have for dinner asparagus, the first vegetable of the season . . ."

Like Frances Leigh on St. Simons, Susan Dabney had "come home to a house denuded of nearly every article of furniture." She wrote of Burleigh, in Mississippi. While her father, Thomas Smith Dabney, had been away on Confederate business in Montgomery for most of the war, the plantation had been stripped of all its cultivating implements. A few mules and a cow constituted the livestock.

"We had brought a few pieces of common furniture from Georgia," she continued, "and a very few necessary articles were bought. In the course of time, some home-made contrivances and comforts relieved the desolate appearance of the rooms, but no attempt was ever made to refurnish the house."

Thus far there had been no apparent change in either the attitude or the work habits of the former slaves: "Those who worked in the fields went out as usual, and cultivated and gathered in the crops. In the house, they went about their customary duties. We expected them to go away, or to demand wages, or at least to give some sign that they knew they were free. But, except that they were very quiet and serious, and more obedient and kind than they had ever been known to be for more than a few weeks, at a time of sickness or other affliction, we saw no change in them.

"At Christmas such compensation was made them for their services as seemed just. Afterwards, fixed wages were offered and accepted. Thomas called them up now and told them as they no longer belonged to him they must discontinue calling him 'master.'

" 'Yes, marster, yes, marster,' was the answer to this. They seem to bring in 'master' and say it oftener than they ever did, was his comment, as he related the occurrence to his children. This was true. The name seemed to grow into a term of endearment."

This affection was expressed even by the blacks on neighboring plantations. Susan could only conclude they were proud to live on the estate of Thomas Dabney, who was almost seventy, and work for him. So with what was left for raising cotton and food, activity and, sometimes, happiness returned to Burleigh.

But not for long. Susan's father one evening announced to his children, "I am a ruined man. The sheriff is downstairs. He has served this writ on me." He had foolishly underwritten several business notes for his friends, and now they were called.

"The Burleigh plantation was put up at auction and sold," Susan wrote, "but the privilege of buying it in a certain time reserved. At this time incendiary fires were common. There was not much law in the land. We heard of the gin houses and cotton houses that were burned in all directions."

One day their gin house with all the cotton inside was burned. This meant now her father had to "borrow the money to buy a postage stamp." It was not surprising when the elder Dabney advised his family. "My children, I shall have nothing to leave you but a fair name." But they all worked and persevered, and little by little began to accumulate a new equity in the plantation.

Almost fourteen years would elapse before Dabney was solvent and then he was nearly on his deathbed.

"The spring has opened," wrote David Schenck, of Lincolnton, North Carolina, "and our people seem invigorated and ready for industrious labor and enterprise." Schenck, a lawyer whose poor health had kept him out of the war, continued on a generally optimistic note, in his diary entry dated March 13: "Our farmers especially are improving their farms and preparing for large crops. Our young men are leaving off idleness and dissipation and seeking employment and labor and all businessmen are adventuring on new projects to improve their fortunes and the material prosperity of the country.

"The Freedmen's Bureau as they become enlightened in the character of the Negro are relaxing their annoyances of the people and the Negroes are fast becoming industrious and civilized. They have here now a flourishing school of 108 scholars taught by a Quaker Yankee who suits them very well. They have also organized a colored Methodist church and are doing as well as their ignorance will allow.

"All would be well with us as we are quiet and unresisting, endeavoring to make the most out of our sad misfortunes but the *Radicals* in Congress are howling like incarnate fiends—taxing their ingenuity and wickedness to invent new modes of torture and insult for us which would soon grind us to powder but for the fine, undaunted stand of President Johnson, who stands thus far adamant against them."

Schenck denounced the Civil Rights Bill from "a mad and Jacobinical Congress" as abolishing "all evil distinctions in the South on account of race of color . . . making their laws [of the states] and judiciary at the mercy of Congress." United States revenue officers "have already drained the county of almost every cent . . . I am still trying to keep soul and body together. I can barely live by the closest economy . . . Our hope now is that the present yield of wheat now being harvested promises to be abundant, and our other crops of corn and oats are also growing finely."

The erstwhile slaves were "working tolerably well and getting remunerative wages, but their want of proper economy and management brings most of them to abject poverty. When sickness comes, they die for want of attention, and there seems no disposition among them to assume the responsibility or care of marriage.

"The next decade will show an alarming decrease in the race, and the work of extermination will be shown in such terms that no one can deny the law of natural destruction to inferior races. The black races will follow the footsteps of his tawny predecessors but his liability to disease and his indolent carelessness will leave but few of his race to be colonized."

Schenck then disgressed: "I am just now repairing my lot, improving my garden, sowing clover, attending to Law, business, etc., etc., which keeps my hands and brains busy day and night. I have but little rest but labor is always sweet when money is the reward, which adds comfort and cheer to the household. I am very happy in quiet life now with my dear wife and interesting children . . ."

Some of the older children in North Carolina were themselves "interesting"—among them Pauline Cameron, of Hillsborough, near Chapel Hill, who was writing to her sister, Anne: "I must beg you to forgive me for not fulfilling my promise before but I have not had an opportunity. I commenced going to school very soon after you left. I take music and French and seven English studies. I am kept very busy nearly all of the afternoon studying. I have just finished the tales of the borders. I like them very much. I am glad to tell you that mother has been better yesterday and today than she has been since she has been sick . . . excuse haste and bad writing . . ."

Six days later Pauline wrote that Dr. J. Jones had arrived "very unexpectedly." This seemed fortuitous since both mother and daughter now were ailing, Pauline with a bad cold: ". . . Mrs. Rowland sent her a basket of the nicest oysters you ever saw already pickled. They were perfectly delightful and just as fat as could be . . . I hope you have enough milk with 16 cows. What are the names of Lillie's pups? How many chickens have you got?"

Sickness this spring continued to be the unwelcome visitor in many if not most households, in all states but especially the Southern. Mary Elizabeth Rives, a thirty-seven-year-old widow who lived on a plantation near Mansfield, Louisiana, wrote in her regularly kept diary, "Time was spent at Bro. Lewis' nursing his little babe. He was very ill indeed. We looked for him to die. Dear little one. His sufferings were intense, pneumonia and inflammation of the bowels. Dr. Bailey with his infinitesimal doses, homeopathy and our grand nursing did wonders, but not our works saved him but God . . .

"I have met with several old friends, been on Canal Street [in New Orleans] several times or more, shopping considerably, spent more money than was absolutely, actually, really necessary. Had a dozen pictures of my own self taken for $25 a dozen."

As March of 1866 neared an end, challenges continued to be experienced in places measurably higher than the average Southern household. For Andrew Johnson, the ides had already passed.

On March 27, the president vetoed the Civil Rights Bill. It had been introduced by a moderate Republican, Senator Lyman Trumbull, of Connecticut. Labeled merely "An Act to protect all persons in the United States in their civil rights, and furnish the means for their vindication," it was far more specific in its details, noting that "all persons of African descent born in the United States" were automatically to be declared citizens. Through its many sections, it not only enumerated their rights but provided relatively harsh penalties for violations.

Johnson observed in his veto message: ". . . All persons born in the United States and not subject to any foreign power, excluding Indians not taxed, are declared to be citizens . . . this provision comprehends the Chinese of the Pacific States, Indians subject to taxation, the people called Gypsies, as well as the entire race designated as blacks, people of color, Negroes, mulattoes, and persons of African blood. Every individual of those races, born in the United States, is by the bill made a citizen . . . It does not purport to declare or confer any other right of citizenship . . .

"The bill in effect proposes discrimination against large numbers of intelligent, worthy and patriotic foreigners, and in favor of the Negro . . . from his previous unfortunate condition of servitude . . . less informed than those who voluntarily came to the country and who were supposedly familiar with the institutions of government, yet had to face an arbitrary five-years' probation before becoming citizens."

Having successfully vetoed only the month before an attempt to expand and prolong the Freedmen's Bureau, Johnson was especially displeased at the "punishing" provisions of the new bill, which would empower agents of the bureau to make arrests. In addition, it would authorize the appointment of special officers and commissioners to bird-dog violations, "even to call to their aid such portion of the land and naval forces of the United States, or of the militia 'as may be necessary to the performance of the duty with which they are charged.' "

This the chief executive branded an "extraordinary power," as he continued: "To me, the details of the bill seem fraught with evil. The white race and the black race of the South have hitherto lived together under the relation of master and slave . . . They stand now each master of itself . . . This [bill] frustrates this adjustment" to a new relation.

"In all our history, in all our experience as a people living under Federal and State law, no such system as that contemplated by the details of this bill has ever before been proposed or adopted . . . It is another step, or rather stride toward centralization and the concentration of all legislative power in the national Government. The tendency of the bill must be to resuscitate the spirit of rebellion, and to arrest the progress of those influences which are more closely drawing around the States the bonds of union and peace."

The bill was passed over his veto within two weeks. The Radicals had been heating up their attack on Johnson not only for his Freedmen's veto but also because of an intemperate, sometimes maudlin speech, or harangue, made extemporaneously on Washington's birthday. He had assailed as traitors the leaders of the party that had elected him to office and singled out such powerful figures as Charles Sumner, Thaddeus Stevens, Ben Wade, other Radical Republicans, and more. Impartially, he had lashed out at those in and out of Congress, North and South, including the orator and abolitionist Wendell Phillips.

Inevitably, the opposition to the president solidified, its focus sharpened. Whereas his foes had earlier called him "a wrong-headed and obstinate man," now he had risen, or sunk, to "a genius in depravity," an "irresolute mule," or, in an opprobrium borrowed from astronomy, a "hole in the sky," a vacuum, a nothing. The New York *Tribune* addressed him as "Judas Johnson," others simply as a traitor. Those who rolled the longer epithets from forked tongues damned him as an "illiterate, coarse, vulgar southerner."

Moreover, he possessed "the face of a demagogue, the heart of a traitor." He was "touched with insanity," also was "corrupt, drunk." All in all, in the realm of vilification, there wasn't much left unsaid.

Led by his arch-enemy, Horace Greeley, the press, with a very few exceptions such as the New York *Times,* was baying after the seventeenth president.

Perhaps it was but part of the backwash of an all-encompassing civil war.

And so the first year after the collapse of the Confederacy ended. It had been marked by mingled progress and reverses, accomplishments and disappointments, compassion and vengeance. The upheaval attending the cessation of so emotional a conflict was profound, far reaching, yet conceivably less than might have been anticipated.

Next to ruins new structures were rising. Beside the charred timbers of barns crops were planted again. Tracks stretched once more over roadbeds that recently had borne only the ashes of ties and twisted travesties of once straight rails. There were fresh graves in village and country cemeteries from New England to the Gulf. But there was also the cry of newborn babies in tens of thousands of households, great and small.

Life was stubborn, durable. If in some hearts loneliness and despair lingered, there was, as well, hope, love, and timeless human needs and longings, together with the simple commonplaces of being.

"I hope you will keep well. We are lonesome but we are getting along very well; and I would not have you to neglect your interest to come home till your business is fully settled," wrote Elizabeth Brown from Atlanta to her husband, Joseph E. Brown, who was rarely in one place for three consecutive days.

"Today and last night has been very rainy and has tried our roof; our bedroom leaked in several places and the rooms above in all the old places. I do hope it will clear off this evening, as it is turning very cold . . .

"John will kill one of the little shoats this eve; it has been so wet that they have been compelled to stay in their house most of the day. I charge them (the children) to be very careful about fires. Andy is living at Uncle William's; it is a good home for him, but I am sorry for such stingy folks to be waited on for nothing. Maria, Alice and Gus work for $120 a year.

"The *Christian Index* comes to me. Did you subscribe for it? If not, I presume you will have to pay for it. It is a very good paper. I still have a very bad cold, but hope when the weather clears off, I will feel better.

"The children are as well as usual and all join me in much love to you. May our Kind Heavenly Father preserve you from all harm. I have written on the blank leaf of your letter; not very good paper, but I trust you may be able to read . . . The children send howdy to the Negroes.

"Ever your own devoted wife . . ."

And to the east, in Savannah, another young wife, alone, was penning: "I am so blue and low spirited that I must relieve my mind by sitting down and having a long talk with you. I went to sleep after the train passed and woke but once, at 6, between that time and 9 o'clock. So I am not tired at all this morning, which I guess is more than you can say. You looked so miserably when you got up this morning that I keep thinking of it and fearing you are ill today. I know you are not well and I am wretched to be away from you. I am sick of being away from you, my love . . ."

So wrote the beautiful, vivacious Nelly Gordon, descendant of one of Chicago's oldest families, the Kinzies. Nelly, thirty-one, had married William Washington Gordon, of about the same age, a Savannah cotton merchant, and spent most of the war in that Georgia port with her two young daughters, while her husband Willy was away fighting with Jeb Stuart's cavalry. When Sherman, who happened to be distantly related to the Kinzies, captured Savannah in December 1864, he not only called on the dark-haired Nelly but helped her return to her parents in Chicago. Families of Confederate officers were, in many cases, compelled to make their homes available to the occupation forces.

Nelly now was back at the familiar Savannah homestead, at the corner of Bull and Oglethorpe, while Willy was traveling in the interest of reestablishing business. He had more orders for cotton than he could possibly fill. She went on, "You don't take care of yourself when I am not with you—and you will certainly be ill. *Please* try to work less and eat and drink more. I hate to be away from you, my own!

"I love you every moment of my life, and I want to be with you always.

"I don't see how I can entertain the idea of going north this fall to meet Mother. If you could pay me a thousand dollars to go now, I would not do it.

"Can't you spare *one* day to me and stay till Monday afternoon next time?

"Now that tiresome worrying affair is not occupying you, you could have more time and less work I should think. You ought to consider my interests and your own, as well as that of the firm. How can I bear to see you get too thin and weak and miserable for slaving at business? No, I *can't*—and I *won't!*

"You must try to recruit, and I must be with you, as soon as I can. Don't you think so, my Darling?

"I wish you would see Jimmy Read and get him to write you the prescription for that *Gentran Tonic* and make Mary Anne go and get it and set it by you at every meal, so that you can remember to take it. I can imagine that you will get this and read it at night; and I wish it were me 3instead of my note. I would love you so, and pet and coddle you. But I can't do it—it makes me mad. Good bye my own dear Love! Please remember how precious you are to your devoted little Wifie . . ."

EPILOGUE

On Monday, April 2, 1866, Andrew Johnson, as president of the United States, did "hereby proclaim and declare that the insurrection which heretofore existed in the States of Georgia, South Carolina, Virginia, North Carolina, Tennessee, Alabama, Louisiana, Arkansas, Mississippi and Florida is at an end and is henceforth to be so regarded." Since its government was not yet formed, Texas was excepted.

It remained for the individual states to reorganize their governments and constitutions then seek readmission to the Union.

The chief executive's legal ghosts reviewed at length the proclamations, commencing with that of April 15, 1861, declaring the seceded states "in a state of insurrection," and the progressive steps taken to crush the rebellion. The writ of habeas corpus, denied with such zeal to Mary Surratt, was restored to the "misguided citizens" of these states. While asserting that "standing armies" or a "military occupation" was "incompatible with the individual rights of the citizens," the proclamation nonetheless did not elaborate on how, when, or at what rate the troops were to be withdrawn from the South.

With peace, the good old summertime was reverting to former connotations and diversions. This first full year without war, the innkeepers of vacation spots for those who could not afford a steamship to Europe dusted the lobbies, painted and freshened their bedrooms, and hung out welcome signs: Saratoga Springs, Lake Champlain, Newport, Long Branch, Cape May, and Atlantic City were among these resorts.

Atlantic City, increasingly gaudy, could accommodate 10,000 vacationers in upwards of seventy hotels—all frame—and numerous small cottages. Those listed as hostelries ranged from the giant United States, boasting

250 rooms at $3.50 a night, and the Congress Hall, almost as large, down to diminutive establishments with a few bedrooms renting at $1 a night. General Grant had a liking for the United States (perhaps because of his own initials), which was built in 1854. It, like the Congress Hall, was distinguished by its turreted plywood corners.

"All the cottages, furnished and unfurnished, have been taken and the renters do not object to paying $500 or $600 for the short period of seven or eight weeks," wrote the correspondent for the New York *Tribune* in June. "The guests, like those at the Chester County House, wander about passages, they gossip on sofas, they take meteorological observations through telescopes, and they anticipate the ringing of the dinner bell.

"Her first class hotels I doubt not are first class. But all that are not first class are sixth class. There is no grade between. But still Atlantic City fills up a very useful place. She is the excursion train watering place of the nation."

The Camden and Atlantic Railroad, in operation only since 1854, lurched between the Philadelphia area and the seashore with doubtful comfort, according to the same reporter: "Sardine boxes convey but a feeble impression of the contiguity that exists between the human sardines on an Atlantic City excursion train. Sometimes the passengers hang themselves by their waist bands (there is such a rush for seats) and reach their destination purple in the face . . . I am convinced that chicken coops and cattle in wagons are utterly effete, threadbare attempts at parallel in describing the tortures of the excursionists who inundate Atlantic City."

Then, as a musing amen, the *Tribune*'s writer concluded, "She is all sand. She has no beautiful inland rivers. She is a poor, plain little creature trying to make the best of herself." "She" did not even have a boardwalk yet; this, along with saltwater taffy, was still a few years on the horizon.

July arrived, the first anniversary of the execution of Mary Surratt.

Others, more lowly placed, also took note this April. For example, there was Virginia Mosby in Warrenton, Virginia: "This day one year ago Gen. Lee surrendered our cause to overwhelming numbers, a day we can never forget. Johnson is doing all to restore our distracted country, but he is beset by a vile clan of radicals that I fear will bring about another cruel war."

This spring, in spite of the "vile clan of radicals," Johnson commenced relenting on the imprisoned Confederates. On April 21, the piece of paper over which Virginia Clay had pleaded, cajoled, and sometimes threatened ever since her husband's incarceration was signed: an order for the release of Clement C. Clay from Fort Monroe. The winsome brunette had been rebuffed repeatedly by Secretary Stanton and Judge Holt. Holt at least, still convinced of Clay's "sinister" shadow behind the assassination, would have preferred to see the Alabama statesman hanged.

Nevertheless, Virginia Clay obtained from General Grant a strong recommendation for her husband's release. Then, by her untiring persistence, she finally impressed Andrew Johnson. He went so far as to compliment her for a recent letter, stating, "It is a most powerful appeal. You have excelled yourself in its production."

Senator James H. Lane had been increasingly depressed ever since his old friend Preston King had jumped off the ferry in New York. The Kansas Republican, who had helped King bar Annie Surratt's access to President Johnson, himself had no history of mental illness. That he had once shot and killed a man and that his wartime commission as brigadier general of volunteers had been revoked after a few months did not necessarily add up to instability.

However, when he returned home in June to attempt, unsuccessfully, to explain his support of Johnson's veto of the Civil Rights Bill, Lane suddenly commenced acting irrationally. In St. Louis, complaining of insomnia, dizziness, melancholia, and other symptoms, he was restrained by a doctor from leaping out of a hotel window. He expressed a morbid fear of death and asked to be admitted to "an insane asylum." His physician, asserting there was no adequate one in the area, assured the legislator that he did not need this drastic treatment anyway. Instead he urged Lane to take a little vacation, see his friends, relax.

He was escorted to the farm of his brother-in-law, McCall. Thinking his patient to be improving, the doctor left. But he had misjudged Jim Lane. On July 1, a Sunday, the senator, discovering a derringer (similar to that employed by Booth) on the mantel, walked with it outside. He sat down, placed the barrel in his mouth, and pulled the trigger. He lingered in a coma until July 11 before expiring.

Thus there had violently arisen a vacancy in the U.S. Senate. Governor Samuel J. Crawford, the last of the "war governors," appointed a little-known Kansas editor, Edmund G. Ross. Although most if not all of the Radical Republicans had never heard of Ross, they believed they could readily control this novice lawmaker.

Some two weeks following Lane's suicide, on July 27, Cyrus Field telegraphed from Heart's Content, Newfoundland, to President Johnson: "Sir: the Atlantic Cable was successfully completed this morning. I hope that it will prove a blessing to England and the United States, and increase the intercourse between our own country and the eastern hemisphere . . ."

At last the *Great Eastern* had succeeded after so much failure. The old cable was dredged up. In a few weeks, the combined transmission of the two had a potential of 1,500 words an hour. The rate, starting at $5 a word, was shortly halved. There was no dearth of messages, especially from the press, enamored with this bonanza. The backlog lengthened by the hour.

But not all news was good this summer. In May, an estimated forty-six blacks had been killed in racial disturbances in Memphis, which had been inspired partly by the presence there of the Third United States Colored Artillery. Without documentation, a New York *Tribune* correspondent wrote of dozens of Negroes—specifically 153—killed in Mississippi and Arkansas since the beginning of the year. Then, on July 30, delegates met in the Mechanics Institute in New Orleans for the stated purpose of remodeling the Louisiana state constitution to hasten suffrage of Negroes. It was actually an illegal reconvening of a convention that had adjourned in 1864.

Simultaneously, a group of some 130 blacks, led by a dentist, Dr. Dostie, marched on the meeting hall, presumably to add pressure to the voting. This in itself was inflammatory to many hot-headed whites who did not themselves possess the vote. Armed with weapons, bars, clubs, and knives, they assembled in a countermob.

The result was much the same as what would result from tossing a torch into a barrel of powder. Wrote the *Annual Cyclopedia:* "Missiles were thrown, shots fired, and finally the Negro crowd scattering wide, ran back toward the building; the great body took refuge in the entrance to the institute, out of which they fired on the police, who fired back in return . . . Soon the firing was transferred from the front of the building to either side, where the Negroes as they appeared were stoned by the crowd outside . . . The Negroes who came out of the front door, as well as those who were dropping from the windows, one by one, were inhumanly attacked and killed."

Confederate flags were unfurled and waved brazenly, in defiance of all of the laws of occupation. Such display only underscored the assumption

that the melee and its inception in die-hard secessionists attacking Union-
ists.

Reporting it, Major General Philip H. Sheridan (who had been in Texas
at the time), commanding the Military Division of the Gulf, declared, "It
was a riot; it was an absolute massacre by the police . . ." He thereby
accused the civil authorities. Dr. Dostie was among the fifty-some killed.
Scores had been injured.

The Radical Republicans, who dumped the blame on the White House
doorstep, thumped that this was but another case in point: Reconstruction
could continue only under the mailed fist.

The hapless president, whether in the right or wrong, was unable to
make friends. His veto of the Colorado Statehood Bill (although sustained) had alienated another 30,000 voters. Desperately, he resolved to
take his case for extreme leniency toward the South to the people. This he
did in the waning summer weeks through a "swing around the circle,"
traveling by train as far west as Chicago. The Radical Republicans (who
would win overwhelmingly in the November elections) orchestrated many
chilly receptions.

Yet Andrew Johnson was not the only driven and disquieted man in
government. Judge Holt himself remained haunted by his memories and
deeds alike. His distress was compounded by the recent admission of and
indictment for perjury of Sanford Conover, one of the Surratt witnesses
whose testimony had proven so devastating. On September 11, in anguish,
Holt wrote to Secretary Stanton: ". . . Charges of the utmost gravity,
affecting my official integrity and conduct, have been preferred against me
. . . to the effect that . . . I suborned testimony which was used upon that
trial and secured the conviction of Mrs. Surratt."

Branding "these accusations" as "utterly false and groundless," Holt
demanded as vindication of his "official honor" that a court of inquiry be
appointed to probe the affair. The trouble was, no one, no governmental
body had charged him with anything. It was what people *thought* that
haunted and tormented him.

The War Department would not assuage him. It curtly replied that the
president was "satisfied with the honesty and fidelity of the Judge Advocate
General." And so the jurist continued in his own private purgatory.

A week later, on the nineteenth, one of the frequent bulletins on the
health of Jefferson Davis was logged in at the War Department from Fort
Monroe: "I respectfully report the health of state prisoner Jefferson Davis

to be much the same as the 16th instant. He complains still of the rheumatic affection of the right shoulder, and also of a sensation of fullness of the head, with a tendency to vertigo."

Nevertheless, according to Surgeon George E. Cooper, Davis's "digestion is comparatively good," and "he sleeps better than heretofore."

There remained others in the South who, like the former Confederate leader, would not admit defeat or that there was anything inherently wrong with secession, and who continued to marvel at why the federal government had been so upset at the rebellion. Among them was Augusta Jane Evans, of Athens, Georgia.

"I do not accept the conclusion of the war as a test of its legitimacy or its expediency," wrote the thirty-one-year-old author of *Beulah* and other novels. "Might often crushes but never makes right. Today—the right of secession is more holy than five years ago. For now it has been sanctified, baptized anew, with the blood of our Legion of Liberty's martyrs. I have an abiding faith that the cause for which we have suffered so much will yet triumph . . . though I shall perhaps be in my quiet grave 'ere it comes."

(The wartime nurse for Confederate casualties who had denounced the Union troops as "hireling hordes of oppression" found that "quiet grave" in 1909, her faith still unfulfilled. But nearly two decades later her name would return to prominence when one of her novels, *St. Elmo,* was produced as a silent film starring John Gilbert, Warner Baxter, and Bessie Love.)

The Indian situation showed no improvement as 1866 ended, quite the opposite. Settlers in Dakota Territory, especially, were under almost constant attack. At Fort Phil Kearny, on December 21, shots were heard after a wagon train had started out for timber. A cavalry force of eighty-one men was hastened from the strongpoint. The soldiers were ambushed by at least 2,000 Sioux, Cheyennes, and some Arapahoes, led perhaps by Chief Red Cloud. Not a trooper survived.

National outrage was renewed. "We must act in vindictive earnestness against the Sioux!" thumped General Sherman. The press called for a return of the Chivington-Connor campaigns of attrition, if not utter extermination. These wishes were partly realized through the replacement of the mild Pope by Major General Winfield Scott Hancock as commander of the Department of the Missouri. On his staff was the dashing Lieutenant Colonel George Armstrong Custer (brevetted a major general during the war).

Soon Hancock's cavalrymen were burning Indian villages, slaughtering their inhabitants, and thus inviting equally savage reprisals. It was unfortunate, Custer would write, that novelists such as James Fenimore Cooper had presented "a false and ill-judged estimate of the Indian character," depicting the Indian as an "innocent, simple-minded being," with other appealing qualities. That General Hancock was forced back on the counterattack was rationalized in part by Custer: "Nature intended him [the Indian] for a savage state; every instinct, every impulse of his soul inclines him to it. He cannot . . . be civilized . . . [and is] guilty of numerous thefts and murders. They [the Cheyennes and Sioux] had attacked him stations of the overland mail route, killed the employees, burned the stations, and captured the stock. Citizens had been murdered in their homes on the frontier of Kansas; murders had been committed on the Arkansas route."

And so the Indian wars continued, well past the midpoint of the nineteenth century.

In many respects more jolting than this bloodshed on the frontier, however, was a verdict by the Supreme Court on December 17, four days before the Fort Phil Kearny massacre. On that date the highest judicial body handed down, in *ex parte Milligan,* the opinion that civilians could not be tried by military tribunals if civil courts were in session. Such armed services commissions were sanctioned early in the war by Lincoln himself. The historic decision meant, immediately, as one observer put it, that the hangings of Mary Surratt, Wirz, and others were "no better than lynchings."

The majority opinion (5–4) written by Justice David Davis, of Maryland, held: "The Constitution of the United States is a law for rulers and people, equally in war and in peace, and covers with the shield of its protection all classes of men, at all times and under all circumstances. No doctrine, involving more pernicious consequences, was ever invented by the wit of man than that any of the provisions can be suspended during any of the great exigencies of government . . . martial law cannot arise from a *threatened* invasion. The necessity must be actual and present; the invasion real, such as effectually closes the [civil] courts . . . Martial rule can never exist where the courts are open, and in the proper and unobstructed exercise of their jurisdiction. It is also confined to the locality of actual war."

The four dissenting jurists, although they generally agreed with the spirit of the decision, held that Congress might want to authorize such commissions in "certain cases." Lambdin P. Milligan, a Confederate supporter, had been arrested in Indiana in 1864 on charges of giving aid and comfort to the enemy. His lawyers, after he had been sentenced to death by the military, applied for a writ of habeas corpus, charging that his constitutional rights to a jury trial had been denied.

Subsequently, President Johnson commuted his sentence to life imprisonment. Now the Supreme Court had set him free.

The chief executive, who far too late recognized the evil of military tribunals and of the suspension of habeas corpus, expressed his satisfaction with the historic ruling. The Radical Republicans, who counted on military panels as a natural bludgeon for imposing their will on the South, bemoaned the loss of this prop. Thaddeus Stevens saw the decision as a "knife of the rebel at the throat of every man who now or ever had declared himself a loyal Union man." Wendell Phillips went so far as to suggest the abolition of the court.

It survived, but in a limping state after a law was passed, over presidential veto, limiting its appellate jurisdiction in cases involving Reconstruction. This the justices acknowledged several months after *Milligan* in *ex parte McCardle,* which concerned a Mississippi newspaper editor who had been arrested for criticizing Reconstruction. The court, bowing supinely to the Radicals, declared it was without jurisdiction in this case.

Thus having pushed the Supreme Court to the ropes, Congress was ready to take on the president. And it did, in 1867, through successive resolutions, charging Andrew Johnson with "usurpation of power" and numerous "high crimes and misdemeanors," including "corruptly using appointing, pardoning and veto" powers. His "treachery" and alleged espousal of the "rebel cause" was at the same time assailed. Even his "morals," or their conceivable lack, did not escape vilification.

The Radicals' barrage, however, was premature; the early impeachment efforts were abortive. Even Horace Greeley's fire-breathing *Tribune* was compelled to counsel moderation.

Finally, the House Judiciary Committee, reporting that there was not "sufficient evidence" to justify so grave an action, passed the matter on to the new Congress, the fortieth.

Many, nonetheless, continued to hold the president guilty of certain "high crimes." The defense attorney William E. Doster, for one, noted, "The character of Mr. Johnson . . . shows more clearly why these people were so summarily hanged. His obstinacy and self-will when opposed by appeals for mercy or magnanimity of sentiment carried him to the opposite extreme of rigor. The suspicion that he might have been one of them made him hasten to show by severity that his hands were clean."

Johnson, irrespective of his culpability or innocence, or of the thrust of his intentions, kept providing ammunition for his ever growing battalions of enemies. In early May 1867 he authorized the transfer of Jefferson Davis from Fort Monroe to civil authorities to answer charges of treason. Arriving in Richmond, in response to a writ of habeas corpus, Saturday morning, May 11, the former president of the Confederacy commented, "I feel like an unhappy ghost visiting this much beloved city."

As his carriage moved through the streets en route to the Spotswood Hotel, there arose a cry, "Hats off Virginians!" Together with the refrain "God bless you!" as a "great concourse of people . . . a sea of heads," according to his wife, Varina, had materialized. Indeed, "room had to be made by the mounted police for the carriages . . . The windows were crowded and even on to the roofs people had climbed. Every head was bared. The ladies were shedding tears."

The reporter for the Richmond *Whig,* who found the crowd somewhat smaller and quieter than Varina Davis indicated, observed that the onetime executive was "pale, very pale, his hair much grayer than when we last saw him and his cheek thin and furrowed. One could see that sickness and sadness and suffering had cast their dark shadow over him."

On Monday, the thirteenth, leaning on the arm of Brigadier General Henry S. Burton, new commandant of Fort Monroe, Davis arrived in federal circuit court, located in the old custom house. This was among the comparatively few government buildings not damaged by the fires. Appropriately, Davis had had his presidential offices there.

Proceedings proved anticlimactic, even as the defendant sat, seeming not to "manifest interest." He was championed by a singular battery of supporters led by Horace Greeley, Cornelius Vanderbilt, and a well-known New York lawyer, Charles O'Conor. Not a one ever had a kind word to say about the secession.

Under the persuasion of these august personages, Judge John C. Underwood somewhat reluctantly agreed to release the prisoner on $100,000 bail. The bond was instantly signed by Greeley, Vanderbilt, and eight other prominent Northerners and Southerners.

At the words from the bench, "The marshal will discharge the prisoner," according to the *Whig,* "as if by sudden shock, the suppressed feelings of the audience broke forth in every part of the hall, and the clapping of hands, the stamping of feet and the huzzahs of hundreds of throats made the hall resound!"

After two years Jefferson Davis was at last a free man. He did not tarry long. That evening he departed with Varina for New York and then Montreal. Never again would he appear as a prisoner in a court of law, nor would the amount of the bond ever be demanded.

The hypothetical case of *United States* v. *Jefferson Davis* had been, in effect, thrown out of court.

Although much of the press approved the president's action in releasing Davis to the civilian courts, a number of substantial dailies did not. The New York *Evening Post,* for example, observed that "the crime of treason" was now shown to the world to be "safe to commit" in the United States. The conservative Hartford *Courant,* Gideon Welles's old paper, wondered aloud how the nation could not hang "even one such traitor" as at least a measure of "holy devotion" to the tens of thousands of Union war dead.

The Philadelphia *Press* bayed along right on the heels of the two, blaming the president for his "infirmity of purpose," while the Radical Republicans rather rejoiced in the faith that Johnson thereby was merely drawing tighter his own noose.

The chief executive, however, would be staggered far more seriously from another source: the resurgence of the Surratt case, which still refused to remain buried. Over Stanton's and Holt's understandable objections, John Surratt had been located and returned from Europe. Here was no mute skeleton in the closet, but a corpus delicti with the inherent ability to snap open the Pandora's box of the whole miserable proceedings.

Mary's son, a slim, sandy-haired youth, went on trial June 10, 1867, in district criminal court, in Washington. This was, of course, a civil procedure in stark contrast to the military tribunal which had dispatched his mother to the gallows. Now twenty-three years old, John had been extradited from Alexandria, Egypt, the previous November. He had been recognized while serving in Rome as, of all things, a papal Zouave, under the name Watson.

The account of John's wanderings and whereabouts during the period surrounding the assassination filled almost the entire two months of the proceedings, which often assumed the aspect of comic opera.

A rabid sympathizer with the South, Surratt surely would have been hanged in 1865—conceivably in place of his mother—had he been apprehended and tried by the commission. Earlier in 1865, he had been privy to Booth's mad scheme to capture Lincoln. When Richmond fell on April 3, Surratt, who was in the Confederacy's capital, fled the city barely in advance of the first Union contingents.

On Friday, April 14, 1865, the night of the assassination, he was at the Brainard House in Elmira, New York, registered as John Harrison. He was reconnoitering the vast Elmira encampment of Confederate prisoners. When, the next morning, he heard fragmentary reports of the assassination, Surratt sent a telegram to Booth in New York. He would avow he knew nothing of his friend's involvement in the crime. In fact he had not been positive that Booth actually was in New York.

Nonetheless, he was worried enough to conclude that the better part of valor was to flee back to his base in Montreal. As for his mother and her mixed bag of boarders, who were known to him, John either did not think about her at all or rationalized that that was *her* lookout.

Surratt boarded the train for Canandaigua, sixty miles to the north. There he registered at the Webster House, again as John Harrison. When, on Monday morning, he read his own name in the paper, then learned of a $25,000 reward on his head, he hastened his flight to Canada. He arrived in Montreal the next day, Tuesday.

He remained there or in the adjacent countryside until September, having made the pragmatic decision that there was nothing he could do about his mother even if he surfaced.

That same month Surratt left for England. After a brief sojourn, he crossed to France before ending up in Italy with the Zouaves. He escaped from Rome to Egypt, only to be captured.

"Our business," declared Edwards Pierrepont, a New York attorney retained as a special prosecutor, "was to bring him [Surratt] to Washington, and that we have done . . . Surratt did come on a train from Elmira and from the depot he went to a barber shop and got shaved . . . I will get him here most beautifully, and so smoothly that you will see him shaved without a quiver." (Surratt wore a goatee as a Zouave.)

With considerable reason, defense counsel Joseph Bradley countered that his client would have had to be "a bird" to move from Elmira to the national capital in the allotted time. It so happened there had been a washout of the railroad bridge over the Susquehanna at Williamsport, Pennsylvania, south of Elmira, during the crucial time between Thursday and Friday. This meant that passengers had to be ferried over the swollen river at Williamsport to continue south to Sunbury, Harrisburg, and Baltimore.

Regular trains were hopelessly delayed or cancelled. Work trains with repair crews, chugging up and down the tracks bordering the river, had clogged the route. Pierrepont used all of his legal ploys to show that the accused was on one of those work trains, or even aboard a single-car "special," used to transport a superintendent of the road. But the trouble was that the attorney could not produce even one single railroader to make positive, unequivocal identification. And, on second thought, the Negro barber, who supposedly shaved the goateed gentleman, admitted this wasn't the man at all.

The case was falling into tatters. In the face of such flimsy and contradictory evidence, it was small wonder that the jury, "nearly equally divided" (8–4 for acquittal), could not deliver a verdict. It was ruled a mistrial. The admitted Confederate agent would be a free man the following year, 1868. Thus had passions cooled in short months.

Yet what had amounted to an exoneration of a disloyal, unsavory, and, in likelihood, cowardly character proved of less consequence than a seemingly casual revelation during Pierrepont's closing address to the jury on August 3. It had come as a rebuttal to a defense taunt that the prosecution was suppressing evidence, such as Booth's diary, which perhaps could free Surratt.

"I hold in my hand the original record," Pierrepont glibly announced; "no other one touched the paper; and when it was suggested by some members of the Commission that in consequence of the age and sex of Mrs. Surratt it might possibly be well to change her sentence to imprisonment for life he [President Johnson] signed the warrant for her death with the paper right before his eyes . . . and there it is . . . !"

Rummaging through the transcripts of the conspiracy trial, Pierrepont had stumbled on the clemency recommendation. Never published, it had remained hidden from the public for two years. Even now it was not put in evidence or read to the jury, merely mentioned in passing.

Still, it was such a damaging document that Judge Holt hurried over later in the day to reclaim it. Surely Holt, Speed, and company had not intended that Pierrepont be quite so open in avowing that the government had secreted nothing.

It hit the press, and the White House, like a bombshell. The Monday, August 5, editions let the nation and the world in on this well-kept secret.

Johnson's reaction was rather predictable. Atop the revelations that Sanford Conover and others had perjured themselves and the connivance on the part of the War Department, this was too much. Stanton must go.

"It is impossible," the president told Gideon Welles, "to get along with such a man in such a position, and I can stand it no longer!"

He seemed to have just the excuse needed to rid himself of one he passionately disliked and distrusted, although he was not alone in this attitude. Johnson asked Stanton to resign. Stanton refused. Then the president suspended him and appointed a reluctant General Grant as interim secretary of war. Johnson would recall of his meeting with "Unconditional Surrender" Grant, "with the hectic smirk peculiar to him [he replied], 'I will of course obey orders.' "

Summarily dumping or trying to jettison Stanton at this particular time did not of itself show whether Johnson knew of the clemency recommendation. He could once have known and then forgotten. Surely he had every motivation to forget.

In spite of the general knowledge that he was an unscrupulous tyrant, the bewhiskered Stanton had survived the war years. He was an administrator and an expeditor. He could make decisions, as General McClellan could not. But now, with peace, his enemies were more consolidated and unequivocal in their judgments: ". . . This duplex figure . . . most marvelous imposter that ever lived or died," was the icy analysis of Welles; "he is imperious to inferiors and abject to superiors . . . with a taste for intrigue, he has been deep in conspiracy . . . a secret opponent of the President's from the commencement of his Administration [bent on] crippling the President on every hand in every way . . . His administration of the War Department cost the country unnecessarily untold millions of money, and the loss of thousands of lives."

Judge Jeremiah S. Black, attorney general under Buchanan, would not concede this "complex" individual's loyalty even to his principal master, Abraham Lincoln. Before Stanton's appointment as war secretary, Black charged, he had cursed "Mr. Lincoln with bitter curses. He called him contemptuous names . . ."

Curiously, perhaps, it was Black, after his appointment as secretary of state during the final few weeks of Buchanan's administration, who obtained Stanton's nomination to succeed him for the same brief interim as attorney general. So now only the Radicals paid court to the dismissed war secretary. In his manifest ruthlessness, they recognized their own handy Robespierre.

In his precipitate act of anger, however, the president went counter to the Tenure of Office Act, which had been passed over his veto in March. This bit of meddling in executive prerogatives specified that presidential appointees could not be removed without the consent of the Senate. Andrew Johnson was initiating a chain reaction—the first boulder of an avalanche, the climax of which he could not foresee or in any manner control, much less stem.

Furthermore, the revelation of the clemency memorandum surely damned any future political ambitions Johnson had entertained. He had made no secret to his intimates that he counted heavily on the support from the reconstructed states.

Now, wrote Colonel Henry Burnett, who had assisted Judge Holt in the conspiracy proceedings, "Over her [Mary Surratt's] execution, a great clamor was raised throughout the country, not only by those who were lately in rebellion, but almost universally by the Roman Catholics. Mr. Johnson heard this clamor and 'his startled ambition grew sore afraid.'

"The press kept referring to the fact that a recommendation for mercy had been signed by a majority of the court; and his new friends and allies were calling upon him with a loud voice to know why he had not heeded the appeal for mercy and saved this hapless woman. Here was a sufficient motive, the motive that changed the whole nature of the man, changed his political thought and attitude, spoiled the purpose of his life."

In Johnson's preoccupation, he had accorded scant thought to a treaty, the Alaska Purchase, placed on his desk May 28, 1867, by Secretary Seward, himself no great favorite of the president's. It had been on the executive agenda since 1861. Johnson signed it anyhow while grumbling that the price, $7.2 million, for that northern wilderness owned by Russia was exorbitant. He could only agree with those who called it Seward's folly or Seward's icebox. At the same time, he wondered whom he could persuade to struggle up to Sitka in October to officiate at the formal transfer. The journey was long, largely by sea.

On January 13, 1868, the Senate voted to reject Johnson's dismissal of his secretary of war, who returned to the department. General Grant was at the same time forbidden to deny Stanton his seat as secretary. The stormy figure nonetheless made no attempt to attend cabinet meetings.

But Stanton's mule stubbornness found its match in Johnson, who prepared formal termination papers for the man he contemplated with ever increasing detestation. If neutrals there remained in the dispute, they could have agreed that Stanton should have followed precedent and tendered his resignation when the new president was sworn in. But the feisty lawyer had not made things easy for the chief executive, in office by reason of an assassination.

Next, Andrew Johnson appointed Major General Lorenzo Thomas as secretary of war. Little known outside of the military, Thomas, a sixty-three-year-old native of Delaware and a West Point graduate, had been adjutant general and had figured during the war in prisoner exchanges.

Thomas, the white-haired honorable soldier, marched over to the War Department on February 21, carrying two letters signed by the president. One curtly informed Stanton that he was fired. The other proclaimed Thomas's appointment. The old officer was completely rebuffed. In fact, Stanton had already barricaded himself in his office, using a sofa for his bed. It was like the war years, when the secretary often ate and slept days at a time in the drab, ill-lit cubicle.

Now, Andrew Johnson had himself supplied the ingredients missing in early impeachment votes. On February 24, the House voted to impeach the president for "high crimes and misdemeanors." After intense debate and bombast, the trial came in the Senate three months later.

"The morning of this memorable May day," wrote the correspondent for the New York *World* Saturday, May 16, 1868, "was one of the loveliest. Its warmth and brightness made the thousands of citizens and strangers to the streets rejoice. The sunshine filtered down on the city through a soft haze hanging over the roofs. The street lamps glowed like electric lights . . . a balmy breeze blowing from the South was beaten by wings of the last returning swallow.

"The Capitol . . . looked as beautiful as a palace in a dream. Along the broad sidewalks and up the picturesque avenues and terraces of the Capitol grounds the flood of human life ascended until noon and after, overflowing the great edifice . . . The whole Capitol resounds everywhere . . ."

Virtually the entire House of Representatives was added to the crush of the galleries. Women with fans and ribbons and diplomats in their particular clothing augmented the color and contrast of this scene.

"The galleries were packed," recalled George W. Julian, a congressman from Indiana, "and an indescribable anxiety was written on every face. Some of the members of the House near me grew pale and sick under the burden of suspense. Such stillness prevailed that the breathing in the galleries could be heard."

As president pro tempore of the Senate, Ben Wade had far more than passing interest in the proceedings. If Johnson were convicted, Wade would become chief executive. It was rumored that he was already assembling a tentative Cabinet.

David Miller Dewitt, a contemporary historian, reported, "The prevailing excitement had reached a pitch of intensity that manifested itself by a stillness that was felt."

At noon, Chief Justice Chase, in the black robes of his office, solemnly called the High Court of Impeachment to order. Former secretary of the Treasury in the Lincoln Cabinet, Salmon Portland Chase was politically ambitious, a Radical Republican by inclination.

Of the fifty-four senators, only one was not in his seat: James W. Grimes, Republican from Iowa, who had suffered a stroke but three days before. The vote of this former Radical Republican was considered essential for acquittal.

A number of the legislators were indisposed or so crippled or enfeebled that they had to be assisted to their chairs. James W. Howard, Republican from Michigan, for one, was borne on a stretcher to the doors of the chamber, then hoisted into his seat. Representative Thaddeus Stevens, of Pennsylvania, who had done so much to bring about impeachment, disabled from birth, was carried in on a small chair. Unwell, too, but ambulatory were Roscoe Conkling, of New York, and Oliver P. Morton, of Indiana.

George F. Edmunds, a Vermont Republican and no friend of the president, moved that the Senate proceed to judgment. William P. Fessenden, of Maine, pleading for time, asked that the vote not be taken until Grimes was present.

Emotionally, Reverdy Johnson, of Maryland, who had unsuccessfully defended Mary Surratt, leapt to his feet to assert, "The Senator is here! I have sent for him. He is downstairs. He will be in the Chamber in a moment!"

And even as Johnson pronounced his last words, Grimes was assisted in, leaning heavily on two aides. Faint and pale, the tall, white-haired senator remained nonetheless impressive.

The chief justice directed the secretary to read the Eleventh Article of Impeachment. It proved to be a rambling philippic revolving primarily around the Tenure of Office Act and Johnson's "denying and intending to deny the power of the said 39th Congress." The president was also accused of attempting "to prevent the execution" of two other congressional acts, one involving army appropriations and the other tailored to promote "the more efficient government of the Rebel States."

The large audience was impatient for the recitation to be done with. All of its members were eminently familiar with the contents. They fidgeted, drummed fingers, and scratched their heads. At last the chief justice arose, grasping the edge of the desk that formed a low rampart before him.

"Call the roll!" he ordered the clerk, who almost in the same charged instant snapped out: "Mr. Anthony!"

Responding in alphabetical order, Henry B. Anthony, former Republican governor of Rhode Island, stood up. He looked pale and even "a little tremulous," according to one of the correspondents present.

"Mr. Senator Anthony, how say you? Is Andrew Johnson, President of the United States, guilty or not guilty of a high misdemeanor as charged in this article?"

Anthony looked squarely at Chief Justice Chase, a personal friend, before replying, "Guilty!"

Amid a "buzz of whispers and the noise of a friction of garments," scribbled the New York *World*, "Mr. Anthony wilted into his seat."

"The roll was called in breathless silence," observed James G. Blaine, a representative from Maine and an opponent of impeachment, "with hundreds of tally papers in the hands of eager observers on the floor and in the gallery, carefully noting each response as given."

It began to appear that there would be no surprises. Simon Cameron, of Pennsylvania, Lincoln's first secretary of war, relieved the tension and evoked laughter when he shouted "guilty!" even before the clerk had finished reading the question. One of Stanton's relatively few friends, Cameron early in the rebellion had advocated freeing and arming the slaves. Cooler heads deemed this too precipitate.

Ten votes for conviction and three for acquittal had been recorded when William Pitt Fessenden, of Maine, was called. Although it was assumed that the distinguished senator, who had served briefly as Treasury secretary, felt favorably toward the president, this tall, spare man, erect but "pale and haggard," stood and said nothing. A new hush spread through the galleries.

Had Fessenden changed his mind?

Then, deliberately, "high and clear," he spoke. "Not guilty!"

There was an audible sigh of relief from the Johnson camp.

He was followed by Joseph F. Fowler, of Tennessee, half claimed by the Radicals although he had admired Johnson when he was military governor of that state. Visibly shaken by emotion, the freshman senator and former professor articulated his response so badly that to some it sounded like "guilty."

Sumner, high priest of the Radicals, was on his feet as if he had been propelled by a great spring, almost shouting, "Did the Court hear his answer?"

Before the chief justice could answer, Fowler cleared his throat to shout out: "*Not* guilty!"

Sumner groaned as he sank back into his chair.

Ever the considerate gentleman, Salmon P. Chase asked James Grimes if he would like to vote while half-reclined in his seat. He would not. Propped by his friends to a wobbly standing position, the Iowa Republican pronounced: "Not guilty."

This was quickly negated by James Howard, of Michigan, also assisted up, who gave a guilty vote.

But Senator John B. Henderson, a forty-two-year-old abolitionist from the long-controversial slave state of Missouri, voted not guilty. This should not have been surprising since he had authored the Thirteenth Amendment, abolishing slavery. Nonetheless, the glowering looks from his state delegation testified that his political career was over and that the heavily bearded senator might be burned in effigy. In fact, he was.

Twenty-four guilty votes and fourteen not guilty had been recorded by the time Edmund G. Ross, of Kansas, was called. In the Senate less than two years, having been appointed to fill the seat left vacant by the suicide of James Lane, Ross was the same age as Henderson and distinguished by a neat beard and rather short hair. Once editor of the Kansas *Tribune,* he had served in the war as a major with the Union Eleventh Volunteer Infantry Regiment of Kansas.

Throughout the voting, Ross had been observed tearing sheets of paper into little strips. They drifted like irregular snowflakes or spring blossoms down from his desk and onto the floor. Surely there was reason for his nervousness.

It was long understood by the Radicals, especially the senior senator from Kansas, Samuel C. Pomeroy, who was almost as rabid as Ben Wade, that Ross's vote could be decisive. As Dewitt summarized it, "This hitherto undistinguished Senator had become the target of every eye; his rooms beset by his radical constituents, associates and friends wild to gain some satisfactory inkling of his mind." He added, "His outgoings and incomings, his companions and his convivialities, his breakfast, his dinner, his lodgings were marked and set down in notebooks; his name speeding over the wires, back and forth, to and from all points of the compass, and ringing from every one's mouth in all quarters of the swarming, simmering, half-delirious capital. Wrapped in the solitude of his own impenetrability, he calmly watched the raging eddies of which he was the center."

Even the chief prosecutor of the impeachment, Benjamin F. Butler, was shaken by the uncertainty of Ross's vote. The South still knew the onetime general and hated him as Beast Butler.

Ross would be quoted as saying that, at this moment, he was "almost literally" peering "down into my open grave."

The chief justice bent forward as the question was read to Edmund Ross, who barely hesitated. In clear but soft conversational tones, he replied, "Not guilty."

The words, DeWitt wrote, "sweep the assembly and, as one man, the hearers fling themselves back into their seats; the strain snaps; the contest ends; impeachment is blown into the air."

The thirty-five votes of guilty balanced against the nineteen (twelve Democrat, seven Republican) of not guilty had proven just one short of the necessary two-thirds majority to convict the seventeenth president and remove him from office. There would have been no appeal.

Ten days later, Johnson was acquitted by the same percentage of two other articles of impeachment. Leaving the eight remaining articles forever in limbo, Justice Chase adjourned the court sine die.

Conceding defeat, Stanton quit his sofa and his refuge in the War Department. He resigned, to resume the practice of law in Washington.

The nation refocused its interest on the next president. In Chicago, on May 20–21, General Grant was the unanimous nominee of the National Union Republican Party. Speaker of the House Schuyler Colfax became his running mate on the fifth ballot.

The plank was evasive on two major issues: Negro suffrage and greenbackism, or the advocacy of paper money not redeemable in gold. The Republicans hoped to placate the North by asserting that the question of suffrage in that section "belonged to the States," never minding that it must be mandatory in the South.

By appropriating Ulysses S. Grant, a prewar Democrat, the Republicans had deprived the opposition of their most likely candidate. Their consolation candidates, Governor Horatio Seymour, of New York, and Francis P. Blair, Jr., of Missouri, the vice presidential nominee, appeared to be weak adversaries.

Then the hero of Appomattox retired to his front porch in Galena, Illinois, to smoke cigars and adamantly refuse any semblance of campaigning. With sturdy disinterest in the party platform, Grant chose only to repeat, when queried, the platitude "Let us have peace."

On July 4, with nothing more to lose, President Johnson proclaimed a general amnesty, pardoning all but Jefferson Davis, who was still, on the books, under indictment. As a matter of fact, the chief executive wanted to absolve the man who had for so long been anathema to him, but his cabinet restrained this desire.

Rumblings of impeachment echoed in the radicals' camp. But what did it matter? The November elections were but four months off, and Johnson was not even a candidate.

The next month, on August 11, Johnson's especial nemesis, Thaddeus Stevens, died of a fever of obscure origins. Crushed by the impeachment court's failure to convict, the Pennsylvania legislator had slumped into a mental and physical decline. Totally unable to accept defeat, he had muttered to his friends that if Johnson could not be removed by law, there was "Brutus's dagger." By provisions of his will, Stevens, in his seventy-seventh year, was buried in a Negro cemetery in Lancaster.

The man of few words who had nonetheless added a new slogan to the American lexicon—"Unconditional surrender!"—proved that he could win by staying home and smoking cigars. Grant was chosen in November by 218–80 electoral votes. The popular vote margin, however, was less than 300,000. Thus given heart, the Republican Congress, before adjourning, passed the Fifteenth Amendment, unequivocally proclaiming that the right to vote should not be denied or abridged on account of race, color, or previous condition of servitude. It would be ratified within the year.

The rights of blacks, however, were effectively being abridged—in great measure through the intimidation of the night riders, murderous vigilantes belonging to several wild-eyed groups springing up like dragons' teeth throughout the South.

Many in the victorious North had to share the blame. For one, Andrew Johnson, in the face of continuing reversals and errors of perception, persisted in oversimplifying the challenges inherent in returning the South to a full role in the federal government. "There is no such thing as reconstruction," he had asserted. "These States have not gone out of the Union. Therefore, reconstruction is unnecessary."

By 1869, Reconstruction, on the contrary, remained real. One of its more noxious by-products was in full cry: the secret self-protection societies, or neighborhood police. Disorder, lack of leadership, excesses on all sides, and conflicting social goals had assured their creation. The Radical Republicans' thirst for vengeance had proven, in rebuttal, a boost to all who still smarted from military defeat.

The Ku Klux Klan, the largest and most flamboyant of these many conclaves, was formed in May 1866 in Pulaski, Tennessee, by a handful of former Confederate soldiers. Starting as a small "fraternal order," it swelled out of proportion to encompass a membership of half a million white-robed and hooded zealots in three years' time. Led by the former ruthless Confederate cavalry general Nathan Bedford Forrest as grand wizard, the Klan dropped all pretense of sociability as it howled for white supremacy, denying blacks civil and political rights through terrorism. When the night riders failed to scare blacks to death, they beat, shot, and hanged them.

A hated target of the Ku Kluxers was the Union League, a patriotic society formed in the North in 1862 and extended to the South during Reconstruction in what turned out to be a vain attempt to get blacks and whites working together for civic betterment. The many leagues were described by Governor R. B. Lindsay, of Alabama, summing up the feelings of his area, as "composed principally of colored men with a sprinkling of whites . . . banded together for the purpose of committing depredations upon the whites."

"On the night of the 5th of May," recalled Elias Hill, a disabled Baptist preacher in South Carolina, "it was between 12 and 1 o'clock when I was awakened and heard the dogs barking and something walking very much like horses. They came in a very rapid manner . . . to my brother's door and attacked his wife and I heard her screaming."

Thus testified the minister before the U.S. Senate Select Committee on the KKK Conspiracy. Then, he said, six masked men burst into his own "little cabin." They threw the bedclothes off and dragged him into the yard, where they questioned him on recent burnings in the neighborhood. Whatever his answer, they hit him.

"They caught my leg and pulled me over the yard and then left me there, knowing I could not walk nor crawl . . . They pointed pistols at me all around my head once or twice as if they were going to shoot me, telling me they were going to kill me . . . He had a horsewhip and he told me to pull up my shirt and he hit me. He told me at every lick, 'hold up your shirt.' I made a moan every time he cut with the horsewhip. I reckon he struck me eight cuts right on the hip bone.

"One of them then took a strap, and buckled it around my neck and said, 'let's take him to the river and drown him!' "

Instead, Hill continued, the men went into the house to command his brother and sister-in-law to pick Elias up and carry him back to his bed. As the woman stooped to lift him, one of the Ku Kluxers struck her with a strap. Then, before they left, they confounded the black family by asking the preacher to "pray for the Ku Klux Klan."

Hill's lips would not move. "I was so chilled with cold and in such pain I could not speak . . ." The blood in his mouth also made it all but impossible to form the words.

"To protect the weak, innocent and defenceless from the indignities, wrongs and outrages of the lawless, the violent, and the brutal," read the code of this "Invisible Empire." But it was not working out quite that way.

Elias Hill's testimony was hardly unique. Sworn statements before the select committee would consume more than 8,000 pages of fine type, in thirteen fat volumes, extending into the early 1870s.

In rebuttal, however, "informed Northerners will concede that the evils of the day justified or excused the Klan's existence," wrote Myrta Lockett Avary. "For my part I believe this country owes a heavy debt to its noiseless white horsemen, shades of its troubled past."

Myrta might, but the government did not choose to "excuse" the Klan. Habeas corpus would be suspended in all states where the Ku Kluxers were active, and more than 1,200 of them would be arrested and convicted. Forrest himself was compelled to disband the night riders. Even so, this and other hate groups stubbornly survived, resisting, like poison ivy, attempts at complete eradication.

If his teeth were, in effect, pulled, Nathan Forrest was unrepentant. He never took an oath of allegiance to the United States.

On March 4, an administration if not quite yet an era ended. This cold, cloudy Thursday, the man who had sighed to Julia, his wife, in November, "I'm afraid I am elected," received the oath from Chief Justice Chase as the eighteenth president of the United States.

The animosity between the outgoing and incoming administrations was unprecedented except for the first presidential bid of Andrew Jackson in 1828. Refusing to ride in the same carriage with Andrew Johnson, Grant, who was garbed in a plain brown suit, went through the inaugural alone, as though he were succeeding no other chief executive. Reciprocating this atmosphere of disdain, Johnson remained closeted in the presidential suite of the Capitol, signing final bills before the fateful hour of 12:00 noon. He made no public appearance that day.

One of the last acts of the discredited president was to pardon Dr. Samuel Mudd. On March 20, 1869, his daughter Nettie wrote, "My father arrived home, frail, weak and sick." Thus ended the ordeal and imprisonment of the hapless country doctor. He had taken charge of Fort Jefferson's hospital in the fall of 1867 following a yellow fever epidemic. This outbreak claimed the lives of the commandant, his wife, the post surgeon and his small son, and others of the garrison and the prisoners, including Michael O'Laughlin, one of the conspirators.

Thirty-eight out of 270 infected had succumbed to a disease that baffled existing medical knowledge. None had associated the ending of the mosquito season with the abatement of an epidemic.

Dr. Mudd had earned, according to the pardon, "the admiration and the gratitude of all who observed and experienced his generous and faithful service to humanity."

Freed from the Dry Tortugas with him were Edward Spangler, the alcoholic stage carpenter, and Samuel Arnold, the childlike admirer of Booth. Neither possessed the capacity even now to understand the charges against him any more than had Payne, Atzerodt, or Herold.

Yet with the return of the Charles County physician, none of the persistent questions as to his complicity in the plot would ever be answered. All that seemed certain to his friends and counsel was that he had dallied with the truth when he denied recognizing Booth the night he set his leg.

Winter turned into spring. On May 10, 1869, a "magnetic ball" was hoisted above the dome of the United States Capitol. In New York, the full choir of Trinity Episcopal Church, at the head of Wall Street, heartily sang the *Te Deum,* even though the day was Monday, not Sunday. Forts rimming New York harbor fired salutes, as similar batteries were booming away in San Francisco. There was a four-mile parade in Chicago. And that evening the skies sparkled and crackled with fireworks in cities and towns throughout the nation.

Obviously, there was a reason for the lusty observances.

Shortly after noon this Monday, under bright, cool skies, at Promontory, Utah, the last spikes of the Union Pacific and Central Pacific had been hammered into place. Contrary to legend, the spikes were iron, not gold. In a land fabled for lawlessness, how long would anything of gold remain where it was?

Largely because of the remoteness of Promontory, fewer than six hundred persons were present. Most who attended came away weary and grumbling about long speeches and even "too much praying."

Soon, travelers would be exploring and experiencing a new America. *Frank Leslie's Illustrated Newspaper* sent along a reporter, who would write: "With Omaha we leave behind us the last suggestions of life in the States, and drink in the first breath of the grandeur and savage freedom of the Plains. Henceforward, our road lies due west, on the straight single track of the Union Pacific; and the train, relaxing its headlong speed . . . runs smoothly and steadily, describing no more oscillating curves, and subject to no erratic jolts and jars.

"The cozy little tables are put up, the portfolios and sketchbooks spread out, and in half an hour the industrious workers of the party are plying pencils and pens as comfortably as though seated at their own desks at home."

In fact, the only sour note was struck, not uncharacteristically, by General Sherman. Unimpressed by the progress of construction, he sniffed that he would not purchase a ticket through to the coast even for his youngest grandchild.

Subsequently, starting out from Chicago, British journalist William Fraser Rae would comment on many aspects of a transcontinental train journey, such as "comfortable beds at night, well-cooked meals," even "the not unmelodious whistle" of the engine in contrast to "the ear-piercing screech" of Britain's trains. At the same time, Rae remarked on the American terminologies, contrasted with those on English trains:

"Railway" for the British "railroad," "line" for "track," "station" for "depot," "checked" for "registered," and indeed "baggage" for "luggage." On the other hand, the "bustle and confusion at most American stations," which he found "greatly in excess" of what might be encountered at "well-managed European" counterparts.

Month by month the fiery decade of the 1860s, with all its disruption and change, was ending. ". . . And now the curtain is rung down and the lights out," wrote Margaret Thorpe, who had journeyed to Fort Monroe "on a cold windy day in February," 1866. "Time is making all things right, is shaping the rough ends, and we of the North and they of the South . . . can never again feel the old bitterness in our hearts, and soon the shame, the strife, the hatred, the grief of the past will seem only as a tale that is told."

But Margaret was penning hopes rather than actualities. Certainly, as Christmas and the New Year approached, Americans had every right to expect a better decade in the 1870s. President Grant, almost ten months into his term, still was accorded the support and goodwill of the people. He continued to sign measures and make appointments that seemed to be endorsed by Congress and the electorate.

In testament, on December 19, he was repaying what he had construed to be a personal debt. Accompanied by Vice President Colfax, Grant called on Edwin Stanton at his nearby K Street residence. It was Sunday, Stanton's fifty-fourth birthday, and the Presidential "Santa's present" was the word that the erstwhile war secretary was being nominated to fill a vacancy on the U.S. Supreme Court.

At the Stanton home, the pair met Representative Samuel Hooper, of Massachusetts, an old friend of Stanton whom the latter had visited on Cape Cod during the summer. Stanton had also spent some time at Mt. Wachusett, near Worcester, hoping to alleviate his chronic asthma and other not fully diagnosed ailments.

Stanton was in generally "cheerful spirits," thought Hooper, although he reclined on a couch during the entire visit. He had been in court the preceding week and was reported to have "ably" argued a case. Of course, Lincoln's cabinet officer, pleased if not entirely surprised at his nomination, did not know President Grant's true feelings for him. The victor at Appomattox would later reminisce in his memoirs about Stanton, "He cared nothing for the feeling of others. In fact, it seemed to be pleasanter to him to disappoint than to gratify."

With speed unprecedented, the Senate confirmed the nomination on Monday, December 20. During the next two days, amid some leavening, there arose an editorial outcry.

"Edwin M. Stanton," observed the New York *World,* "the pettifogger and bully who is thus elevated to the bench is still suffering from nervous prostration brought on by the avenging shades of his victims, Mrs. Surratt and the Andersonville prisoners. They are always present to his sin-burdened conscience and it is questionable if his mind will ever be sufficiently restored to permit him to assume the duties of the new position."

The writer referred, of course, to the hard War Department stance of not trading prisoners with the Confederates. In this position, however, Stanton had not been disputed by General Grant.

"The country will learn with regret of the nomination and prompt confirmation," seconded the *National Intelligencer.* "The name of Stanton is, perhaps, more hated by the American people than that of any other living man. To associate his name with justice is a cruel mockery and a crying shame. The bloodiest and most cruel incidents of the war were of his enactment, and every page in the history of his public life is of a character that should have marked him as most unfit for this position. Such men have arisen in other revolutions, and have served the purposes of the hour, but in the calm of peace which has succeeded they have been condemned to their just retribution, and their names execrated by all mankind."

The St. Louis *Republican* barked, "Upon his judicial ermines will rest the ineffaceable stain of an innocent woman's blood—a stain which no congressional enactment, no party claptrap can wash away."

On the other hand, the New York *Times* could not find encomiums enough. The editorial writer praised Stanton for "honorable public service and conspicuous ability and worth . . . sturdy integrity, his intellectual acumen and force and his unswerving patriotism."

The New York *Tribune* opined that "no single man except Abraham Lincoln and possibly Ulysses S. Grant deserves a larger share of the national gratitude, or will fill in history a more honorable place."

One might have reasonably speculated that the scribes from both New

York journals could have been lavishing praise upon some entirely different person in an entirely different time frame.

On Wednesday, the twenty-second, Stanton quit his couch and walked out under cold, leaden skies to pay his respects to President Grant at the White House. It was the time of year for official calls at the executive mansion. Apparently, the health of the justice-designate permitted this stroll of some four blocks. No other visitors expressed any surprise to see him there.

The next day, Thursday, the twenty-third, there was reported to have been a mysterious visit to the house on K Street. Colonel William P. Wood, who had been superintendent of Old Capitol prison, came, presumably, to wish his erstwhile chief a merry Christmas and congratulate him on his appointment. The subject turned to the conspiracy trial, and Stanton allegedly exclaimed, "The Surratt woman haunts me so that my nights are sleepless and my days miserable!" (Quoted from the Washington *Gazette* by the author Otto Eisenschiml, the comment cannot be independently corroborated, nor can the particular issue of the newspaper located.)

That Thursday night, Edwin Stanton sickened. This was most unexpected since he had trudged over to the White House only the day before. Surgeon General Barnes and Stanton's pastor, the Reverend T. A. Starkey, of the Epiphany Episcopal Church, were summoned about midnight. With these two at Stanton's bedside together with members of his family, Lincoln's war secretary succumbed at 3:00 A.M. on Friday, December 24, Christmas Eve.

Barnes certified that his patient had died of congestive heart failure, complicated by asthma. But was this diagnosis correct? How could a man at death's door have faced a raw December morning for his Christmas call at the executive mansion only hours before?

If a heart attack or asthma had not claimed him, what had?

Stanton's corpse was soon laid to rest, but not so the rumors that had speedily arisen. They were fueled, in measure, by his widow's secretiveness. His body never left the upstairs bedroom in which he had expired. It was believed not to have been embalmed (which had become almost customary during the Civil War) and certainly underwent no autopsy. It was removed directly to a mahogany coffin, lightly trimmed with silver. The lid was tightly screwed on in Ellen Stanton's presence.

"No reverent or irreverent gazing on the features of the dead was permitted," wrote the correspondent of the New York *Times*. "The last leave taking of the family was done in secret."

What might have been a simple desire for privacy would assume suspicious, sinister proportions. He had committed suicide by cutting his throat, else why were his remains so assiduously cloaked from view? This was the most prevalent speculation on the part of those who refused to believe Dr. Barnes's verdict of natural causes.

Some recalled the suicide, in 1846, of Dr. Darwin Stanton, the brother of the controversial secretary in Lincoln's cabinet.

The health of Edwin Stanton was sufficiently poor, however, that one was not compelled by the suddenness of his passing to reach for other causes such as suicide or foul play. Certainly more symbolic than the manner of reason for Stanton's demise was the fact that this figure who had so dominated a decade had made his singularly dramatic exit in its closing hours.

Now the 1860s, with all their hate and raw violence, were at once history. This in itself seemed improbable.

The end of a decade, however, was far from the conclusion of Reconstruction. Scholars would find it measurably easier to date the accomplishments of the physical reconstruction than those of the moral. They would fill fat volumes, chronicling the industrialization of the South in the 1880s and telling of the glistening new tracks and fast trains at the turn of the century, along with the advent of tall buildings in once decimated cities, especially in Atlanta.

When General Sherman dared return to the scene of his greatest conquest—more than a decade later—a local editor felt safe in musing that the illustrious military figure had been "a little careless with fire."

During the Spanish-American War, in 1898, a number of Confederate veterans, even if a bit less spry than in the 1860s, marched side by side with their onetime Yankee adversaries. This happenstance in itself lent further unreality to the decade of civil strife. "A palace in a dream," wrote the correspondent for the New York *World* of the Capitol the morning of the impeachment trial. When Sherman had marched out of Atlanta, he paused on the heights to look back and observe of the campaign that it had become "like the memory of a dream," fragile, ephemeral, unlikely.

Memories of the Civil War and the months following it are also of the stuff of gossamer. Yet the legacies, both good and evil, persist like a paradox to this day.

POSTSCRIPT

King, Lane, Stanton—each associated in his own way with the Lincoln assassination, the circumstances of the passing of each not fully clarified. One other would himself be associated with violence. Major Rathbone, who briefly wrestled with Booth, would marry Clara Harris, then murder her in a fit of madness. He lived out his days in an insane asylum.

But Stanton?

Stanton "might have made an uncommonly bad associate justice of the Supreme Court." So wrote the lawyer and indefatigable diarist George Templeton Strong. As an obituary, it was a profound understatement.

If Strong was frustrated in attempting to assimilate this dominant figure of the 1860s, he was—and remains—in ample company. The man and his acts have eluded a succession of biographers, even as Stanton eluded Johnson's efforts to banish him from his cabinet. To this day there is no critical agreement on whether Stanton was hero, despot, or—if it can be imagined—something in between. Those who have labeled him eccentric might have been among his mildest detractors.

This author, for one, has paused many times before the granite obelisk in Oak Hill Cemetery, located in the fashionable Georgetown section of the national capital. There reposes the dust of Lincoln's secretary of war and of Ellen Stanton, who survived him by only four years. Though entering the azalea-covered precincts to visit the graves of his own relatives, the writer wonders what secrets are entombed beneath the ivy surrounding the impressive Stanton monument.

Although he finds it not easy to believe that the man who a century ago made Washington tremble was himself involved in the so-called Lincoln plot, he nonetheless continues to ponder the wellspring of the man's vindictive fury. This is a matter of record. Just what might Mary Surratt, for one, have known that made Stanton so determined to exterminate her?

Might the two ever have been acquainted, if but slightly? If so, where and under what circumstances? Could this have been another "Did Johnson know Booth?" riddle. What about the pages missing from the Booth diary?

Was there some real motivation, other than the man's basic cruelty, for muzzling the defendants, hooding them, denying them their right to testify in their own defense?

There is well-documented evidence of Stanton's near psychotic grief occasioned by the death of his first wife. That he kept the ashes of his infant daughter in a metal case in his bedroom hinted, some believed, that Stanton was a necrophile. But these emotions and acts early in life are not proof in themselves of suicidal tendencies.

History merely informs us that Edwin Stanton made certain that a woman would be hanged. But its pages are brittle. Too many are stuck together, or missing. The trail is cold. An inquest on Lincoln's secretary of war still concludes with question marks, in bold face.

In the shades of Oak Hill, one might hope that this stormy, enigmatic, troubled figure has at last found his peace.

DRAMATIS PERSONAE

ANDREWS, ELIZA "FANNY"—young lady of Washington, Georgia.

ANDREWS, SIDNEY—journalist.

ARNOLD, SAMUEL A.—tried for conspiracy in Lincoln's assassination.

ATZERODT, GEORGE A.—tried for conspiracy in Lincoln's assassination.

AVARY, MYRTA LOCKETT—Virginia author.

BAKER, COLONEL LAFAYETTE—chief of the National Secret Service Bureau.

BARNES, SURGEON GENERAL JOSEPH K.—prominent at Lincoln's deathbed and at conspiracy trial.

BENJAMIN, JUDAH P.—Confederate cabinet member.

BINGHAM, JOHN—assistant judge advocate at conspiracy trial.

BOOTH, JOHN WILKES—Lincoln's assassin.

BOTTS, JOHN MINOR—Unionist in Richmond.

BOUGHTON, WILLIS—diarist of Sheffield, Illinois.

BOWLES, SAMUEL—journalist.

BOYD, BELLE—alleged Confederate spy.

BRECKINRIDGE, JOHN CABELL—Confederate general and cabinet member.

BROOKS, ABBIE—schoolteacher in Tennessee.

BROOKS, NOAH—Washington journalist.

BROWN, JOSEPH E.—Georgia politician and former governor.

BURNETT, COLONEL HENRY—special judge advocate.

BUTLER, MAYOR GENERAL BENJAMIN—prosecutor at Johnson's impeachment.

CAMERON, PAULINE—schoolgirl in North Carolina.

CAMERON, SIMON—Lincoln's first secretary of war.

CAMPBELL, CALLAWAY—Georgia businessman.

CAMPBELL, JUDGE JOHN A.—Richmond leader.

CARY, CONSTANCE—young belle of Richmond.

CHAMBERLAIN, MAJOR GENERAL JOSHUA L.—Union officer and author.

CHASE, CHIEF JUSTICE SALMON P.—presided at Johnson's impeachment.

CHESNUT, MARY BOYKIN—diarist of South Carolina.

CHIPMAN, COLONEL NORTON P.—prosecutor of Henry Wirz.

CHIVINGTON, COLONEL J. M.—fought Indians.

CHRISTIAN, ASBURY—Richmond writer.

CLAIBORNE, DR. JOHN H.—Petersburg physician.

CLAMPITT, JOHN W.—Mary Surratt's counsel.

CLAY, CLEMENT—onetime U.S. senator from Alabama and Confederate emissary to Canada.

CLAY, VIRGINIA—wife of Clement and author.

COBB, HOWELL—former Georgia governor and brigadier general, Confederate army.

COBB, MARY ANN—wife of Howell and writer.

COLFAX, SCHUYLER—vice president under Grant.

CONGER, LIEUTENANT EVERETT—captured Booth.

CONNOR, BRIGADIER GENERAL PATRICK E.—headed Indian campaign.

CONOVER, SANFORD—perjurer, witness at conspiratacy trial.

COPP, COLONEL ELBRIDGE J.—with Third New Hampshire Infantry.

CORBETT, SERGEANT BOSTON—shot Booth.

COX, MAJOR GENERAL JACOB D.—headed occupation forces in Carolinas.

CRAWFORD, N. J.—friend of Howell Cobb.

CROCKER, CHARLES—Central Pacific founder.

CUMMING, KATE—nurse and author.

CUSTER, MAJOR GENERAL GEORGE A.—postwar commander of Seventh Cavalry Regiment as lieutenant colonel.

CUTTS, ADELE—Stephen Douglas's widow.

DABNEY, SUSAN—Mississippi plantation chronicler.

DANA, CHARLES A.—assistant secretary of war.

DAVIS, JEFFERSON—president of the Confederacy.

DAVIS, VARINA—wife of the president.

DENNETT, JOHN RICHARD—correspondent for *The Nation*.

DEWITT, DAVID MILLER—historian of the nineteenth century.

DODGE, MAJOR GENERAL GRENVILLE—chief engineer of the Union Pacific and corps commander during the battle for Atlanta.

DOSTER, WILLIAM E.—former provost marshal of the District of Columbia, defense counsel for accused conspirators.

DOUGLAS, COLONEL HENRY KYD—of Stonewall Brigade.

EDMONDSTON, CATHERINE ANN—writer, of North Carolina.

EGGLESTON, COLONEL BEROTH B.—commander at Atlanta.

ELKINS, BRIGADIER GENERAL JAMES A.—member of conspiracy trial commission.

ELLIOTT, LIEUTENANT JOSEPH TAYLOR—*Sultana* survivor.

ELTINGE, CAPTAIN PETER—stationed in Atlanta.

EVANS, AUGUSTA JANE—Georgia author.

EWING, THOMAS—defense counsel at conspiracy trial.

FERGUSON, ARTHUR N.—Union Pacific surveyor.

FLUDD, ELIZA—Charleston resident.

FOSTER, BRIGADIER GENERAL ROBERT S.—member of conspiracy trial commission.

GARDNER, ALEXANDER—photographer.

GOBRIGHT, LAURENCE A.—Associated Press correspondent.

GORDON, NELLY—Savannah belle.

GRANT, GENERAL ULYSSES S.—commander-in-chief of Union armies and later president of the United States.

GREELEY, HORACE—publisher of New York *Tribune*.

GREENHOW, ROSE O'NEAL—Confederate spy in Washington.

GURLEY, DR. PHINEAS D.—Lincoln's pastor.

HANCOCK, MAJOR GENERAL WINFIELD SCOTT—commander in District of Columbia.

HARDIE, BRIGADIER GENERAL JAMES A.—inspector general in the War Department.

HARNDEN, LIEUTENANT COLONEL HENRY—of First Wisconsin Cavalry, pursuer of Jefferson Davis.

HARRIS, JOEL CHANDLER—author, of Georgia.

HARRIS, BRIGADIER GENERAL T. M.—member of conspiracy trial commission.

HARRISON, BURTON—aide to Davis.

HARTRANFT, MAJOR GENERAL JOHN F.—provost in Washington, D.C.

HEROLD, DAVID—tried for conspiracy in Lincoln's assassination.

HOLT, JUDGE JOSEPH—judge advocate general in the Bureau of Military Justice. He held, as well, the temporary rank of brigadier general.

HOOKER, MAJOR GENERAL JOSEPH—marshal in chief of the funeral procession in Springfield, Illinois, and onetime commander of the Army of the Potomac.

HOPKINS, MARK—Central Pacific founder.

HOWARD, MAJOR GENERAL OLIVER OTIS—former corps commander before Atlanta, in attendance at Lincoln funeral, also appointed head of Freedman's Bureau.

HOWE, BRIGADIER GENERAL ALBION P.—member of conspiracy trial commission.

HUFFMAN, JAMES—returned from a Union prison to his home in Virginia.

HUNTER, MAJOR GENERAL DAVID—presided over conspiracy trial commission.

HUNTINGTON, COLLIS P.—Central Pacific founder.

JOHNSON, ANDREW—president of the United States.

JOHNSON, SENATOR REVERDY—helped defend Mary Surratt, veteran Maryland legislator.

JOHNSTON, GENERAL JOSEPH E.—surrendered Confederate Army of Tennessee.

JONES, CHARLES COLCOCK JR.—Savannah lawyer.

KAUTZ, MAJOR GENERAL AUGUST V.—member of conspiracy trial commission.

KEAN, ROBERT GARLICK HILL—department head in the Confederate War Department, Richmond.

KECKLEY, ELIZABETH—former slave, in the White House.

KING, PRESTON—former Senator, Johnson associate.

LAMAR, GEORGE W.—Georgian.

LANE, SENATOR JAMES H.—Kansan, associate of Johnson.

LEALE, DR. CHARLES A.—physician, at Ford's Theatre.

LEE, ROBERT E.—general in chief of Confederate armies and commander Army of Northern Virginia.

LEIGH, FRANCES BUTLER—Sea Islands plantation owner.

LINCOLN, ABRAHAM—president of the United States.

LLOYD, JOHN—witness at conspiracy trial.

LOMAX, VIRGINIA—confined in Old Capitol prison.

LUBBOCK, GOVERNOR FRANK—aide to Davis.

LYON, COLONEL WILLIAM P.—on occupation duty, Texas.

MALLORY, STEPHEN R.—Confederate navy secretary.

McCOOK, BRIGADIER GENERAL EDWARD M.—on duty in Atlanta.

MINTY, COLONEL ROBERT H. G.—commanded Second Division, Cavalry Corps, Military Division of the Mississippi, in pursuit of Davis.

MOORE, CAPTAIN JAMES M.—reported on Andersonville.

MORRIS, B. F.—wrote of Lincoln burial.

MOSBY, VIRGINIA—wife of Colonel John S. Mosby.

MUDD, DR. SAMUEL—tried for conspiracy in Lincoln's assassination.

MUDD, SARAH—wife of Dr. Mudd.

MURPHY, ISAAC—governor of Arkansas.

MUSSEY, COLONEL REUBEN D.—President Johnson's secretary.

O'LAUGHLIN, MICHAEL—tried for conspiracy in Lincoln's assassination.

PALMER, CAPTAIN HENRY E.—in Powder River campaign.

PATTERSON, MARTHA—Johnson's daughter.

PAYNE, LEWIS—tried for conspiracy in Lincoln's assassination.

PETO, SIR MORTON—English visitor, economist.

PIERPOINT, FRANCIS H.—interim governor of Virginia.

PIERREPONT, EDWARDS—special prosecutor.

POPE, MAJOR GENERAL JOHN—commanded Department of the Northwest.

PORTER, BRIGADIER GENERAL HORACE—aide to Grant.

PRITCHARD, COLONEL BENJAMIN D.—commanded Fourth Michigan Cavalry, in Davis pursuit.

PRYOR, SARA—resident of Petersburg and friend of Lee.

RAE, WILLIAM FRASER—British journalist.

RATHBONE, MAJOR HENRY R.—guest in Lincoln's theater box.

RAWLINGS, HANNAH GARLICK—Orange County, Virginia, resident.

REAGAN, JOHN H.—Confederate postmaster.

REARDON, FRANK—Union Pacific employee.

REID, WHITELAW—reporter, Cincinnati *Gazette*.

RICHARDS, CAROLINE COWLES—Canandaigua, New York, resident.

RIVES, MAY ELIZABETH—Mansfield, Louisiana, resident.

ROBSON, KATE HESTER—Georgia girl.

ROSS, EDMUND G.—senator, filled Lane's term.

RUSSELL, WILLIAM H.—British reporter.

SCHENCK, DAVID—North Carolinian.

SCHURZ, CARL—prominent lawyer and major general.

SEDDON, JAMES A.—Confederate war secretary.

SEMMES, RAPHAEL—Confederate admiral and captain of raider *Alabama*.

SEWARD, WILLIAM H.—secretary of state.

SHERIDAN, GENERAL PHILIP—postwar commander of Military Division of the Gulf.

SHERMAN, GENERAL WILLIAM T.—postwar commander, Military Division of the Mississippi.

SHOTWELL, RANDOLPH—North Carolinian, prisoner of war.

SIMPSON, THE REVEREND MATTHEW—Methodist Episcopal bishop who delivered the Lincoln eulogy.

SPANGLER, EDWARD—tried for conspiracy in Lincoln's assassination.

SPEED, JAMES—attorney general.

STANFORD, LELAND—Central Pacific founder.

STANTON, EDWIN M.—secretary of war.

STEPHENS, ALEXANDER H.—Confederate vice president.

STEVENS, THADDEUS—representative from Pennsylvania, Radical Republican.

SUMNER, CHARLES P.—senator from Massachusetts, Radical Republican.

SURRATT, ANNIE—daughter of Mary Surratt. Known also as "Anna."

SURRATT, JOHN—son of Mary Surratt.

SURRATT, MARY—boardinghouse keeper, tried for conspiracy in Lincoln's assassination.

TAYLOR, LIEUTENANT GENERAL RICHARD "DICK"—one of the last Confederate commanders to surrender, visitor to Johnson.

TAYLOR, COLONEL WALTER—aide to Lee.

TERRY, MAJOR GENERAL ALFRED H.—commanded occupation forces in Richmond.

THOMAS, MAJOR GENERAL LORENZO—secretary of war, briefly, under Johnson.

THOMPSON, JACOB—Confederate emissary to Canada.

THOMPSON, LIEUTENANT MILLETT S.—on duty in occupied Richmond.

THOMPSON, WILLIAM SYDNOR—in Marietta, Georgia.

THORPE, MARGARET—schoolteacher, Fort Magruder, Virginia.

TOMPKINS, COLONEL C. H.—member of conspiracy trial commission.

TOOMBS, ROBERT A.—briefly Confederate secretary of state and, later, brigadier general.

TOWNSEND, GEORGE ALFRED—reporter, New York *World*.

TRENHOLM, ALFRED—Confederate Treasury secretary.

TROWBRIDGE, JOHN T.—reporter, from Hartford, Connecticut.

TRUMAN, BEN C.—emissary of Johnson's.

VANDERBILT, CORNELIUS—shipping magnate.

WADDELL, CAPTAIN JAMES—commanded Confederate raider *Shenandoah*.

WADE, REPRESENTATIVE BENJAMIN—Radical Republican, from Ohio.

WALLACE, MAJOR GENERAL LEWIS (LEW)—member of conspiracy trial commission.

WALTER, THE REVEREND JACOB A.—priest who pleaded for Mary Surratt.

WEICHMANN, LOUIS—testified at conspiracy trial.

WEISS, SUSAN ARCHER—young lady of Richmond.

WELLES, GIDEON—secretary of the navy.

WILSON, MAJOR GENERAL JAMES H.—Sherman's cavalry corps commander who organized pursuit of Jefferson Davis.

WIRZ, CAPTAIN HENRY—Andersonville prison commander.

WYLIE, JUDGE ALEXANDER—Washington jurist.

ACKNOWLEDGMENTS

The author first must give credit where credit is due: to Mary Hoehling, co-author of the successful predecessor book (still in print) *The Day Richmond Died*. She aided in the genesis of this manuscript variously: typing, proofing, suggesting, a helpmate in countless ways above and beyond the call of duty. She did confess that she went through the agonies, vicariously, so many times with the unfortunate, martyred Mary Surratt that she began to feel she was right there, with her, on the gallows.

Mary Hoehling, especially, contributed her charming and inspirational presence to the author's many and sometimes lengthy journeys in search of this often elusive yesterday in American history.

At the same time, he wishes to express appreciation to quite a number of others who supported his labors and made this work possible. Among them:

Rodney Armstrong, director and librarian, Boston Athenaeum; also Lisa Bachman, reference librarian.

Laurel G. Bowen, curator of manuscripts, Illinois State Historical Society.

Robert L. Byrd, assistant curator, William B. Perkins Library, Duke University.

Margaret Cook, curator of manuscripts and rare books, Earl Gregg Swem Library, College of William and Mary.

Anthony Dees, director, Georgia Historical Society.

Kathryn DeGraff, special collections librarian, DePaul University, Chicago. Ms. DeGraff searched assiduously for the missing Washington *Gazette* in the Otto Eisenschiml papers, which might have unlocked at least some of the mystery surrounding Stanton's final hours.

Richard Drew, recently retired photo curator of the American Petroleum Institute, and his successor, Lenore E. Alexander. The pictorial collection under their aegis treats not petroleum alone but is also a window on life and mores in the post–Civil War United States: even in Pithole!

Thomas A. Durant, picture librarian of the National Park Service, U.S. Department of the Interior. The library is a vast treasure of America of two centuries, transcending scenics alone.

Franklin M. Garrett, historian, Atlanta Historical Society. This distinguished scholar materially aided the author with an earlier book, *Last Train from Atlanta*.

J. Larry Gulley, manuscripts librarian, University of Georgia libraries; also David Hammond, library assistant.

Josephine L. Harper, reference archivist, State Historical Society of Wisconsin. Ms. Harper has assisted the author for some time in other projects.

Elizabeth Lessard, librarian, Manchester (New Hampshire) Historic Association. Ms. Lessard was one of a number of librarians and researchers in the North queried by the author in search of testimony left by returning Union soldiers.

Linda M. Matthews, reference archivist, Emory University, and Dr. Dan Carter, Mellon Professor of History, Emory University.

The late William M. E. Rachal, editor, Virginia Historical Society. Bill Rachal was a longtime friend and helpmate of the author, who assisted especially in the research of *The Day Richmond Died*. His death is mourned, in particular, by scholars throughout the South.

James H. Richards, Jr., librarian, Gettysburg College.

Richard A. Schrader, reference archivist, Southern Historical Collection, University of North Carolina. When the late, famed Dr. James W. Patton was its curator, the collection furnished major grist for the author's work on the siege of Atlanta.

J. Ronald Shumate, manager of industry communications, Association of American Railroads. His role, through the vehicle of the rails, is much that of Dick Drew's, of the American Petroleum Institute.

Allen H. Stokes, manuscript division, South Carolinian Library, University of South Carolina.

John Thompson, a respected San Diego attorney, who aided the author in matters associated with his own expertise.

Louis L. Tucker, director, Massachusetts Historical Society.

John E. Witherbee, research specialist, Union Pacific Railroad, Omaha, who found the unusual diary material on the building of the tracks.

REFERENCES

Note: Sources are listed only under the first chapter in which they were cited. They appear in the order in which they were cited.

FOREWORD

Cary, Constance (Mrs. Burton Harrison). *Recollections Grave and Gay*. New York: Scribner, 1911.

Leyburn, John. "The Fall of Richmond." *Harper's New Monthly Magazine,* vol. 33, 1886.

Rawlings, Hannah Garlick. Letter to her sister, Clarissa. *Virginia Magazine of History and Biography,* vol. 75, 1967.

Stanard, Mary Newton. See references for April.

Lamar, George W. Papers. University of Georgia Libraries.

Quotations from these and others are also to be found in Hoehling, A. A. and Mary. *The Day Richmond Died*. San Diego: A. S. Barnes, 1981. (Reissued as *The Last Days of the Confederacy*. New York: Fairfax, 1986.)

The general facts and figures in the foreword are to be found in many histories and encyclopedias, such as:

Commager, Henry Steele, ed. *Documents of American History*. New York: Appleton-Century-Crofts, 1958.

Dunning, William Archibald. *The Civil War and Reconstruction*. New York: Macmillan, 1904.

McPherson, Edward. *The Political History of the United States of American During the Period of Reconstruction*. Washington, D.C.: Solomons and Chapman, 1875.

. . . or, the readable Bowers, Claude G. *The Tragic Era*. Boston: Houghton Mifflin, 1929.

Bettersworth, John K. *Confederate Mississippi*. Baton Rouge: Louisiana State University Press, 1943.

House of Representatives. "The Wreck of the Railways." In *House Report 34*, 39th Cong., 2d sess., 1865. The principal Southern rail systems contributed to this congressional document.

Appleton's Annual (subsequently referenced), 1865, contains further statistics on the railroads.

1865

April

Taylor, Colonel Walter H. *General Lee, His Campaigns in Virginia*. Norfolk: Nusbaum, 1906.

Dispatches of Merriam, William H. Various articles in New York *Herald*. From April 16, 1865.

Southall, John. "Recollections of the Evacuation of Richmond." *Confederate Veteran*, vol. 37, 1929. Includes the return of General Lee.

Pollard, Edward A. *Southern History of the War*. New York: Richardson, 1866.

Stanard, Mary Newton. *Richmond, Its People and Its Story*. Philadelphia: Lippincott, 1923. Quotes Julia Page Pleasants.

The assassination of President Lincoln is the subject of countless books, articles, memoirs, and official records. Though many were consulted, they are far too numerous to list. These are specifically referenced in the chapter:

Tanner, James. Account of Lincoln on his deathbed. *American Historical Review*, vol. 9, 1924.

Vincent, Thomas M. "Abraham Lincoln and Edwin M. Stanton." Address to Grand Army of the Republic, Burnside Post 8, Department of the Potomac, April 25, 1889.

Leale, Dr. Charles A. "Lincoln's Last Hours." Military Order of the Loyal Legion, February 1909.

Eisenschiml, Otto. *Why Was Lincoln Murdered?* Boston: Little, Brown, 1937.

Grant, Ulysses S. *Personal Memoirs.* 2 vols. New York: Webster, 1886.

Welles, Gideon. *Diary.* Boston: Houghton Mifflin, 1911.

Flower, Frank A. *Edwin McMasters Stanton.* Akron, Ohio: Saalfield, 1905.

Roscoe, Theodore. *Web of Conspiracy.* Englewood Cliffs, New Jersey: Prentice Hall, 1959.

Dana, Charles A. *Recollections of the Civil War.* New York: Appleton, 1898.

Washington newspapers: *Constitutional Union, Evening Star,* and *National Intelligencer.* From April 15, 1865.

Documents from the trial of the accused conspirators, to be referenced subsequently, also bear on the assassination.

Lewis, Lloyd. *Sherman, Fighting Prophet.* New York: Harcourt Brace Jovanovich, 1932.

Sherman, William T. *Memoirs of William T. Sherman.* vol. 2. New York: Appleton, 1875.

Johnston, Joseph Eggleston. *Narrative of Military Operations.* New York: Appleton, 1874.

Davis, Jefferson. *The Rise and Fall of the Confederate Government.* New York: Yoseloff, 1958.

Davis, Varina Howell. *Jefferson Davis.* New York: Belford, 1890.

McElroy, Robert. *Jefferson Davis, the Unreal and the Real.* New York: Harper & Row, 1937.

Durkin, Joseph T. S. J. *Stephen R. Mallory, Confederate Navy Chief.* Chapel Hill: University of North Carolina Press, 1954.

Mallory, Stephen R. "Last Days of the Confederate Government." *McClure's.* 1900. Published twenty-seven years after his death.

Chesnut, Mary Boykin. *A Diary from Dixie.* Myrta Avary, ed. New York: Appleton, 1905.

Andrews, Eliza Frances. *The Wartime Journal of a Georgia Girl.* New York: Appleton, 1908.

Cumming, Kate. *Gleanings from Southland.* Birmingham, Alabama: Roberts, 1895.

Clopton, Virginia Clay. *A Belle of the Fifties.* New York: Doubleday, 1904.

Richards, S. P. Diary. Atlanta Historical Society.

Richards, Caroline Cowles. *Village Life in America 1852–'72*. New York: Holt, 1913.

Burnett, Colonel Henry L. Account of Washington after the assassination, the conspiracy trial, and observations on personalities including Andrew Johnson and Edwin Stanton. Military Order of the Loyal Legion. April 3, 1889.

Poore, Ben Perley. *Perley's Reminiscences of 60 Years in the National Metropolis*. Tecumseh, Michigan: Mills, 1866.

Brooks, Noah. *Washington D.C. in Lincoln's Time*. New York: Century, 1895.

Nicolay, John G., and John Hay. *Abraham Lincoln: A History*. New York: Century, 1890.

Nicolay, John G. Papers. Library of Congress.

Semmes, Admiral Raphael. *Service Afloat*. New York: Kennedy, 1903. His several editions commenced with London imprints immediately following the war.

Baker, L. C. *History of the United States Secret Service*. Philadelphia: privately printed, 1867.

———. *Spies and Traitors*. Philadelphia: Potter, 1894.

Townsend, George Alfred. *The Life, Crime and Capture of John Wilkes Booth*. New York: Dick and Fitzgerald, 1865.

Berry, Chester D. *Loss of the Sultana*. Lansing, Michigan: Thorp, 1892.

Elliott, Joseph Taylor and others. "The *Sultana* Disaster." *Indiana Historical Society Magazine*, vol. 5, 1913.

Elliott, James. *Transport to Disaster*. New York: Holt, Rinehart & Winston, 1962.

Michael, Lieutenant William H. C. Paper speculating on sabotage of the *Sultana*. Nebraska Commandery of the Loyal Legion. Vol. 1, 1902.

Hoehling, A. A. *Damn the Torpedoes!* Winston-Salem, North Carolina: Blair, 1989. Chapter on *Sultana*.

Pryor, Sara. *My Day: Reminiscences of a Long Life*. New York: Macmillan, 1909.

History of the 127th New York Infantry. Comments of Colonel William Gurney. Privately printed. No date.

May

Morris, B. F., compiler. *Memorial Record of the Nation's Tribute to Abraham Lincoln*. Washington, D.C.: Morrison, 1865.

Note: News events such as the rewards offered for Jefferson Davis and others are found in newspapers and magazines of the times as well as *Appleton's Annual*

Cyclopaedia and Register of Important Events of the Year, 1861–1903. These are listed elsewhere in the References (see under August).

Christian, W. Asbury. *Richmond Past and Present.* Richmond: Jenkins, 1912.

Thompson, Millett S. *Thirteenth Regiment of New Hampshire Volunteer Infantry.* Boston: Houghton Mifflin, 1888.

Claiborne, John Herbert. *Seventy-five Years in Old Virginia.* Washington, D.C.: Neale, 1904.

Cox, Major General Jacob D. Papers. Atlanta Historical Society.

Chamberlain, Joshua L. *The Passing of the Armies.* New York: Putnam, 1915.

Ambler, Charles H. *Francis H. Pierpont.* Chapel Hill: University of North Carolina Press, 1937.

Williamson, James J. *Prison Life in the Old Capitol.* West Orange, New Jersey: privately printed, 1911.

Ross, Ishbel. *Rebel Rose.* New York: Harper & Row, 1954.

Campbell, Helen Jones. *The Case for Mrs. Surratt.* New York: Putnam, 1943.

Butler, J. George. *Some Incidents in the Trial of President Lincoln's Assassins.* Paper delivered before the Commandery of the State of New York, Military Order of the Loyal Legion. New York: Appleton, 1891.

Holt, Joseph. Papers. Library of Congress.

Townsend, George Alfred. *Campaigns of a Non-Combatant.* New York: Blelock, 1866.

Davis, Varina Howell. *Jefferson Davis.* New York: Belford, 1890.

Harnden, Henry. "The First Wisconsin Cavalry at the Capture of Jefferson Davis." *State Historical Society of Wisconsin Magazine,* vol. 14, 1898.

Harnden, Henry. *The Capture of Jefferson Davis.* Madison, Wisconsin: Tracy Gibbs, 1898.

Reagan, John H. *Memoirs.* Walter F. McCaleb, ed. Washington, D.C.: Neale, 1906.

Wilson, James H. *Under the Old Flag.* New York: Appleton, 1912.

Lawton, G. W. "Running at the Heads." *Atlantic Monthly,* September 1865. Article on the capture of Jefferson Davis.

Stephens, Alexander H. *Recollections.* New York: Doubleday, 1910.

Browning, Orville Hickman. *Diary.* Theodore Calvin Pease and James G. Randall, eds. Springfield, Illinois: Historical Society, 1925.

Porter, Brigadier General Horace. *Campaigning with Grant.* Bloomington: Indiana University Press, 1897.

Copp, Colonel Elbridge J. *Reminiscences of the War of the Rebellion*. Nashua, New Hampshire: Telegraph, 1911.

Lewis, Lloyd. *Sherman, Fighting Prophet*. New York: Harcourt Brace Jovanovich, 1932.

Greenhow, Rose O'Neal. *My Imprisonment and the First Year of Abolition Rule in Washington*. London: Bentley, 1863.

June

Boughton, Willis. "Drover Days, or Pioneer Life in Illinois, 1862–1876." Unpublished memoirs. Illinois State Historical Society.

Schurz, Carl. *Reminiscences*. Vol. 3. New York: McClure, 1907.

Reid, Whitelaw. *After the War: A Southern Tour*. Cincinnati: Moore, Wilstach and Baldwin, 1866.

Dennett, John Richard. *The South as It Is*. New York: Viking, 1965. From articles published in *The Nation*.

Schuckers, J. W. *Life and Public Service of Salmon P. Chase*. New York: Appleton, 1874.

Trowbridge, J. T. *The South: A Tour of Its Battle-Fields and Ruined Cities, A Journey through the Desolated States, and Talks with the People*. Hartford, Connecticut: Stebbins, 1866.

Rhodes, Edwin R. Papers. Georgia Historical Society. Also W. H. Sauls's papers.

Lee, Robert E., ed. *Recollections and Letters of General Lee*. New York: Doubleday, 1924.

Horan, James D., ed. *CSS Shenandoah: The Memoirs of Lieutenant Commanding James I. Waddell*. New York: Crown, 1960.

Waddell, Lieutenant James I. Diaries. In *Official Records of the Union and Confederate Navies*. Series I, vol. 3, "Operations of the Cruisers—Confederate."

Note: A significant, sizable collection in the National Archives pertains to the Lincoln assassination under the heading *Court Martial of the Lincoln Conspirators*. Leading a list of documents is the official transcript of the trial, running to about 5,000 pages in longhand, records of the judge advocate general, and other War Department papers. Names and quotations not otherwise attributed in these pages likely are to be found in these vast files (record group 153).

The key for Archives searchers is the "Old Military" section.

House of Representatives. *House Report 104,* 39th Cong., 1st sess. See also the

Congressional Globe, forerunner of the *Congressional Record,* for the 39th and 40th congresses.

Barnes, W. H. *History of the 39th Congress.* New York: Harper & Row, 1868.

Bishop, Jim. *The Day Lincoln Was Shot.* New York: Harper & Row, 1955.

Oldroyd, Osborn H. *The Assassination of Abraham Lincoln.* Washington, D.C.: Oldroyd, 1901.

Poore, Ben Perley. *The Conspiracy Trail for the Murder of the President.* 3 vols. Boston: Tilton, 1865–66.

Douglas, Henry Kyd. *I Rode with Stonewall.* Chapel Hill: University of North Carolina Press, 1940.

Pitman, Benn, comp. *The Assassination of President Lincoln and the Trial of the Conspirators.* Cincinnati: Moore, Wilstach and Baldwin, 1865.

Clampitt, John W. "The Trial of Mrs. Surratt." *North American Review,* vol. 131, no. 286, 1880.

Sandburg, Carl. *Abraham Lincoln—The War Years.* Vol. 4. New York: Harcourt Brace Jovanovich, 1939.

Weichmann, Louis J. *A True History of the Assassination.* Floyd E. Risvold, ed. New York: Knopf, 1975.

Doster, William E. *Lincoln and Episodes of the Civil War.* New York: Putnam, 1915.

Johnson, Reverdy. Papers. Library of Congress.

Thomas, Benjamin Platt, and Harold H. Hyman. *Stanton.* New York: Knopf, 1962.

Milton, George Fort. *The Age of Hate: Johnson and the Radicals.* New York: Coward McCann, 1930.

Edwin R. Rhodes and W. H. Sauls recollections. Georgia Historical Society.

Note: Relative to the entry of Brigadier General Edward M. McCook, of the Fourth Division, U.S. Cavalry: As with most army and navy figures quoted in this book, if not specifically referenced, his observations will be found in *Official Records of the Union and Confederate Armies, War of the Rebellion.*

This monumental project, initiated by a joint congressional resolution in 1866, did not terminate until 1901. During this period, the U.S. Government Printing Office produced 129 volumes, grouped into four series. Its smaller naval consumption (already referenced), treats on some of the same subjects and includes many of the same participants.

Curiously, the references to the immediate postwar events, such as conditions in the South, the capture of Booth, the alleged conspirators' trial, and the Indian campaigns, are sprinkled throughout the four series.

The serious researcher must study the comprehensive general index for specific entries. Since the primary purpose of this study is not a textbook, full citations as to series, parts, volumes, pages, and dates are out of the question.

Sanborn, Margaret. *Robert E. Lee, the Complete Man*. Philadelphia: Lippincott, 1967.

Leech, Margaret. *Reveille in Washington, 1860–1865*. New York: Harper & Row, 1941.

July

Keckley, Elizabeth. *Behind the Scenes*. New York: Carleton, 1868.

Jones, James S. *Life of Andrew Johnson*. Greeneville: East Tennessee, 1901.

Thomas, Lately. *The First President Johnson*. New York: Morrow, 1968.

Walter, Rev. Jacob. "A True Statement of Facts Regarding the Surratt Case." *Catholic Review,* August 29, 1891; also read before the Catholic Historical Society, May 25, 1891.

Hardie, Brigadier General James A. Papers. Library of Congress.

Tucker, Glenn. *Hancock the Superb*. New York: Bobbs Merrill, 1960.

Goodrich, Frederick E. *Life of Winfield Scott Hancock*. Boston: Russell, 1886.

DeWitt, David Miller. *The Judicial Murder of Mary E. Surratt*. Baltimore: Murphy, 1895.

MaxField, Captain Albert. *The Story of One Regiment, the 11th Maine*. Privately printed, 1896.

Hamilton, J. G. de Roulhac, ed. *The Papers of Randolph Shotwell*. vol. 2. Raleigh: North Carolina Historical Commission, 1931.

Huffman, James. *Ups and Downs of a Confederate Soldier*. New York: Rudge, 1940.

Mosby, Virginia. Diary. Alderman Library, University of Virginia. This splendid library holds many published works of the period, including a complete set of the *Confederate Veteran*.

Holt, Joseph. Vindication of . . . Washington, D.C.: privately printed, 1866. This is the sole source of the Colonel Mussey quote.

Riddle, A. *Life of Benjamin F. Wade*. Cleveland: Williams, 1886.

Moore, Guy W. *The Case of Mary Surratt*. Norman: University of Oklahoma Press, 1954.

Butler, Benjamin F. *Butler's Book*. Boston: Thayer, 1892.

Note: John Clampitt, previously cited, is the source of the John Brophy quote.

August

Lining, Dr. Charles. "The Cruise of the *Shenandoah*." *Tennessee Historical Magazine,* vol. 8, 1924.

Horn, Stanley F. *Gallant Rebel, the Fabulous Cruise of the CSS* Shenandoah. New Brunswick, New Jersey: Rutgers University Press, 1947.

Appleton's Annual Cyclopaedia and Register of Important Events of the Year. New York: Appleton, 1861–1903. Numerous entries for 1865–66. This work is almost as remarkable as the *Official Records* (which see under June). Indisputably the ancestor of modern books of the year and information almanacs and digests, *Appleton's,* with its ever curious editors, covered a broad spectrum from agriculture in the Midwest to exploration in Africa. Contained are some well-written accounts, quoted, or merely lifted, of such events as the surrender at Appomattox and the assassination.

Russell, William H. *The Atlantic Telegraph*. London: Day, 1866.

Field, Henry M. *History of the Atlantic Telegraph*. New York: Scribner, 1867.

The *Great Eastern* and the Cable." *Atlantic Monthly,* November 1865.

Wood, John Taylor. "Escape of the Confederate Secretary of War." *Century Magazine,* vol. 47, 1893.

Butler, Pierce. *Judah P. Benjamin*. Philadelphia: Jacobs, 1891.

Meade, Robert Douthat. *Judah P. Benjamin, Confederate Statesman*. New York: Oxford University Press, 1943.

Evans, Eli N. *Judah P. Benjamin: The Jewish Confederate*. New York: Free Press, 1988.

Nepveux, Ethel Trenholm Seabrook. *George Alfred Trenholm, the Company That Went to War*. Charleston, South Carolina: privately printed, 1973. It has been speculated that this bold and sometimes dashing figure was the inspiration for Rhett Butler in *Gone With the Wind*. Only the late author, however, could answer this musing.

Craven, John J. *Prison Life of Jefferson Davis*. New York: Carleton Press, 1866.

"Ladies of Abbeville." South Caroliniana Library, University of South Carolina.

Brown, Joseph E. Papers. University of Georgia Libraries. A vast collection. Also the Howell Cobb collection.

Taylor, Richard. *Reconstruction under Johnson*. New York: Appleton, 1879.

Mudd, Nettie, ed. *The Life of Dr. Samuel A. Mudd*. New York and Washington, D.C.: Neale, 1906.

September

Botsford, Henry. *The Valley of Oil*. New York: Hastings House, 1946.

Conn, Frances G., and Shirley S. Rosenberg. *The First Oil Rush*. New York: Meredith, 1967.

Darrah, William Culp. *Pithole, the Vanished City*. Gettysburg, Pennsylvania: privately published, 1972.

Miller, Ernest C. *Oil Mania*. Philadelphia: Dorrance, 1941.

Giddens, Paul H. *Pennsylvania Petroleum, 1750–1872*. Titusville: Pennsylvania Historical and Museum Commission, 1947.

Note: The American Petroleum Institute has available a documentary film on Pithole.

Weiss, Susan Archer. *The Home Life of Poe*. New York: Broadway, 1907.

Avary, Myrta Lockett. *Dixie after the War*. New York: Doubleday, 1906.

Freeman, Douglas Southall. *Robert E. Lee, a Biography*. 4 vols. New York: Scribner, 1935.

Horn, Stanley F. *The Robert E. Lee Reader*. New York: Bobbs-Merrill, 1949.

Lee, Robert E., ed. *Recollections and Letters of General Lee*. New York: Doubleday, 1924.

Thompson, Kate (Mrs. Jacob). Correspondence. Howell Cobb collection, University of Georgia Libraries.

General background information, including old illustrations, was provided by Washington and Lee University, the onetime Washington College, of Lexington, Virginia.

October

Lyon, Adelia C. *Reminiscences of the Civil War: Compiled from the War Correspondence of Colonel William P. Lyon*. San Jose, California: privately printed, 1896.

Brooks, Abbie. Diary. Atlanta Historical Society.

McPherson, Edward. *The Political History of the United States of America during the Period of Reconstruction.* Washington, D.C.: Solomons and Chapman, 1875.

Note: Figures on education are derived from several sources, including the Census Bureau, Freedmen's Bureau, congressional documents, *Appleton's Annual,* contemporary encyclopedias, and numerous newspapers.

Andrews, Sidney. *The South Since the War.* Boston: Ticknor & Fields, 1866.

Robson, Kate Hester. Papers. Atlanta Historical Society.

Fludd, Eliza. Papers and letters. William R. Perkins Library, Duke University.

Harris, Joel Chandler. *Stories of Georgia.* New York: American Book Co., 1896.

Note: Relative to General Grant's report on army strength, the subjects of demobilization, Reconstruction, operations on the Western frontier (including the Indian Wars), are covered in an extensive bibliography at the U.S. Army Military History Institute, Carlisle Barracks, Pennsylvania.

Jones, Charles Colcock. Papers. University of Georgia Libraries.

November

Documentation on Andersonville prison (now a national monument some fifty miles southwest of Macon, Georgia) is almost as voluminous as that on the Lincoln assassination. The principal reference in the *Official Records* is under "Prisons" and "Prisoners," which includes a somewhat abridged transcript of the trial of the commandant, Captain Wirz (series II, vol. 8, 1899). Various congressional documents treat the subject including no. 23, 40th Cong., 2d sess., 1867.

The following is but a sampling of the many books written on the subject, including memoirs:

Chipman, General Norton P. *The Tragedy of Andersonville.* Sacramento: privately printed, 1911.

Futch, Ovid L. *History of Andersonville Prison.* Gainesville: University of Florida Presses, 1968.

Hesseltine, William H. *Civil War Prisons.* Columbus: Ohio State University Press, 1930.

Howe, Thomas H. *Adventures of an Escaped Union Prisoner from Andersonville.* San Francisco: Crocker, 1886.

McElroy, John. *This Was Andersonville.* Privately printed, 1879.

Moore, John W. *History of North Carolina*. Vol. 2. Raleigh, North Carolina: Alfred William, 1880.

Ransom, John L. *Andersonville Diary*. Auburn, New York: privately printed, 1881.

Younger, Edward, ed. *Inside the Confederate Government: The Diary of Robert G. H. Kean, Head of the Bureau of War*. New York: Oxford University Press, 1957.

Stibbs, John Howard. *Andersonville and the Trial of Henry Wirz*. Iowa City, Iowa: Clio Press, 1911.

Mogelever, Jacob. *Death to Traitors: The Story of General Lafayette Baker*. New York: Doubleday, 1960.

Rutherford, William. Letter about the death of Mary Willis Erwin. Cobb collection, University of Georgia Libraries.

Johnson, Andrew, and Edwin Stanton. State papers. Library of Congress.

December

McRae, John, and George Sherrill. Correspondence. Cyrus H. McCormick collection of documents on farm machinery. State Historical Society of Wisconsin.

Boorstin, Daniel J. *The Americans: The Democratic Experience*. New York: Random House, 1973. Especially allusions to the "uniformity system."

Peto, Sir S. Morton. *Resources and Prospects of America*. Philadelphia: Lippincott, 1866.

Parton, James. "History of the Sewing Machine." *Atlantic Monthly*, May 1867.

Eltinge, Peter, and E. W. Webster. Papers. William R. Perkins Library, Duke University.

Thompson, William Sydnor, and Elisha Lowery. Papers. Robert R. Woodruff Library for Advanced Studies, Emory University.

Campbell, Charles and Callaway. Papers. College of William and Mary.

Ayer, Lewis Malone, and Charles Heyward. Papers. South Caroliniana Library, University of South Carolina.

Edmondston, Catherine Ann. *Journal of a Secesh Lady*. Raleigh, North Carolina: Division of Archives and History, 1979.

Columbia *Phoenix* newspapers. South Caroliniana Library, University of South Carolina.

1866

January

Park, William Lee. *Pioneer Pathways to the Pacific*. Clare, Michigan: Clare Aire, 1935.

Ferguson, Arthur N. Diary. Union Pacific Archives. Also various papers, clippings, maps, and so forth.

Bowles, Samuel. *Across the Continent*. New York: Hurd and Houghton, 1968.

Early History of Fremont, Nebraska. Fremont, Nebraska: Pathfinder Press, no date. A collection of bound articles.

Kraus, George. *High Road to Promontory*. Palo Alto, California: American West, 1969.

Galloway, John Debo. *The First Transcontinental Railroad*. New York: Simmons Boardman, 1950.

"Across the Continent." *Frank Leslie's Illustrated Newspaper,* September 1877.

Dodge, Grenville. *Battle of Atlanta and Other Campaigns*. Council Bluffs, Iowa: Iowa Monarch, 1911.

Note: Letters and further manuscript material of General Dodge are held in the collections of the Historical, Memorial, and Art Building, Des Moines, Iowa.

Palmer, Captain Henry E. "The Powder River Campaign." Nebraska State Historical Society, 1887.

Hafen, Leroy R. *Powder River Campaigns*. Glendale, California: Clark, 1961.

February

Thorpe, Margaret. Diary. College of William and Mary.

Note: Although the exact location of Sara Pryor's Cottage Farm eluded Richmond and Petersburg historians, a small roadside marker in the latter city indicates the site of one of Lee's field headquarters. Since Pryor attested that the general used Cottage Farm, the spot may be one and the same. Neither soul would feel much at home there today. It has become the locale of gasoline stations on asphalt pavements, fast food establishments, and video shops.

U.S. Congress. Joint Committee on Reconstruction. *Report*. 39th Cong. Washington: Government Printing Office, 1866.

Brock, William R. *An American Crisis: Congress and Reconstruction 1865–1867*. New York: St. Martin's, 1963.

U.S. Senate. *Ex. Doc. 43*. 39th Cong., 1st sess. Ben C. Truman's report to the president. April 9, 1866.

Thomas, Ella Gertrude (Clanton). Papers. University of Georgia Libraries.

Leigh, Frances Butler. *Ten Years on a Georgia Plantation*. London: Bentley, 1883.

March

Lines, Jennie and Sylvanus. Papers. University of Georgia Libraries.

Smedes, Susan Dabney. *A Southern Planter*. New York: Pott, 1899.

Collins, Anne Cameron, Mary Elizabeth Rives, and David Schenck. Papers. Southern Historical Collection, University of North Carolina.

Trumbull, Horace. *The Life of Lyman Trumbull*. Boston: Houghton Mifflin, 1913.

Krug, Mark M. *Lyman T. Trumbull, Conservative Radical*. New York: Barnes, 1965.

Allen, James Stewart. *Reconstruction: The Battle for Democracy (1865–1876)*. New York: International, 1937.

Baker, G. G. *Andrew Johnson and the Struggle for Presidential Reconstruction (1865–1868)*. Boston: Heath, 1966.

Beale, Howard Kennedy. *The Critical Year: A Study of Andrew Johnson and Reconstruction*. New York: Ungar, 1958.

Gordon family. Papers. Georgia Historical Society. Especially the letter of Nelly.

EPILOGUE

Burgess, John W. *Reconstruction and the Constitution*. New York: Scribner, 1902.

Rae, William F. *Westward by Rail*. New York: Appleton, 1871.

Bailes, Kendall E. *Rider on the Wind: Jim Lane of Kansas*. Shawnee Mission, Kansas: Wagon Wheel Press, 1962.

Sheridan, General Philip. *Personal Memoirs of P. H. Sheridan*. Vol. 2. New York: Webster, 1883.

Evans, Augusta Jane (Wilson). Papers. University of Georgia Libraries.

Fidler, William Perry. *Augusta Jane Evans: A Biography*. University: University of Alabama Press, 1951.

Custer, George A. *Wild Life on the Plains*. St. Louis: Sun, 1883.

Dabney, Virginius. *Richmond, the Story of a City*. New York: Doubleday, 1976.

Pierrepont, Edwards August. *The Trial of John H. Surratt*. Washington, D.C.: Government Printing Office, 1867.

Brigance, William Norwood. *Jeremiah Sullivan Black, a Defender of the Constitution.* London: Oxford University Press, 1934.

Wilson, Henry. *A Contribution to History, Edwin M. Stanton.* Series of papers by the Hon. J. S. Black. Easton, Pennsylvania: Cole, Morwitz, 1871.

Pratt, Fletcher. *Stanton: Lincoln's Secretary of War.* Westport, Connecticut: Greenwood Press, 1953.

As in the case of the Lincoln assassination and Andersonville, documents on the Andrew Johnson impeachment accumulate to millions of words, in addition to official records in the *Congressional Globe* and Senate documents, including *Proceedings in the Trial of Andrew Johnson . . . before the Senate of the United States, 1868.* The matching House Report is no. 7, 40th Cong., 1st sess., 1868.

Smith, Gene. *High Crimes and Misdemeanors.* New York: Morrow, 1977.

Blaine, James G. *Twenty Years in Congress.* Norwich, Connecticut: Bill, 1886.

DeWitt, David Miller. *The Impeachment and Trial of Andrew Johnson.* New York: Macmillan, 1903.

David, Donald E. *Inside Lincoln's Cabinet: The Civil War Diaries of Salmon Portland Chase.* New York: Longman, 1954.

Julian, George W. *Political Recollections.* Chicago: Jansen McClurg, 1884.

McCall, Samuel. *Thaddeus Stevens.* Boston: Houghton Mifflin, 1899.

Callender, E. B. *Thaddeus Stevens, Commoner.* Boston: Williams, 1882.

Ross, Edmund. *History of the Impeachment of Andrew Johnson.* Privately printed, 1868.

Stryker, Lloyd Paul. *Andrew Johnson, a Study in Courage.* New York: Macmillan, 1929.

Kennedy, John F. *Profiles in Courage.* New York: Harper & Row, 1955.

Jellison, Charles A. *Fessenden of Maine.* Binghamton, New York: Syracuse University Press, 1962.

Badeau, Adam. *Grant in Peace, a Personal Memoir.* Hartford, Connecticut: Scranton, 1887.

Headley, J. T. *The Life and Travels of General Grant.* Philadelphia: Hubbard, 1879.

U.S. Congress. *Ku Klux Conspiracy.* Joint Select Committee. 42d Cong. Washington, D.C.: Government Printing Office, 1872.

Strong, George Templeton. *The Diary of George Templeton Strong.* Allan Nevins, ed. New York: Macmillan, 1952.

Fleming, Walter L. *Documentary History of Reconstruction*. 2 vols. Cleveland: Clark, 1906.

ALSO BEAR IN MIND

Adams, Henry. *Education of Henry Adams*. Boston: Houghton Mifflin, 1918.

Avery, I. W. *History of Georgia*. New York: Brown & Derby, 1881.

Bailyn, Bernard, and others. *The Great Republic: A History of the American People*. Boston: Little, Brown, 1977.

Belz, Herman. *Reconstructing the Union: Theory and Policy during the Civil War*. Ithaca, New York: Cornell University Press, 1969.

Blay, John S. *After the Civil War A Pictorial Profile of America from 1865 to 1900*. New York: Crowell, 1960.

Crook, William H. *Through Five Administrations*. New York: Harper & Row, 1907. Crook was a presidential bodyguard given the night off by Lincoln before he left for Ford's Theatre.

Oberholtzer, E. P. A. *A History of the United States Since the Civil War*. 5 vols. New York: Macmillan, 1917.

Broomall. *Speech of Hon. J. M. Broomall of Pennsylvania Delivered in House of Representatives January 8, 1867*. Washington, D.C.: McGill & Witherow, 1867.

Garrett, Franklin. *Atlanta and Environs*. New York: Lewis Historical, 1954.

Hamilton, J. G. de Roulhac. *Reconstruction in North Carolina*. Raleigh, North Carolina: Edwards and Broughton, 1906.

Gobright, L. A. *Recollections of Men and Things at Washington*. Philadelphia: Claxton, Remsen and Haffelfinger, 1869. This Associated Press reporter was aboard the funeral train.

Hoehling, A. A. *Last Train from Atlanta*. New York: Yoseloff, 1958.

———. *Thunder at Hampton Roads*. Englewood Cliffs, New Jersey: Prentice-Hall, 1976.

McCarthy, Charles H. *Lincoln's Plan of Reconstruction*. New York: McClure, Phillips, 1901.

Nevins, Allen. *Study in Power*. New York: Scribner, 1953.

Reed, Wallace P. *History of Atlanta, Georgia*. Atlanta: Moss, 1889.

Rowland, Dunbar, ed. *Jefferson Davis, Constitutionalist*. Jackson, Mississippi: Department of Archives and History, 1923.

A surprising number of books have been written about that stormy figure Charles Sumner, the earliest being:

Storey, Moorfield. *Charles Sumner*. Boston: Houghton Mifflin, 1900.

Shotwell, Walter G. *The Life of Charles Sumner*. New York: Crowell, 1910.

Lewis, Lloyd. *Myths after Lincoln*. New York: Harcourt Brace, 1929.

Libraries consulted, not previously listed, include the Martin Luther King (District of Columbia Public): Library of Congress (card catalog files as distinct from the Manuscript Division); Maine State; New York Public; Montgomery County (Md.) Public; and the Sarasota County Public libraries.

Other magazines referenced include the *Century, Illustrated London News, Lippincott's, Harper's* (both weekly and monthly), and *Pennsylvania Magazine of History*.

Newspapers cited include:

Atlanta *Intelligencer*

Baltimore *Sun*

Boston *Daily Advertiser*

Boston *Journal*

Charleston *Daily Courier*

Chicago *Tribune*

New York *Herald*

New York *Times*

New York *Tribune*

New York *World*

Philadelphia *Inquirer*

Philadelphia *Press*

Philadelphia *Times* (in 1879, it published a collection of its war reports which appeared in the Weekly *Times* as "Annals of the War")

Richmond *Whig* (as reestablished)

Savannah *Herald*

St. Louis *Republican*

Washington *Chronicle*

Constitutional Union (Washington)

The Evening Star (Washington)

National Intelligencer (Washington)

INDEX